JavaScript Deep Dive
Modern Development Practices

Contents

Introduction

JavaScript is a versatile and powerful programming language that has become an essential tool for web development. This book, "JavaScript Deep Dive: Modern Development Practices," is designed to provide a comprehensive and detailed exploration of JavaScript, catering to both beginners and experienced developers seeking to deepen their understanding of the language.

JavaScript was created by Brendan Eich in 1995 and has since evolved significantly. It started as a simple scripting language to add interactivity to web pages but has grown into a full-fledged programming language capable of developing complex web applications, server-side applications, and even mobile applications. The language's flexibility and continuous development have ensured its relevance in the ever-changing landscape of web development.

The primary objective of this book is to equip readers with a thorough understanding of JavaScript's core concepts and modern development practices. This book covers fundamental topics such as variables, data types, operators, and control structures, as well as more advanced topics like asynchronous programming, event handling, and modules. Each chapter is meticulously crafted to build on earlier sections, ensuring a natural progression of knowledge.

We begin with an introduction to JavaScript, delving into its history, the basic syntax and structure of the language, and its role in web development. Understanding the context and evolution of JavaScript sets the foundation for comprehending its current capabilities and future potential.

The next chapters cover essential programming constructs such as variables, data types, operators, and control structures. These concepts form the backbone of JavaScript and are crucial for writing functional and efficient code. The book guides readers through these topics with clear explanations and practical examples, ensuring a solid grasp of the fundamentals.

Functions and scope are vital aspects of JavaScript programming, and the book dedicates an entire chapter to these topics. Functions allow for modular and reusable code, while scope determines the accessibility of variables. Mastery of these concepts is necessary for writing clean and maintainable code.

Objects and prototypes are central to JavaScript's object-oriented capabilities. This book provides an in-depth exploration of creating and manipulating objects, understanding prototypes, and leveraging inheritance. These concepts are fundamental for constructing complex data structures and implementing robust programming patterns.

The Document Object Model (DOM) is the interface between JavaScript and web documents. This book offers comprehensive coverage of the DOM, including traversing and manipulating elements, handling events, and integrating JavaScript with HTML and CSS. Proficiency in the DOM is essential for building dynamic and interactive web pages.

Event handling is a critical aspect of web development, as it allows JavaScript to respond to user interactions. The book covers various event types, adding and removing event listeners, and best practices for managing events efficiently. A solid understanding of event handling is necessary for creating responsive and user-friendly applications.

Asynchronous JavaScript is pivotal for modern web applications, enabling non-blocking operations and improving performance. This book delves into the intricacies of callbacks, promises, and the async/await syntax, providing practical examples and best practices. Mastery of asynchronous programming is essential for building efficient and responsive applications.

Modules and modern JavaScript features are explored to keep readers updated with the latest advancements in the language. The book covers the ES6 module system, modern syntax features, and tools for transpiling and bundling JavaScript code. Familiarity with these concepts is crucial for staying current in the rapidly evolving world of JavaScript development.

In conclusion, "JavaScript Deep Dive: Modern Development Practices" aims to provide readers with a deep and comprehensive understanding of JavaScript. By covering fundamental concepts and advanced topics, this book serves as a valuable resource for anyone looking to master JavaScript and apply it to modern web development. With clear explanations, practical examples, and a structured approach, readers will be well-equipped to tackle real-world programming challenges and build sophisticated applications.

Chapter 1

Introduction to JavaScript

This chapter provides a comprehensive overview of JavaScript, starting with its history and evolution. It explains what JavaScript is and its fundamental role in web development. The chapter guides readers through setting up a development environment, writing their first JavaScript program, and understanding the basic syntax and structure of the language. It also covers the significance of ECMAScript standards, differences between JavaScript in the browser and on the server, as well as debugging and testing practices, laying a solid foundation for further exploration of the language.

1.1 The History of JavaScript

JavaScript, a cornerstone of modern web development, was created in 1995 by Brendan Eich while he was working at Netscape Communications Corporation. Initially a 10-day project, JavaScript was first released in the Netscape Navigator 2.0 browser under the name "Mocha", which was later changed to "LiveScript" before finally settling on "JavaScript". The name "JavaScript" was coined as part of a marketing agreement between Netscape and Sun Microsystems, who wished to capitalize on the popularity of Java, another prominent programming language at the time.

JavaScript was designed to be a lightweight, interpreted scripting language with a syntax loosely based on Java but with simpler, more flexible semantics. It was created to make web pages more dynamic and interactive without the need for server-side programming, allowing for immediate feedback and richer user interfaces.

Shortly after its release, JavaScript underwent standardization due to the growing competition between different web browsers. In 1996, Netscape submitted JavaScript to ECMA International, resulting in the first edition of the ECMAScript standard in 1997. ECMAScript serves as the standardized specification upon which JavaScript is based, ensuring cross-browser compatibility and ongoing evolution of the language.

JavaScript development continued to advance rapidly. By 1999, ECMAScript 3 was released and became the foundation for many modern JavaScript features, including regular expressions, better string handling, and exception handling. However, the subsequent ECMAScript 4 proposal, which included numerous complex changes, was ultimately abandoned due to disagreements in the development community.

The years following saw a focus on stability and incremental improvement, leading to the eventual release of ECMAScript 5 in 2009. ECMAScript 5 introduced several critical features such as strict mode, which enforces a more disciplined coding style and helps catch common coding errors, and the JSON format, which became the de facto standard for data interchange on the web.

The most significant leap forward came with ECMAScript 6, also known as ECMAScript 2015 (ES6), finalized in 2015. ES6 included major additions like classes, modules, arrow functions, Promises, generators, and the let and const keywords, which allowed developers to write cleaner, more modular, and more efficient code. This version catalyzed the wide adoption of modern JavaScript programming practices.

In recent years, ECMAScript has shifted to an annual release schedule, with each new edition introducing incremental but meaningful improvements. Notable features added post-ES6 include async/await for better asynchronous programming, additional built-in libraries such as Map and Set, and enhancements to the language's capabilities such as optional chaining and nullish coalescing operations.

The ongoing evolution of JavaScript ensures it remains relevant in the ever-changing landscape of web technologies. This adaptability has cemented JavaScript's role not just in the browser, but also in server environments through platforms like Node.js, allowing for full-stack development using a single language. JavaScript's history is a testament to its resilience and essential nature in modern web development.

Understanding this history provides context for the diverse and powerful capabilities JavaScript offers today, highlighting the language's journey from a simple scripting tool to a robust and versatile programming language.

1.2 What is JavaScript?

JavaScript is a high-level, interpreted programming language that conforms to the ECMAScript specification. Initially designed to make web pages dynamic and interactive, JavaScript has significantly evolved, becoming a pivotal technology in modern web development. It is an essential component of the web development triad along with HTML and CSS. HTML structures the content on the web page, CSS styles it, and JavaScript brings it to life.

JavaScript's syntax is heavily influenced by Java and C, which has led to its widespread adoption due to the familiarity and ease of learning for developers already proficient in these languages. It is dynamically typed, supports object-oriented, imperative, and functional programming styles, making it versatile for various applications, from simple form validations to complex server-side applications using environments like Node.js.

JavaScript is executed by the browser, which includes a JavaScript engine. For instance, Google Chrome employs the V8 engine, Firefox uses SpiderMonkey, and Microsoft's Edge runs Chakra. These engines interpret and execute JavaScript code, enabling dynamic manipulation of web page elements without requiring a page reload.

```
// Example: A simple JavaScript code to display an alert box
alert("Hello, world!");
```

The 'alert' function, as shown above, is part of the global JavaScript object and provides a straightforward way to display a message box to the user.

JavaScript operates based on the Document Object Model (DOM), a hierarchical representation of web pages. The DOM allows JavaScript to access and manipulate HTML elements programmatically. For example, changing the text of a paragraph with a specific id can be achieved easily with JavaScript:

```
// Example: Changing the content of an HTML element
document.getElementById("demo").innerHTML = "Hello, JavaScript!";
```

In addition to client-side scripting, JavaScript has made significant strides on the server side with the advent of Node.js. Node.js is a runtime environment that allows JavaScript to be executed outside of a web browser, making it possible to build scalable and efficient server-side applications. Node.js leverages the V8 engine and includes a rich set of libraries to handle various functionalities like file system I/O, networking, and more.

JavaScript's ecosystem is further enriched by a plethora of libraries and frameworks such as React, Angular, and Vue.js for front-end development, and Express.js for back-end development. These tools allow developers to create robust, maintainable, and performant applications with less effort and more consistency.

```
// Example: Using a JavaScript library (jQuery) to hide an element
$(document).ready(function(){
  $("#hideButton").click(function(){
    $("#demo").hide();
  });
});
```

In the example above, jQuery, a popular JavaScript library, simplifies DOM manipulation and event handling, demonstrating how libraries can streamline JavaScript development.

JavaScript is an asynchronous programming language. It supports asynchronous operations through mechanisms such as callbacks, promises, and the 'async'/'await' syntax. These features allow developers to write non-blocking code, which is essential for maintaining performance and responsiveness in web applications.

```
// Example: Using Promise for asynchronous operation
let promise = new Promise(function(resolve, reject) {
  // Simulate a network request
  setTimeout(function() {
    resolve("Data fetched successfully!");
  }, 2000);
});

promise.then(function(value) {
  console.log(value); // Output: Data fetched successfully!
});
```

JavaScript's ability to run asynchronously ensures that resource-intensive operations such as API requests or file I/O do not block the execution of other code, contributing to a smoother user experience.

In addition to its technical capabilities, JavaScript is standardized through the ECMAScript specification, which ensures consistency and compatibility across different implementations. ECMAScript defines the core features and functionality of the language, while JavaScript extends these features to cater specifically to web development needs.

Given its versatility, ubiquity, and continually evolving nature, JavaScript remains a fundamental cornerstone in modern software development, driving innovation and fostering the creation of diverse applications across various domains of technology.

1.3 Setting Up the Development Environment

To efficiently write, test, and debug JavaScript code, setting up a development environment is a crucial initial step. This section outlines the necessary tools and steps involved in creating a conducive JavaScript development environment.

1. Text Editor or Integrated Development Environment (IDE)

Choosing the right text editor or IDE is the first step. Popular options include:

- **Visual Studio Code (VS Code)**: A free, powerful editor with extensive plugins and support for JavaScript development.
- **Sublime Text**: A lightweight, fast editor with robust plugin support.
- **Atom**: Developed by GitHub, offering extensive customization and collaboration features.
- **WebStorm**: A comprehensive commercial IDE with advanced features for JavaScript development.

Example of installing Visual Studio Code:

```
# Download the installer from https://code.visualstudio.com/
# For Windows: Run the downloaded .exe file
# For macOS: Open the .dmg file and drag VS Code to the Applications folder
# For Linux: Follow the instructions on the website to use the package manager for
    your distribution
```

2. Node.js and npm

Node.js is a JavaScript runtime built on Chrome's V8 JavaScript engine that allows you to run JavaScript on the server side. npm (Node

Package Manager) is bundled with Node.js and is used for managing JavaScript packages.

Download and install Node.js from https://nodejs.org/. After installation, verify the installation by running the following commands in the terminal:

```
node -v
npm -v
```

```
v16.x.x  # Node.js version
8.x.x    # npm version
```

3. Version Control System (Git)

Using a version control system like Git helps manage changes to your codebase. Git is widely used, and its integration with services like GitHub, GitLab, and Bitbucket is essential for collaborative development.

Install Git from https://git-scm.com/ and verify by executing:

```
git --version
```

```
git version 2.32.x
```

4. Browser Developer Tools

Modern browsers come with built-in developer tools that aid in JavaScript development. Google Chrome and Mozilla Firefox are recommended for their powerful developer tools.

To access developer tools:

- Google Chrome: Right-click on a webpage and select "Inspect", or press 'Ctrl+Shift+I' on Windows/Linux or 'Cmd+Opt+I' on macOS.
- Mozilla Firefox: Right-click on a webpage and select "Inspect Element", or press 'Ctrl+Shift+I' on Windows/Linux or 'Cmd+Opt+I' on macOS.

The Console tab within these tools is particularly useful for running JavaScript code snippets and debugging.

5. Setting Up a Basic Project Structure

Creating a well-organized project structure is pivotal for maintainability. A typical JavaScript project structure might include:

```
project-root/
 src/ # Source files
   index.js # Main JavaScript file
   components/ # Sub-directory for JS components
 dist/ # Distributable (built) files
 node_modules/ # Project dependencies (created by npm)
 .gitignore # Files to be ignored by Git
 package.json # Project metadata and dependencies
 README.md # Project documentation
```

6. Initializing a Node.js Project

In the terminal, navigate to your project directory and run:

```
npm init
```

This command initializes a new Node.js project, creating a 'package.json' file where you can specify project metadata and dependencies. Follow the prompts to set up the project or use:

```
npm init -y
```

for default settings.

7. Installing Essential Packages

Install packages essential for development such as linters, formatters, and build tools. Example with 'eslint' and 'prettier':

```
npm install --save-dev eslint prettier
```

Setup configuration files for these tools, such as '.eslintrc.js' for ESLint:

```
module.exports = {
    env: {
        browser: true,
        es2021: true,
    },
    extends: [
        'eslint:recommended',
        'prettier',
    ],
    parserOptions: {
        ecmaVersion: 12,
        sourceType: 'module',
    },
    rules: {
    },
};
```

8. Configuring the Development Environment

Once all tools are installed, configure your IDE or text editor for optimal workflow:

- **VS Code Settings**: Configure settings.json to integrate ESLint and Prettier.
- **Extensions**: Install useful extensions like 'ESLint', 'Prettier', 'Debugger for Chrome' in VS Code.

Example 'settings.json' for VS Code:

```
{
    "editor.formatOnSave": true,
    "editor.codeActionsOnSave": {
        "source.fixAll.eslint": true
    }
}
```

With the development environment properly set up, developers can now focus on writing efficient and error-free JavaScript code. The tools and configurations outlined in this section provide a solid foundation for robust JavaScript development practices.

1.4 Your First JavaScript Program

In this section, we will guide you through writing, understanding, and executing your first JavaScript program. This process entails setting up a working environment, writing code, and interpreting the output. This practical experience will cement fundamental concepts and provide a starting point for more complex tasks.

To begin, ensure you have a text editor or an Integrated Development Environment (IDE) installed. Common choices include VSCode, Sublime Text, and Atom. For this example, we will utilize VSCode due to its advanced features and widespread use.

Create a new folder for your project, and within this folder, create a file named `index.html`. This HTML file will host your JavaScript code. Then, create a second file called `script.js`, where your JavaScript code will reside. The directory structure should look as follows:

```
my\_first\_js\_project/

    index.html
    script.js
```

Open `index.html` in your text editor and populate it with the following content.

Listing 1.1: HTML template for running JavaScript

```
<!DOCTYPE html>
<html lang="en">
<head>
    <meta charset="UTF-8">
    <meta name="viewport" content="width=device-width, initial-scale=1.0">
    <title>JavaScript Program</title>
</head>
<body>
    <h1>Hello, JavaScript!</h1>
    <script src="script.js"></script>
</body>
</html>
```

Here, we set up a basic HTML structure. The `<script>` tag at the bottom of the body references the `script.js` file, where our JavaScript code will execute in the context of this HTML page.

Next, open `script.js` and add the following JavaScript code:

```
console.log("Hello, world!");
```

Listing 1.2: Your First JavaScript Program

This code utilizes the `console.log` function to print the string "Hello, world!" to the browser's console, an essential tool for debugging and monitoring the output of JavaScript code.

To view the output, open `index.html` in a web browser. To accomplish this in VSCode, you can right-click on the `index.html` file in the file explorer and select "Open with Live Server" if you have the Live Server extension installed. Alternatively, navigate to the folder in your file explorer and double-click `index.html` to open it in your default web browser.

Once the HTML page is opened in the browser, access the browser's Developer Tools. In Google Chrome, this can be done by right-clicking the page, selecting "Inspect," and then navigating to the "Console" tab. Here, you should see the output from your JavaScript code:

```
Hello, world!
```

This signifies that your JavaScript code executed successfully. Understanding the `console.log` function is crucial, as it allows you to print messages and inspect variable values, facilitating the debugging and development process.

Next, let's expand your first program by manipulating the Document Object Model (DOM). In `index.html`, add a new HTML element inside the body, just below the `<h1>` tag:

```
<p id="greeting"></p>
```

Now, update `script.js` with the following JavaScript code to change the text content of this paragraph element:

```
document.getElementById("greeting").textContent = "Welcome to the world
    of JavaScript!";
```

The `document.getElementById` function selects the HTML element with the specified ID, allowing you to modify its properties. The `textContent` property sets or returns the text content of the specified node.

Refresh the browser window to see the change. The paragraph element should now display the text:

```
Welcome to the world of JavaScript!
```

The simple actions of logging messages to the console and manipulating the DOM are foundational in JavaScript programming. Understanding these basics prepares you for more advanced topics, allowing you to create interactive web pages and applications. Additionally, observing the direct impact of your code reinforces the connection between syntax and functionality, facilitating deeper comprehension of JavaScript's capabilities and enhancing your programming proficiency.

1.5 JavaScript Syntax and Structure

Understanding the syntax and structure of JavaScript is essential for harnessing its full potential in web development. JavaScript syntax is the set of rules that define a correctly structured JavaScript program, while the structure pertains to how code is organized and written to perform specific tasks effectively.

Basic Syntax:

JavaScript code is composed of statements. A statement is an instruction executed by the web browser. JavaScript statements can be simple or compound and typically end with a semicolon. For example:

```
// A simple statement
var greeting = "Hello, World!";
```

In the above example, `var greeting = "Hello, World!";` is a single statement that declares a variable named `greeting` and assigns it a string value.

Blocks and Scope:

JavaScript allows statements to be grouped together inside blocks, which are denoted by curly braces {}. Blocks define scope, which is crucial for understanding variable accessibility within your code.

```
// A compound statement with a block
function greet() {
 var greeting = "Hello, World!";
 console.log(greeting);
}
```

Here, the variable `greeting` is scoped within the function `greet` and is not accessible outside of it.

Identifiers:

Identifiers are names given to variables, functions, and other entities in JavaScript. They must begin with a letter, underscore (_), or a dollar sign ($), and can contain alphanumeric characters. Identifiers are case-sensitive.

Keywords and Reserved Words:

JavaScript uses keywords that are reserved for controlling the structure and the flow of a program. Some common keywords include `if`, `else`, `while`, `for`, `return`, and `function`. These cannot be used as identifiers.

Comments:

Comments are used for adding notes and explanations within the code, improving readability. JavaScript supports both single-line and multi-line comments:

```
// This is a single-line comment

/*
This is a multi-line comment
which spans multiple lines
*/
```

Data Types:

JavaScript is a dynamic language, meaning that variables can hold any type of value without needing explicit type declarations. Major data types in JavaScript include:

- `Number`: Represents both integer and floating-point numbers.
- `String`: Represents textual data.

- `Boolean`: Represents logical entities, `true` or `false`.
- `Object`: Represents key-value pairs and more complex structures.
- `Undefined`: Indicates a variable declared but not yet assigned a value.
- `Null`: Represents the intentional absence of any object value.

```
var age = 25; // Number
var name = "John Doe"; // String
var isStudent = true; // Boolean
var person = {firstName: "John", lastName: "Doe"}; // Object
var notDefined; // Undefined
var empty = null; // Null
```

Operators:

JavaScript provides a variety of operators for performing operations on variables and values. These include:

- Arithmetic Operators: +, −, ∗, /, `extbackslash extpercent`.
- Assignment Operators: =, +=, −=, ∗=, /=.
- Comparison Operators: ==, ===, !=, !==, >, <, >=, <=.
- Logical Operators: &&, ||, !.

```
var sum = 10 + 5; // 15
var product = 4 * 5; // 20
var isEqual = (sum == product); // false
var andCondition = (isEqual && true); // false
```

Control Structures:

Control structures in JavaScript dictate the flow of execution. Common control structures include conditional statements and loops.

```
// If statement
if (age > 18) {
 console.log("Adult");
} else {
 console.log("Minor");
}

// For loop
for (var i = 0; i < 5; i++) {
 console.log(i);
}
```

```
// While loop
var count = 0;
while (count < 5) {
 console.log(count);
 count++;
}
```

Functions:

Functions are reusable blocks of code that perform a specific task. They are defined using the `function` keyword followed by a name, parameter list, and a function body.

```
function add(a, b) {
 return a + b;
}

var sum = add(5, 10); // 15
```

Functions can also be assigned to variables and passed as arguments to other functions, reflecting JavaScript's first-class function properties.

Arrays:

Arrays are used to store multiple values in a single variable. They are zero-indexed and can hold mixed data types.

```
var colors = ["red", "green", "blue"];
console.log(colors[0]); // red
```

Objects:

Objects are collections of key-value pairs and are fundamental to JavaScript's functionality. They can encapsulate properties and methods.

```
var person = {
 firstName: "John",
 lastName: "Doe",
 age: 30,
 greet: function() {
 console.log("Hello, " + this.firstName);
 }
};

person.greet(); // Hello, John
```

This thorough understanding of JavaScript's syntax and structure forms the foundation for writing and comprehending more sophisticated code. By mastering these elements, developers can effectively utilize JavaScript's capabilities in creating dynamic and interactive web applications.

1.6 Evolution of JavaScript: ECMAScript

Understanding the evolution of JavaScript requires delving into ECMAScript, the standardized scripting language specification upon which JavaScript is based. ECMAScript is maintained by ECMA International, a standards organization for information and communication systems. The evolution of ECMAScript directly influences the capabilities of JavaScript, enabling developers to utilize modern features and improvements in the language.

ECMAScript 1 and 2: Foundations The standardization process began in 1997 with the release of ECMAScript 1 (ES1). This initial version outlined the basic syntax and structure of the language. It provided the necessary foundation for consistent language behavior across different implementations. ECMAScript 2 (ES2), released in 1998, mainly focused on aligning the specification with ISO/IEC 16262 and introducing minor adjustments without significant language changes.

ECMAScript 3: The First Major Update ECMAScript 3 (ES3), introduced in 1999, brought about a multitude of enhancements and new features. Key additions included:

- Regular expressions for pattern matching.
- Improved string manipulation capabilities.
- Exception handling with `try`, `catch`, and `finally` blocks.
- The introduction of control statements such as `do-while`.

ES3 formed the basis of JavaScript implementations for many years and established features that are still utilized in modern JavaScript.

ECMAScript 4: Abandoned Draft The road to ECMAScript 4 (ES4) was notably contentious. Development began in the early 2000s, aiming to introduce significant changes, including:

- Class-based inheritance.
- Strong typing.
- Optional static type checking.

However, due to disagreements within the development community, ES4 was ultimately abandoned. The failure to reach a consensus led to the next stable release, ECMAScript 5.

ECMAScript 5: Revival and Innovation Released in 2009, ECMAScript 5 (ES5) revived and rejuvenated JavaScript development with notable advancements:

- Strict mode, introduced with `"use strict";`, enforced better coding practices and error checking.
- Enhanced object handling with `Object.create`, `Object.defineProperty`, and other methods.
- Array methods such as `map`, `reduce`, `forEach`, `filter`, and `some`.
- JSON support with built-in `JSON.parse` and `JSON.stringify`.

ES5 significantly improved JavaScript's robustness and performance, laying the groundwork for more complex web applications.

ECMAScript 6: The Modern Era ECMAScript 6 (ES6), known also as ES2015, is often considered the most transformative update in the history of JavaScript, introduced in 2015. Major features include:

- `let` and `const` for block-scoped variable declarations.
- Arrow functions providing a concise syntax for writing functions.
- Promises enabling better asynchronous programming control.
- Template literals for easier string interpolation and multi-line strings.
- Class syntax to support object-oriented programming paradigms.
- Modules allowing the import and export of code between files.
- Enhanced object literals, destructuring assignments, and more.

The introduction of these features revolutionized JavaScript, making it more powerful and expressive.

Subsequent ECMAScript Versions Continuing the trend of annual updates, the ECMAScript standard has consistently introduced incremental features and improvements:

- ECMAScript 2016 (ES7): Brought `Array.prototype.includes` and the `**` operator for exponentiation.
- ECMAScript 2017 (ES8): Added features like `async/await` for simplifying asynchronous code and `Object.entries/Object.values` methods.
- ECMAScript 2018 (ES9): Included asynchronous iteration with `for-await-of` and the `Promise.finally` method.
- ECMAScript 2019 (ES10): Introduced `Array.prototype.flat`, `Array.prototype.flatMap`, and `Object.fromEntries`.
- ECMAScript 2020 (ES11): Brought `BigInt` for large integer representations, `Promise.allSettled`, and optional chaining.
- ECMAScript 2021 (ES12): Introduced logical assignment operators and `String.prototype.replaceAll`.

The steady evolution of ECMAScript has not only expanded JavaScript's feature set but also ensured that it remains relevant and capable of meeting modern development requirements. As ECMAScript continues to evolve, developers gain access to tools and functionalities that drive innovation and efficiency in web development.

1.7 JavaScript in Web Development

JavaScript is a cornerstone technology in web development, and its role is pivotal in enabling dynamic and interactive web applications. JavaScript allows developers to manipulate the Document Object Model (DOM), handle events, validate data, communicate with web servers, and much more. This section delves into these aspects, providing detailed explanations and examples to solidify understanding.

Manipulating the DOM:

The DOM is a programming interface for web documents. It represents the page so that programs can change the document structure, style, and content. JavaScript can access and modify the DOM, thus enabling dynamic content updates without requiring a full page reload.

To access DOM elements, JavaScript provides several methods, such as `getElementById`, `getElementsByClassName`, `querySelector`, and `querySelectorAll`.

```
let element = document.getElementById('myElement');
let elements = document.getElementsByClassName('myClass');
let singleElement = document.querySelector('.myClass');
let multipleElements = document.querySelectorAll('.myClass');
```

Listing 1.3: Accessing DOM Elements

Once a DOM element is referenced, JavaScript can alter its properties, apply styles, or even modify its structure by adding or removing elements.

```
element.innerHTML = 'New content'; // Change inner HTML
element.style.color = 'blue'; // Apply style
element.setAttribute('class', 'newClass'); // Change attribute
```

Listing 1.4: Modifying DOM Elements

Handling Events:

Events represent actions that occur in the browser, such as clicks, key presses, or mouse movements. JavaScript enables the registration and handling of these events, allowing developers to create responsive interfaces. Event listeners can be attached to DOM elements to execute JavaScript code when specified events occur.

```
element.addEventListener('click', function() {
    console.log('Element clicked!');
});
```

Listing 1.5: Adding Event Listeners

Common events include `click`, `mouseover`, `mouseout`, `keydown`, and `submit`. Proper event handling enhances user interaction and improves the overall user experience.

Data Validation:

JavaScript is often employed for client-side form validation to ensure that the data entered by users conforms to expected formats before it is sent to the server. This can help prevent errors and reduce the load on the server.

```
function validateForm() {
```

```
    let name = document.forms['myForm']['name'].value;
    if (name === '') {
        alert('Name must be filled out');
        return false;
    }
    return true;
}
document.getElementById('myForm').onsubmit = validateForm;
```

Listing 1.6: JavaScript Form Validation

Asynchronous Communication:

JavaScript supports asynchronous operations through the use of `XMLHttpRequest` and the Fetch API, enabling web pages to communicate with servers without reloading. This technique is known as AJAX (Asynchronous JavaScript and XML).

```
let xhr = new XMLHttpRequest();
xhr.open('GET', 'data.json', true);
xhr.onload = function() {
    if (this.status == 200) {
        console.log(JSON.parse(this.responseText));
    }
}
xhr.send();
```

Listing 1.7: Using XMLHttpRequest for AJAX

With the Fetch API, the syntax becomes more modern and promises-based, offering cleaner and more readable code.

```
fetch('data.json')
    .then(response => response.json())
    .then(data => console.log(data))
    .catch(error => console.error('Error:', error));
```

Listing 1.8: Using Fetch API for AJAX

JavaScript's ability to dynamically update content, handle events, validate input, and communicate asynchronously with servers makes it indispensable in modern web development. Ensuring a firm grasp of these functionalities will greatly enhance the capability to develop interactive and efficient web applications.

1.8 JavaScript Engines and Runtime Environments

JavaScript engines are crucial components in the execution of JavaScript code. They are specialized programs that read, interpret, and execute JavaScript code. The efficiency and performance of these engines significantly impact the overall experience of running JavaScript applications. The most renowned JavaScript engines include Google's V8, Mozilla's SpiderMonkey, Apple's JavaScriptCore, and Microsoft's Chakra.

The V8 engine, a cornerstone of Google's Chrome browser and the Node.js runtime, compiles JavaScript to native machine code before executing it, enhancing the runtime performance. The SpiderMonkey engine, used by Mozilla's Firefox, and JavaScriptCore, used by Apple's Safari, follow similar paradigms with certain optimizations specific to their environments. Microsoft's Chakra engine, embedded within Microsoft Edge and Internet Explorer, offers its unique optimizations and execution models.

JavaScript engines can be characterized by their Just-In-Time (JIT) compilation techniques. These techniques involve an initial parsing phase where the JavaScript code is parsed into an Abstract Syntax Tree (AST). Subsequently, the engine translates the AST into intermediate representations (IR), which are then optimized and compiled into machine code just in time for execution. This process allows for real-time optimizations based on the code's execution profile, enhancing performance dynamically.

```
function add(a, b) {
    return a + b;
}
console.log(add(2, 3)); // Outputs: 5
```

In the above JavaScript snippet, the function `add` and its invocation would be parsed into an AST. The engine performs constant folding optimization, recognizing that `2` and `3` are constant values, and optimizes the addition operation at compile-time.

JavaScript runtime environments encompass more than just the engine. They include a set of libraries, APIs, and runtime resources available to JavaScript code. In browsers, this environment includes the Document Object Model (DOM), Web APIs like `fetch`, `XMLHttpRequest`, and `localStorage`, as well as various event-handling mechanisms. Server-side JavaScript environments like Node.js provide modules for file system access, networking, and child processes.

The Event Loop is a critical component of JavaScript runtime environments, enabling asynchronous execution. JavaScript executes in a single-threaded manner but handles asynchronous operations using the Event Loop, which allows non-blocking behavior. The Event Loop continuously checks the call stack to see if it's empty and polls the callback queue for pending tasks to push onto the call stack.

```
console.log("Start");

setTimeout(() => {
    console.log("Callback");
}, 1000);

console.log("End");
```

Execution output:

```
Start
End
Callback
```

In the above example, the `setTimeout` function schedules the callback to be executed after 1000 milliseconds. The initial messages "Start" and "End" are logged immediately, while the "Callback" message is deferred and executed once the call stack is clear, exhibiting the non-blocking nature of the Event Loop.

Microtask and Macrotask queues further define the Event Loop. Microtasks, which include promises and certain `MutationObserver` callbacks, are treated with higher priority and are executed before any rendering is performed. Macrotasks, such as `setTimeout` and `setInterval`, are scheduled for subsequent cycles of the event loop.

```
Promise.resolve().then(() => {
    console.log("Microtask");
});

setTimeout(() => {
    console.log("Macrotask");
}, 0);

console.log("Synchronous");
```

Execution output:

```
Synchronous
Microtask
Macrotask
```

Integrating with various runtime environments, engines like V8 leverage the available resources to optimize performance. For example, in Node.js, V8 capitalizes on asynchronous I/O operations, concurrency, and efficient memory management to provide a robust platform for server-side applications.

JavaScript engines also manage garbage collection, vital for optimal memory usage. V8, for instance, employs a generational garbage collection strategy with different spaces for objects based on their lifetimes (young generation and old generation). It periodically runs garbage collection processes to reclaim memory occupied by unreachable objects.

Understanding JavaScript engines and runtime environments is essential for writing efficient, performant code and leveraging the full potential of JavaScript in both browser and server settings. By grasping the underlying mechanisms and execution models, developers can make informed decisions to optimize their applications effectively.

1.9 JavaScript in the Browser vs. on the Server

JavaScript can be executed in two principal environments: the web browser and the server. Understanding the distinctions between these environments is crucial for developing efficient and effective JavaScript applications. This section meticulously explores these differences, enabling developers to optimally leverage JavaScript in both contexts.

JavaScript in the browser, often referred to as client-side JavaScript, runs directly within the user's web browser. The primary interaction here is through the Document Object Model (DOM), which represents the structure of a web page. JavaScript can manipulate the DOM to create dynamic user interfaces, validate user inputs, and handle events such as clicks, form submissions, and keyboard inputs. The core functionality revolves around enhancing the user experience by making web pages interactive and responsive. Browsers like Chrome, Firefox, Safari, and Edge include built-in JavaScript engines (e.g., V8 for Chrome, SpiderMonkey for Firefox) that parse, compile, and execute JavaScript code.

Consider a simple example where JavaScript is used to change the content of an HTML element when a button is clicked:

```
<!DOCTYPE html>
```

```
<html>
<body>

<h2>Example of Client-Side JavaScript</h2>
<p id="demo">Hello World!</p>
<button type="button" onclick="changeContent()">Click Me!</button>

<script>
function changeContent() {
  document.getElementById("demo").innerHTML = "Hello JavaScript!";
}
</script>

</body>
</html>
```

In this example, the 'changeContent' function accesses the DOM, identifies the element with the 'id' "demo", and modifies its content. This demonstrates the power of JavaScript in the browser to create engaging and interactive web pages.

Server-side JavaScript, most commonly executed in environments like Node.js, operates outside the browser on a web server. Unlike client-side JavaScript, it does not have direct access to the DOM or browser-specific APIs such as 'window' and 'document'. Instead, server-side JavaScript focuses on back-end operations, which may include database interactions, handling HTTP requests and responses, and performing server-side logic.

Node.js, powered by the V8 engine, is a popular environment for executing server-side JavaScript. It allows developers to use JavaScript for both front-end and back-end development, promoting a unified language across the entire application stack. Below is an example of a simple Node.js server that responds with "Hello World!" when accessed:

```
const http = require('http');

const hostname = '127.0.0.1';
const port = 3000;

const server = http.createServer((req, res) => {
  res.statusCode = 200;
  res.setHeader('Content-Type', 'text/plain');
  res.end('Hello World\n');
});

server.listen(port, hostname, () => {
  console.log(`Server running at http://${hostname}:${port}/`);
});
```

When this code is executed, Node.js creates an HTTP server that listens on the specified port and hostname. Upon receiving a request, it responds with a plain text "Hello World" message.

Key Differences

- **Execution Context**:
  - **Client-side**: Runs in the browser, often interacting with the DOM and browser APIs.
  - **Server-side**: Runs on a server environment, handling back-end operations.
- **Environment**:
  - **Client-side**: Limited by the browser's sandbox environment, ensuring security and isolation from the operating system.
  - **Server-side**: Has access to the file system, network, and other operating system functionalities, offering more control but requiring careful management of security and resource usage.
- **Libraries and APIs**:
  - **Client-side**: Access to browser-specific APIs (e.g., 'window', 'document', 'localStorage').
  - **Server-side**: Access to server-side modules and APIs (e.g., 'fs' for file system operations, 'http' for handling web requests).
- **Performance**:
  - **Client-side**: Performance is affected by the user's browser and device capabilities. Heavy computations should be avoided as they can slow down the user interface.
  - **Server-side**: Typically has more computational power and memory, but must manage multiple concurrent requests efficiently.
- **Security**:
  - **Client-side**: Runs in a restricted environment to prevent security vulnerabilities like Cross-Site Scripting (XSS).

- **Server-side**: Requires robust security measures to protect against threats such as SQL Injection, Cross-Site Request Forgery (CSRF), and others.

Practical Considerations

When developing a full-stack web application, understanding the roles of client-side and server-side JavaScript is essential. Client-side JavaScript enhances user interaction and responsiveness, making applications more engaging. Server-side JavaScript handles the core business logic, database interactions, and ensures that client requests are processed efficiently.

Consider a scenario where you develop a web application that allows users to register, log in, and view their profile. The client-side JavaScript would handle form validation, real-time user feedback, and DOM manipulation for a smooth user experience. The server-side JavaScript would manage user authentication, session handling, database queries, and sending the appropriate data to the client.

The seamless interaction between client-side and server-side JavaScript not only promotes a better separation of concerns but also enhances maintainability and scalability. Each layer of the application can be developed, tested, and scaled independently while still working together to form a cohesive and performant system.

By leveraging the strengths of JavaScript in both environments, developers can build robust, dynamic, and scalable applications that meet modern web development needs.

1.10 Debugging and Testing JavaScript Code

Debugging and testing are critical aspects of software development, ensuring that applications function as intended and maintain robustness. This section delves into the methodologies, tools, and best practices for debugging and testing JavaScript code. Mastering these techniques is essential for developing reliable, maintainable software.

Debugging JavaScript Code

The process of debugging involves identifying and resolving issues within the code. Effective debugging allows developers to understand the root cause of a problem and apply appropriate solutions to prevent recurrence. JavaScript provides several tools and methodologies to facilitate debugging.

Using the Browser Developer Tools

Modern web browsers are equipped with powerful developer tools designed to assist in debugging JavaScript. These tools typically include a JavaScript console, a source code debugger, and performance analysis features.

```
console.log('Initializing application...');
const sum = (a, b) => a + b;
console.log('Sum of 5 and 3:', sum(5, 3));
```

Listing 1.9: Logging output to the console

```
Initializing application...
Sum of 5 and 3: 8
```

The `console.log()` method is ubiquitous for outputting data to the console during development and is particularly useful for simple debugging and tracing code execution.

Setting Breakpoints and Examining Variables

To perform more in-depth debugging, setting breakpoints in the source code is highly effective. Breakpoints allow developers to pause the execution of the script at a specified line of code, observe the call stack, and inspect the values of variables.

To set a breakpoint in most browser developer tools, open the "Sources" panel, find the desired line, and click on the line number. When execution hits the breakpoint, the browser will pause, and you can investigate the current state of the application.

```
function calculateArea(radius) {
    const pi = 3.14159;
    const area = pi * radius * radius; // Set breakpoint here
    return area;
}

const result = calculateArea(10);
console.log('Area:', result);
```

Listing 1.10: Example Function with a Breakpoint

```
Area: 314.159
```

The Debugger Statement

In addition to setting breakpoints through the developer tools UI, the `debugger` statement in JavaScript can force the execution to pause if the browser's developer tool is open.

```
function calculateCircumference(radius) {
    const pi = 3.14159;
    debugger; // Execution will pause here if developer tools are open
    const circumference = 2 * pi * radius;
    return circumference;
}

const circumferenceResult = calculateCircumference(10);
console.log('Circumference:', circumferenceResult);
```

Listing 1.11: Using the Debugger Statement

```
Circumference: 62.8318
```

Testing JavaScript Code

Testing ensures that code performs correctly under various conditions. Two primary types of testing are commonly used in JavaScript: unit testing and integration testing.

Unit Testing

Unit tests focus on verifying the functionality of individual components or functions. This granularity allows developers to identify bugs early in the development cycle. Popular frameworks for unit testing JavaScript include Jest, Mocha, and Jasmine.

Consider the following example using Jest:

```
// sum.js
function sum(a, b) {
    return a + b;
}
module.exports = sum;

// sum.test.js
const sum = require('./sum');

test('adds 1 + 2 to equal 3', () => {
    expect(sum(1, 2)).toBe(3);
});
```

Listing 1.12: Example Unit Test with Jest

```
PASS  ./sum.test.js
  adds 1 + 2 to equal 3 (5ms)
```

Integration Testing

Integration tests examine the interactions between different parts of an application, ensuring that modules work together as expected. Tools like Selenium, Cypress, and Puppeteer are widely used for this purpose.

Using Cypress, an integration test might look like the following:

```
// Sample.spec.js
describe('My First Test', () => {
    it('Visits the Kitchen Sink', () => {
        cy.visit('https://example.cypress.io')
        cy.contains('type').click()
        cy.url().should('include', '/commands/actions')
        cy.get('.action-email').type('fake@email.com')
            .should('have.value', 'fake@email.com')
    })
})
```

Listing 1.13: Example Integration Test with Cypress

```
My First Test
    Visits the Kitchen Sink (1234ms)
```

Automating Tests with Continuous Integration

Consistency and reliability in testing can be enhanced through Continuous Integration (CI). CI tools like Jenkins, Travis CI, and GitHub Actions automate the execution of tests as part of the development workflow, ensuring that each code change is verified by existing tests.

For a project utilizing GitHub Actions, a sample workflow configuration might be:

Listing 1.14: GitHub Actions Workflow for Running Tests

```
name Node.js CI

on [push, pull_request]

jobs
  build

    runs-on ubuntu-latest

    strategy
      matrix
        node-version [12.x, 14.x, 16.x]

    steps
    - uses actions/checkout@v2
    - name Use Node.js ${{ matrix.node-version }}
      uses actions/setup-node@v2
      with
```

```
    node-version ${{ matrix.node-version }}
  - run npm install
  - run npm test
```

For robust and maintainable JavaScript applications, adopting debugging and testing best practices is crucial. These processes help identify and rectify defects, ensure code correctness, and maintain software quality throughout its lifecycle.

Chapter 2

Variables and Data Types

This chapter delves into the foundational concepts of variables and data types in JavaScript. It covers the declaration of variables using var, let, and const, and explains the different data types, both primitive and complex. The chapter explores type conversion, coercion, and the implications of variable scope and hoisting. Additionally, it addresses constants, immutability, and the usage of template literals and string interpolation. By understanding these core topics, readers will be equipped to manage data effectively in their programs.

2.1 Introduction to Variables

In any programming language, variables serve as fundamental building blocks. They allow for the storage and manipulation of data, which is crucial for performing various computational tasks. In JavaScript, variables are used to store data values that the program can reference and manipulate.

JavaScript provides three primary methods for declaring variables: `var`, `let`, and `const`. Each of these has distinct characteristics and behaviors that are important to understand for effective programming practices.

```
// Declaring variables using var, let, and const
var exampleVar = "This is a var variable";
let exampleLet = "This is a let variable";
```

```
const exampleConst = "This is a const variable";
```

Variable Naming Conventions

When naming variables in JavaScript, it is important to follow certain conventions to maintain code readability and prevent potential errors. Here are the key rules for naming variables:

- Variable names must start with a letter, underscore (_), or dollar sign ($).
- Subsequent characters can also include digits (0-9).
- Variable names are case-sensitive, meaning `varName` and `varname` would be considered different variables.
- Names should be descriptive and concise, typically using camelCase for readability.

```
// Valid variable names
let userName = "Alice";
let $userAge = 25;
let _userCity = "New York";
let user_data = "Data";

// Invalid variable names
// let 123name = "Bob"; // Error: Names cannot start with digits
// let user-age = 30; // Error: Hyphens are not allowed
```

Variable Declaration

The process of declaring a variable involves specifying the variable name and assigning an initial value. If the initial value is not provided, JavaScript assigns `undefined` as the default value.

```
let uninitializedVar;
console.log(uninitializedVar); // Output: undefined
```

Dynamic Typing

JavaScript is a dynamically typed language, meaning that variables do not have a fixed type. This allows a variable to hold a value of any data type at any point in time.

```
let dynamicVar = 15; // Initially a number
dynamicVar = "Now a string"; // Now a string
dynamicVar = true; // Now a boolean
```

Variable Scope

The scope of a variable refers to its accessibility within different parts of a program. JavaScript supports function scope and block scope. Variables declared with `var` are function-scoped, while those declared with `let` and `const` are block-scoped. Block scope means that the variable is limited to the block in which it is defined (e.g., within {} brackets).

```
function testScope() {
    var functionScoped = "I'm accessible throughout the function";
    if (true) {
        let blockScoped = "I'm only accessible within this block";
        const anotherBlockScoped = "Same block limitation";
        console.log(blockScoped); // Output: I'm only accessible within
            this block
    }
    console.log(functionScoped); // Output: I'm accessible throughout the
        function
    // console.log(blockScoped); // Error: blockScoped is not defined
}
```

Hoisting

Hoisting is JavaScript's default behavior of moving declarations to the top of the current scope (function or global). This means that variable and function declarations are processed before any code is executed. However, `let` and `const` are not hoisted in the same way as `var`; they are hoisted to the top of the block but are not initialized.

```
console.log(hoistedVar); // Output: undefined
var hoistedVar = 10;

// console.log(hoistedLet); // Error: Cannot access 'hoistedLet' before
    initialization
let hoistedLet = 20;
```

Proper understanding and usage of variables in JavaScript are crucial for writing effective and error-free code. Grasping these fundamental concepts are essential for delving deeper into the intricacies of JavaScript programming.

2.2 Declaring Variables with var, let, and const

In JavaScript, variables serve as containers for storing data values. The ability to declare and manipulate variables is fundamental to any programming endeavor. JavaScript provides three primary keywords for variable declaration: `var`, `let`, and `const`. Understanding their differences, characteristics, and appropriate use cases is essential for effective and efficient code development.

var Keyword

The `var` keyword is the oldest way to declare variables in JavaScript and was introduced in ECMAScript 1. Variables declared using `var` have function scope, meaning they are accessible throughout the entire function in which they are declared. They are also subject to hoisting, a behavior where variable declarations are moved to the top of their enclosing scope during the compilation phase. Consider the following example:

```
function exampleVar() {
    console.log(name); // Output: undefined
    var name = 'Alice';
    console.log(name); // Output: Alice
}

exampleVar();
```

Even though the `name` variable appears to be used before its declaration, JavaScript internally "hoists" the declaration to the top of the function scope. The variable's value, however, remains undefined until the assignment is evaluated. This hoisting behavior can lead to unintentional bugs that are hard to diagnose.

let Keyword

The `let` keyword, introduced in ECMAScript 6 (ES6), addresses some of the limitations and problematic behaviors of `var`. Variables declared with `let` have block scope, meaning they are only accessible within the block (enclosed by curly braces) where they are defined. This scoping behavior enhances readability and maintains a clear boundary of variable use. Additionally, `let` variables are not hoisted in the same manner as `var`, instead they reside in a "temporal dead zone" from the start of the block until their declaration.

```
function exampleLet() {
    console.log(name); // ReferenceError: name is not defined
    let name = 'Bob';
    console.log(name); // Output: Bob
}

exampleLet();
```

In this case, attempting to access `name` before its declaration results in a `ReferenceError`, as opposed to the undefined output observed with `var`. This makes it clear that the variable is not yet initialized, thereby preventing unintended errors.

const Keyword

The `const` keyword, also introduced in ES6, is used to declare variables that are intended to remain constant u2013 their values should not change through re-assignment after the initial assignment. Like `let`, `const` variables have block scope. However, there are additional constraints:

- A `const` variable must be initialized at the time of declaration.
- The value of a `const` variable cannot be reassigned.

```
function exampleConst() {
    const birthYear = 1990;
    // birthYear = 2000; // Uncaught TypeError: Assignment to constant
        variable.
    console.log(birthYear); // Output: 1990
}

exampleConst();
```

Attempting to reassign a `const` variable results in a `TypeError`. It is important to note that while primitive values are immutable, objects assigned to `const` variables can still be modified:

```
const person = { name: 'Carol' };
person.name = 'David';
console.log(person.name); // Output: David
```

Although the reference to the `person` object is constant and cannot be changed, the object's properties can be modified. This characteristic underscores the distinction between constancy of reference versus constancy of value.

Throughout JavaScript development, selecting the appropriate keyword for variable declaration is crucial. While `var` offers legacy compatibility, modern practices recommend `let` and `const` for their predictable scoping and error-resistant behaviors. The choice between `let` and `const` largely hinges on whether the variable's value is intended to remain unchanged, thereby ensuring optimal code stability and readability.

2.3 Understanding Data Types

JavaScript, as a dynamic and interpreted language, categorizes values into various data types. Understanding these data types is foundational for effective programming as it guides how data is stored, processed, and retrieved. JavaScript has several built-in data types, classified into two primary categories: primitive and complex.

Primitive data types include:

- Number
- String
- Boolean
- Undefined
- Null
- Symbol
- BigInt

Complex data types encompass:

- Object
- Function, a subtype of Object
- Array, also a subtype of Object

Number: JavaScript features a single number type, which includes both integer and floating-point numbers conforming to the IEEE 754 standard. The built-in `Number` object provides capabilities to handle operations such as conversions and parsing.

```
let integer = 42;
let floatingPoint = 3.14;
```

String: Strings in JavaScript are immutable sequences of UTF-16 code units. They are used to represent textual data and support a variety of methods for manipulation.

```
let greeting = "Hello, World!";
let name = 'Ada Lovelace';
```

Boolean: This type has only two values: `true` and `false`. They are primarily used in control flow structures.

```
let isJavaScriptFun = true;
let isCodingTiring = false;
```

Undefined: A variable that has been declared but not assigned a value is of type `undefined`.

```
let someVariable;
console.log(someVariable); // output: undefined
```

```
undefined
```

Null: The `null` type represents the intentional absence of an object value. It is considered one of JavaScript's primitive values.

```
let noValue = null;
```

It is important to note that `typeof null` returns `"object"` due to a bug that traces back to JavaScript's first implementation.

```
console.log(typeof null); // output: object
```

```
object
```

Symbol: Introduced in ECMAScript 2015, a `Symbol` is a unique and immutable primitive value. They are often used to create unique property keys for objects.

```
let uniqueSymbol = Symbol('unique');
console.log(uniqueSymbol); // output: Symbol(unique)
```

```
Symbol(unique)
```

BigInt: A larger integer type allowing safe calculations beyond the `Number.MAX_SAFE_INTEGER` (`2^{53} - 1`).

```
let bigNumber = BigInt(1234567890123456789012345678890);
console.log(bigNumber); // output: 1234567890123456789012345678890n
```

```
1234567890123456789012345678890n
```

In contrast, complex data types are reference types. Among them, `Object` types are central. An `Object` is a collection of properties, where a property is an association between a name and a value.

```
let person = {
   firstName: "Alan",
   lastName: "Turing",
   age: 42
};
```

Arrays, a type of object, are used to store ordered collections of elements.

```
let numbers = [1, 2, 3, 4, 5];
```

Functions, another subtype of objects, are first-class objects in JavaScript. Besides being callable entities, they can possess properties and methods.

```
function greet(name) {
   return `Hello, ${name}`;
}
```

Understanding the distinctions between these types is crucial because operations and functions behave differently depending on the type of their operands. For example, adding two numbers results in arithmetic addition, whereas adding a number to a string concatenates.

```
let resultNumber = 5 + 5; // 10
let resultString = "5" + 5; // "55"
```

This comprehension is pivotal when performing type conversions, managing memory, and optimizing performance. Additionally, the awareness of differences between primitive and complex types assists in predicting outcomes of equality checks and mutation behaviors.

2.4 Primitive Data Types

In JavaScript, primitive data types represent simple, immutable types of data. There are six primitive data types: `undefined`, `null`, `boolean`, `number`, `string`, and `symbol`. These data types are immutable, meaning that their values cannot be changed once they are created. To understand how each type works, let us delve into their characteristics and use cases.

Undefined: The `undefined` type is assigned to variables that have been declared but not initialized. When a variable is declared without a value, it automatically holds `undefined`.

```
// Example
let x;
console.log(x); // Output: undefined
```

Null: The `null` type represents the intentional absence of any object value. It is explicitly assigned to a variable to indicate that it has no value.

```
// Example
let y = null;
console.log(y); // Output: null
```

Boolean: The `boolean` type has only two possible values: `true` and `false`. Boolean values are commonly used in control flow statements like `if` conditions and loops.

```
// Example
let isAdult = true;
let hasLicense = false;
console.log(isAdult); // Output: true
console.log(hasLicense); // Output: false
```

Number: The `number` type represents both integer and floating-point numbers. JavaScript uses a double-precision 64-bit format as specified by the IEEE 754 standard.

```
// Example
let age = 25; // Integer
let price = 19.95; // Floating-point
console.log(age); // Output: 25
console.log(price); // Output: 19.95
```

Note that JavaScript has a special value called `NaN`, which stands for "Not-a-Number". It is used to represent a value that is not a legal number.

```
// Example
let result = 0 / 0;
console.log(result); // Output: NaN
```

String: The `string` type is used to represent textual data. Strings in JavaScript are immutable and can be enclosed in single quotes (' '), double quotes (" "), or template literals (` `).

```
// Example
let name = 'John Doe';
let greeting = "Hello, World!";
let templateLiteral = `This is a template string.`;
console.log(name); // Output: John Doe
console.log(greeting); // Output: Hello, World!
console.log(templateLiteral); // Output: This is a template string.
```

Strings also support various methods for manipulating text, such as concatenation, slicing, and searching within the string.

```
// Example
let text = 'JavaScript';
let concatenated = text + ' ' + 'Language';
console.log(concatenated); // Output: JavaScript Language
console.log(text.slice(0, 4)); // Output: Java
console.log(text.includes('Script')); // Output: true
```

Symbol: The `symbol` type is a unique and immutable primitive value that is often used to identify object properties uniquely. Symbols are created using the `Symbol()` function.

```
// Example
let sym1 = Symbol('identifier1');
let sym2 = Symbol('identifier2');
console.log(sym1 === sym2); // Output: false
```

Though symbols are not commonly used in everyday JavaScript programming, they become essential when working with certain advanced topics like enhancing object property enumeration or creating private properties.

It is noteworthy that primitive types are compared by value, not by reference. When two primitives have the same value, they are considered equal.

```
// Example
let num1 = 100;
let num2 = 100;
let str1 = 'hello';
let str2 = 'hello';
console.log(num1 === num2); // Output: true
console.log(str1 === str2); // Output: true
```

By understanding primitive data types and their characteristics, you lay a strong foundation for managing and manipulating data in JavaScript.

2.5 Complex Data Types

Complex data types in JavaScript include objects and arrays. They are capable of holding multiple values in a single variable. Understanding their characteristics and behavior is fundamental to effective JavaScript programming.

Objects. An object is a collection of properties, and a property is an association between a name (or key) and a value. A property's value can be a function, which is known as a method. JavaScript objects are dynamic, meaning that properties can be added and deleted at runtime.

```
let person = {
    firstName: "John",
    lastName: "Doe",
    age: 30,
    fullName: function() {
        return this.firstName + " " + this.lastName;
    }
};

// Accessing properties
console.log(person.firstName); // Outputs: John
console.log(person["lastName"]); // Outputs: Doe

// Calling method
console.log(person.fullName()); // Outputs: John Doe

// Adding a property
person.email = "john.doe@example.com";

// Deleting a property
delete person.age;

console.log(person);
```

```
{
    firstName: "John",
    lastName: "Doe",
    fullName: function() { return this.firstName + " " + this.lastName; },
    email: "john.doe@example.com"
}
```

Arrays. An array is a special type of object used for storing ordered collections of values. These values can be of any data type, including other arrays and objects.

```
let fruits = ["Apple", "Banana", "Cherry"];

// Accessing array elements
console.log(fruits[0]); // Outputs: Apple

// Adding an element
fruits.push("Date");

// Removing an element
let lastFruit = fruits.pop(); // Removes and returns the last element

console.log(fruits); // Outputs: ["Apple", "Banana", "Cherry"]
```

```
[
    "Apple",
    "Banana",
    "Cherry"
]
```

Nested Objects and Arrays. Complex data structures can include nested objects and arrays, which allow for more sophisticated data organization.

```
let company = {
   name: "Tech Corp",
   employees: [
      { name: "Alice", position: "Developer" },
      { name: "Bob", position: "Designer" }
   ],
   address: {
      street: "123 Main St",
      city: "Tech City"
   }
};

// Accessing nested objects and arrays
console.log(company.employees[0].name); // Outputs: Alice
console.log(company.address.city); // Outputs: Tech City
```

```
Company Name: Tech Corp
First Employee: Alice
Company City: Tech City
```

Iterating Over Objects and Arrays. Iteration is a common task when working with complex data types. For arrays, we typically use loops like `for`, `forEach`, `map`, and `for...of`. For objects, the `for...in` loop is often used to iterate over properties.

```
// Iterating over an array
let numbers = [1, 2, 3, 4, 5];
for (let i = 0; i < numbers.length; i++) {
   console.log(numbers[i]);
}
```

```
// Using forEach
numbers.forEach(function(number) {
    console.log(number);
});
```

```
1
2
3
4
5
```

```
// Iterating over an object
let car = {
    brand: "Toyota",
    model: "Corolla",
    year: 2020
};

for (let key in car) {
    console.log(key + ": " + car[key]);
}
```

```
brand: Toyota
model: Corolla
year: 2020
```

Manipulating Complex Data Types. JavaScript provides several methods to manipulate objects and arrays, enabling effective data management and transformation.

```
// Cloning objects
let original = { a: 1, b: 2 };
let copy = Object.assign({}, original);
copy.b = 3;

console.log(original); // Outputs: { a: 1, b: 2 }
console.log(copy); // Outputs: { a: 1, b: 3 }

// Merging objects
let obj1 = { a: 1 };
let obj2 = { b: 2 };
let merged = { ...obj1, ...obj2 };

console.log(merged); // Outputs: { a: 1, b: 2 }
```

```
original: { a: 1, b: 2 }
copy: { a: 1, b: 3 }
merged: { a: 1, b: 2 }
```

As we can see, JavaScript's complex data types offer powerful ways to organize and manipulate data. Through objects and arrays, it is possible to build intricate and highly functional data structures.

2.6 Type Conversion and Coercion

Type conversion and coercion are fundamental concepts in JavaScript that affect how data is manipulated and utilized in different contexts. Understanding these concepts is crucial for avoiding unexpected behaviors and bugs in your programs.

Type conversion (also known as type casting) is the explicit transformation of one data type into another. JavaScript provides built-in methods to perform this type of conversion. For example, you can convert a string containing numeric characters into a number.

```
// Explicit type conversion (type casting)
let strNumber = "123";
let num = Number(strNumber); // converts string to number
console.log(num); // Output: 123
```

In the example above, the `Number()` function explicitly converts the string `"123"` to the numeric value `123`. Similarly, the `String()` function can be used to convert a number into a string.

```
let num = 456;
let strNumber = String(num); // converts number to string
console.log(strNumber); // Output: "456"
```

JavaScript also provides methods for converting values to booleans using `Boolean()`.

```
let value1 = Boolean(1); // true
let value2 = Boolean(0); // false
let value3 = Boolean("Hello"); // true
let value4 = Boolean(""); // false
```

In contrast to type conversion, type coercion is the implicit transformation of one data type to another by the JavaScript engine. This can happen when operators are used on mismatched types. For example, the addition operator can coerce a number into a string if one of the operands is a string.

```
let result1 = '5' + 3; // '53' (string coercion)
let result2 = '5' - 3; // 2 (number coercion)
```

In the example `result1`, the number `3` is coerced into the string `'3'` and then concatenated with `'5'`, resulting in `'53'`. In `result2`, the string `'5'` is coerced into the number `5` before performing the subtraction.

Type coercion often occurs in situations involving equality comparisons, especially with the == operator, which performs type conversion before comparison. The === operator, however, does not perform type conversion and compares both value and type.

```
let a = '5';
let b = 5;

console.log(a == b); // true (type coercion)
console.log(a === b); // false (no type coercion)
```

Coercion can involve complex rules. For instance, using + with a string on either side results in string concatenation, whereas using -, *, or / on string operands tries to convert them to numbers. Other types like `null` and `undefined` also have specific coercion rules.

```
console.log(null == 0); // false
console.log(null == undefined); // true
console.log(undefined == 0); // false
console.log('5' * 2); // 10 (string coerced to number)
console.log('five' * 2); // NaN (cannot convert to number)
```

JavaScript has a concept known as "truthy" and "falsy" values, which determines how non-boolean values are coerced into boolean types. Falsy values include `0`, `""` (empty string), `null`, `undefined`, `NaN`, and `false`. All other values are considered truthy.

```
if (0) {
   console.log("This will not execute");
}

if ("") {
   console.log("This will not execute");
}

if ("hello") {
   console.log("This will execute");
}

if (42) {
   console.log("This will execute");
}
```

Understanding type conversion and coercion helps in writing more predictable and robust JavaScript code. It allows developers to foresee and prevent possible pitfalls caused by implicit type changes. These core concepts enable more predictable and reliable control over the behavior of the types in the program, ensuring that variables and expressions behave as expected in various operations and contexts.

2.7 Variable Scope and Hoisting

Scope in JavaScript defines the accessibility of variables, objects, and functions in various parts of the code. Understanding the scope of a variable is crucial in managing its lifecycle and preventing unintended side effects. JavaScript has two types of scope: global scope and local scope. Local scope can be further divided into function scope and block scope, based on where the variable is declared.

A variable declared outside any function or block is in the global scope and can be accessed from anywhere in the code. Conversely, variables declared within a function are in the function scope and can only be accessed within that function. Variables declared with `let` or `const` inside a block (e.g., within braces `{}`) are in the block scope.

```
var globalVar = "I am a global variable";

function exampleFunction() {
    var functionScopedVar = "I am function scoped";
    if (true) {
        let blockScopedVar = "I am block scoped";
        console.log(blockScopedVar); // I am block scoped
    }
    console.log(functionScopedVar); // I am function scoped
    // console.log(blockScopedVar); // ReferenceError: blockScopedVar is not
        defined
}

exampleFunction();
console.log(globalVar); // I am a global variable
// console.log(functionScopedVar); // ReferenceError: functionScopedVar is not
    defined
```

The example above demonstrates the distinction between global, function, and block scope. Accessing a variable outside its scope will result in a `ReferenceError`.

Hoisting is JavaScript's default behavior of moving declarations to the top of their containing scope during the compilation phase. It only hoists the declarations, not the initializations. Variable and function declarations that are hoisted can lead to unexpected behaviors, especially with the `var` keyword since `let` and `const` are not initialized until their definition is evaluated.

```
console.log(hoistedVar); // undefined
var hoistedVar = "I am hoisted";

function hoistedFunction() {
    console.log("I am a hoisted function");
}

hoistedFunction(); // I am a hoisted function
```

```
// console.log(notHoistedLet); // ReferenceError: cannot access 'notHoistedLet'
    before initialization
let notHoistedLet = "I am not hoisted";

// console.log(notHoistedConst); // ReferenceError: cannot access 'notHoistedConst'
    before initialization
const notHoistedConst = "I am not hoisted";
```

In this code, the declaration of `hoistedVar` is moved to the top of its scope, but its initialization remains at its original location. Thus, when `console.log(hoistedVar)` is called, it returns `undefined`. Function declarations are also hoisted, allowing them to be invoked before their declarations in the code.

```
var x = 1;
a(); // logs 10
b(); // TypeError: b is not a function

function a() {
  console.log(10);
}

var b = function() {
  console.log(20);
};
```

In the above example, the function `a` is hoisted, but `b` is treated as a regular variable assignment. Thus, calling `b` before its assignment results in a TypeError because `b` is initially `undefined`.

Block-scoped variables declared with `let` and `const` are not subject to hoisting in the same way. They enter a "temporal dead zone" from the start of their enclosing block until they are initialized. During this period, any reference to the variable will result in a `ReferenceError`.

```
{
   // console.log(temporalVar); // ReferenceError: Cannot access 'temporalVar'
        before initialization
   let temporalVar = 'I am not hoisted';
   console.log(temporalVar); // I am not hoisted
}
```

Understanding these principles aids in writing robust, predictable code. Missteps in variable scope and hoisting can lead to elusive bugs, thus a firm grasp of these concepts is crucial for effective JavaScript programming.

2.8 Constants and Immutability

In JavaScript, constants are declared using the `const` keyword, which stands for constant. Once a variable is defined with `const`, it cannot be reassigned. This immutability is a crucial concept for maintaining data integrity and predictable program behavior. However, it's important to understand the nuances of immutability when working with complex data types.

```
const PI = 3.14159;
PI = 3.14; // This will throw an error
```

Listing 2.1: Declaring a constant in JavaScript

In the above code snippet, attempting to reassign a value to `PI` after it has been declared will result in a TypeError. This property of constants ensures that their value remains constant through the execution of the program.

Despite the immutability of `const` declarations, this does not imply that the value itself is immutable, particularly when dealing with complex data types such as objects and arrays. While the variable binding is immutable, the contents of the object or array it references can still be modified.

```
const car = { brand: 'Toyota', model: 'Corolla' };
car.model = 'Camry'; // This is allowed
car = { brand: 'Honda', model: 'Civic' }; // This will throw an error
```

Listing 2.2: Mutable contents of a constant object

In this example, while the object `car` itself cannot be reassigned to a different object, the properties of `car` can still be changed.

To achieve truly immutable data structures, such as those used in functional programming paradigms, additional techniques or libraries (e.g., Immutable.js) are often employed. By default, JavaScript does not provide built-in mechanisms for deep immutability.

Next, consider arrays, which behave similarly when declared as constants.

```
const colors = ['red', 'blue', 'green'];
colors.push('yellow'); // This is allowed
colors = ['purple', 'orange']; // This will throw an error
```

Listing 2.3: Mutable contents of a constant array

The array `colors` can have elements added or removed, as `push` is a method operating on the contents of the array and not the binding itself. However, reassigning `colors` to a new array is not permitted.

An important aspect to consider is the immutability of primitive and complex data types:

- **Primitive data types** such as numbers, strings, and booleans are inherently immutable. Once created, their value cannot be changed.
- **Complex data types** such as objects and arrays can have their internal structure changed even when declared as constants.

A practical use case for constants in JavaScript is to define configuration values, magic numbers, or any data that should not change throughout the lifespan of the program. Consider the example where an API endpoint is defined as a constant:

```
const API_BASE_URL = 'https://api.example.com/v1/';
fetch(`${API_BASE_URL}users`)
  .then(response => response.json())
  .then(data => console.log(data));
```

Listing 2.4: Using constant for configuration

Declaring `API_BASE_URL` as a constant ensures that the base URL for API requests remains unchanged, adding reliability to the code.

To prevent accidental modification of the contents of objects while maintaining immutability, JavaScript provides `Object.freeze()` and `Object.seal()` methods:

```
const user = { name: 'Alice', age: 25 };
Object.freeze(user);
user.age = 30; // This will be ignored in strict mode or throw an error
```

Listing 2.5: Freezing an object to prevent modifications

Here, the `Object.freeze()` method ensures that no properties of the `user` object can be modified. Attempting to change `user.age` does nothing in non-strict mode or throws an error in strict mode.

While dealing with immutable data structures, it is often beneficial to adopt functional programming techniques. Functions that do not cause side-effects and do not mutate their arguments can lead to more predictable and easier-to-understand code. Methods like `Array.map()`,

Array.filter(), and Array.reduce() serve as examples of such functional programming techniques:

```
const numbers = [1, 2, 3, 4];
const doubled = numbers.map(n => n * 2); // [2, 4, 6, 8]
```

Listing 2.6: Using functional methods to maintain immutability

The original numbers array remains unchanged, and a new array doubled is created with the results of the map() operation.

Understanding constants and immutability in JavaScript lays the groundwork for writing more reliable, maintainable, and bug-free code. It ensures that certain values remain unchanged throughout the execution of a program, providing clarity in the behavior of such variables. This principle is foundational for structuring robust programs, particularly in the context of evolving JavaScript applications and libraries like React, where immutability plays a central role in state management and rendering optimization.

2.9 Template Literals and String Interpolation

Template literals, introduced in ECMAScript 6, represent a significant enhancement in the way strings are handled in JavaScript. Unlike traditional single or double-quoted strings, template literals are enclosed by backticks (" `"), introducing the capability for multiline strings and embedded expressions through string interpolation.

Template literals present several advancements over classic string definitions. With template literals, developers can create strings that span multiple lines without requiring concatenation or newline characters ('\n'). This ability simplifies reading and maintaining the code.

```
let multilineString = `This is a string
that spans multiple
lines.`;
console.log(multilineString);
```

```
This is a string
that spans multiple
lines.
```

One of the most powerful features of template literals is the capability to embed expressions using the ${...} syntax. This approach is known as string interpolation. Using interpolation, variables and expressions can be directly inserted within a string, enhancing readability and expressivity.

```
let a = 5;
let b = 10;
console.log(`The sum of $\{a\} and $\{b\} is $\{a + b\}.`);
```

```
The sum of 5 and 10 is 15.
```

The ${...} form evaluates the expression contained within the braces at runtime, and the result is then concatenated into the surrounding string. This behavior negates the need for complex string concatenations and improves both performance and clarity of the code.

Expressions

Within template literals, any valid JavaScript expression can be embedded using the ${...} syntax. This includes variables, arithmetic operations, function calls, and even complex expressions.

```
let user = { name: 'Alice', age: 25 };
console.log(`User $\{user.name\} is $\{user.age\} years old.`);
```

```
User Alice is 25 years old.
```

Nesting Template Literals

Template literals can also be nested within expressions, allowing for dynamic construction of complex strings. This feature can be particularly useful when generating HTML or constructing query strings.

```
let items = ['apple', 'banana', 'cherry'];
let list = `
<ul>
  $\{items.map(item => `<li>$\{item\}</li>`).join('')\}
</ul>
`;
console.log(list);
```

```
<ul>
  <li>apple</li><li>banana</li><li>cherry</li>
</ul>
```

In this example, the ‘map‘ function iterates over each item in the ‘items‘ array and generates an ‘<li>‘ element for each. The resulting array is then joined into a single string without additional separators, culminating in a formatted HTML unordered list.

Tagged Templates

Template literals also support a construct known as tagged template literals. Tag functions provide a mechanism to customize the construction of template literals by processing and modifying the raw string and interpolation values before they are combined. This feature can be used for a variety of purposes, such as escaping characters in unsafe strings or translating messages into different languages.

The syntax for tagged templates involves prefixing the template literal with a function name that will act as the tag processor.

```
function tag(strings, ...values) {
    console.log(strings);
    console.log(values);
    return strings[0] + values.join('');
}

let output = tag`Hello, $\{user.name\}!`;
console.log(output);
```

```
["Hello, ", "!"]
["Alice"]
Hello, Alice!
```

In this example, the 'tag' function is invoked with two arguments: an array of literal string segments ('strings') and an array of evaluated interpolation values ('values'). This allows the function to properly reconstruct the final string or apply any required transformations.

Raw Strings

Within tagged template literals, the 'String.raw' method can be used to obtain the raw string representation of the template literal, disregarding the usual processing of escape sequences. This feature is especially useful for strings containing file paths or regular expressions where escape characters should be retained.

```
let path = `C:\Users\$\{user.name\}\Documents`;
console.log(path); // Incorrect due to escape sequence processing
let rawPath = String.raw`C:\Users\$\{user.name\}\Documents`;
console.log(rawPath); // Correctly displays the raw path
```

```
C:UsersAliceDocuments
C:\Users\Alice\Documents
```

The second console output demonstrates that ‘String.raw‘ properly retains the backslashes, preserving the intended path format.

Understanding the functionality and applications of template literals and string interpolation equips developers with robust tools for dynamic string handling, leading to more readable and maintainable JavaScript code.

2.10 Working with Numbers and BigInt

JavaScript primarily utilizes the ‘Number‘ data type to represent numerical values. The ‘Number‘ type in JavaScript is a double-precision 64-bit binary format IEEE 754 value. This format enables the representation of both integers and floating-point numbers. It is essential to understand the various operations that can be performed on numbers, the precision limitations, and the introduction of the ‘BigInt‘ data type for handling arbitrarily large integers.

Mathematical operations can be performed on numbers using common arithmetic operators such as ‘+‘, ‘-‘, ‘*‘, ‘/‘, and ‘

```
// Example of basic arithmetic operations
let a = 10;
let b = 4;
console.log(a + b); // Output: 14
console.log(a - b); // Output: 6
console.log(a * b); // Output: 40
console.log(a / b); // Output: 2.5
console.log(a % b); // Output: 2
```

In addition to basic arithmetic, JavaScript provides a ‘Math‘ object which contains a variety of mathematical functions and constants. For example:

- ‘Math.pow(x, y)‘ computes x^y.
- ‘Math.sqrt(x)‘ computes the square root of x.
- ‘Math.abs(x)‘ returns the absolute value of x.
- Constants such as ‘Math.PI‘ for π.

```
// Example of using Math object functions
let x = 16;
console.log(Math.pow(x, 2)); // Output: 256
```

```
console.log(Math.sqrt(x)); // Output: 4
console.log(Math.abs(-x)); // Output: 16
console.log(Math.PI); // Output: 3.141592653589793
```

Precision and Limitations

A critical aspect of working with the 'Number' data type is understanding its precision limitations. In JavaScript, the precision of floating-point arithmetic is restricted by the IEEE 754 standard, which can lead to rounding errors in some calculations. For example:

```
// Floating-point precision issues
console.log(0.1 + 0.2); // Output: 0.30000000000000004
console.log(0.3 - 0.1); // Output: 0.19999999999999998
```

This behavior is inherent to the way floating-point arithmetic is handled in binary systems. Therefore, when dealing with financial calculations or other scenarios requiring high precision, it is advisable to use libraries such as 'big.js' or 'decimal.js' that offer arbitrary-precision arithmetic.

The 'BigInt' Data Type

To handle integers larger than the 'Number' type can safely represent (`Number.MAX_SAFE_INTEGER`), JavaScript introduced the 'BigInt' data type. 'BigInt' allows the representation of whole numbers larger than $2^{53} - 1$ and provides arbitrary magnitude and precision for integer calculations.

A 'BigInt' is created by appending 'n' to the end of an integer literal or using the 'BigInt' constructor:

```
// Creating BigInt values
let bigInt1 = 1234567890123456789012345678901234567890n;
let bigInt2 = BigInt("1234567890123456789012345678901234567890");
console.log(bigInt1); // Output: 1234567890123456789012345678901234567890n
console.log(bigInt2); // Output: 1234567890123456789012345678901234567890n
```

Arithmetic operations on 'BigInt' values are similar to those on 'Number' values:

```
// Arithmetic operations with BigInt
let a = 1234567890123456789012345678901234567890n;
let b = 1234567890123456789012345678901234567890n;
console.log(a + b); // Output: 2469135780246913578024691357802469135780n
console.log(a - b); // Output: 0n
console.log(a * b); // Output: A very large BigInt
```

```
console.log(a / b); // Output: 1n
console.log(a % b); // Output: 0n
```

It is crucial to note that mixing 'BigInt' and 'Number' types in arithmetic operations will throw an error due to the differing precision and representation. Explicit type conversion is required:

```
// Mixing BigInt and Number types
let num = 10;
let bigInt = 10n;
console.log(bigInt + BigInt(num)); // Output: 20n
console.log(Number(bigInt) + num); // Output: 20
```

This section has covered the essentials of working with 'Number' and 'BigInt' data types in JavaScript. Understanding the basics of arithmetic operations, precision limitations of floating-point numbers, and the utilization of 'BigInt' for large integers provides a robust foundation for effectively managing numerical data in JavaScript programming.

2.11 Booleans and Comparison Operations

Booleans are one of the fundamental data types in JavaScript, representing logical values. A Boolean can only have one of two values: `true` or `false`. These values are integral to control structures like `if` statements, loops, and other conditional logic. Understanding how to utilize Booleans effectively, alongside comparison operations, is essential for making decisions in your code.

Booleans are typically the result of comparison operations, which compare two values and return a Boolean value. JavaScript provides a variety of comparison operators, including:

- == (Equality)
- === (Strict Equality)
- != (Inequality)
- !== (Strict Inequality)
- > (Greater than)
- >= (Greater than or equal to)
- < (Less than)
- <= (Less than or equal to)

Equality (==) and Strict Equality (===)

The == operator compares two values for equality, performing type coercion if necessary. For example:

```
console.log(5 == '5'); // true
console.log(true == 1); // true
console.log(false == 0); // true
```

Here, JavaScript converts the string `'5'` to the number `5` before making the comparison, which results in `true`. Similarly, `true` is coerced to `1` and `false` to `0`.

In contrast, the === operator, known as the strict equality operator, compares both the value and the type without performing any type coercion:

```
console.log(5 === '5'); // false
console.log(true === 1); // false
console.log(false === 0); // false
```

In these cases, the comparisons result in `false` because the types of the values being compared do not match.

Inequality (!=) and Strict Inequality (!==)

The != operator checks if two values are not equal, again performing type coercion if necessary:

```
console.log(5 != '5'); // false
console.log(true != 1); // false
console.log(false != 0); // false
```

The !== operator, meanwhile, operates similarly to the strict equality operator, checking both value and type without coercion:

```
console.log(5 !== '5'); // true
console.log(true !== 1); // true
console.log(false !== 0); // true
```

Greater than and Less than Operators

The greater than (>) and less than (<) operators compare numeric values directly. When applied to values of other types, type coercion occurs. For strings, the comparison is based on lexicographic order (dictionary order).

```
console.log(10 > 5); // true
```

```
console.log('apple' < 'orange'); // true
console.log('apple' > 'Apple'); // true (case-sensitive comparison)
console.log('5' > 2); // true ('5' coerced to number 5)
```

Greater than or Equal to and Less than or Equal to Operators

The greater than or equal to (>=) and less than or equal to (<=) operators function similarly to their non-equal counterparts, adding equality to the comparison:

```
console.log(10 >= 5); // true
console.log(5 >= 5); // true
console.log(2 <= 3); // true
console.log(3 <= 3); // true
```

Boolean Logic and Compound Comparisons

JavaScript also supports Boolean logic operators that allow for combining multiple comparisons. These include:

- && (Logical AND)
- || (Logical OR)
- ! (Logical NOT)

The logical AND (&&) operator returns `true` only if both operands are `true`:

```
console.log(true \&\& true); // true
console.log(true \&\& false); // false
console.log(false \&\& false); // false
console.log(5 > 3 \&\& 10 < 20); // true
```

The logical OR (||) operator returns `true` if at least one of the operands is `true`:

```
console.log(true || false); // true
console.log(false || false); // false
console.log(5 > 10 || 20 < 30); // true
```

The logical NOT (`!`) operator negates the value of its operand, converting `true` to `false` and vice versa:

```
console.log(!true); // false
console.log(!false); // true
console.log(!(5 > 3)); // false
```

By understanding and correctly applying Booleans and comparison operations, developers can create robust and efficient conditional logic in their JavaScript programs. The ability to logically evaluate scenarios and make decisions based on various conditions is a cornerstone of programming.

2.12 Special Values: Null, Undefined, and NaN

In JavaScript, there are several special values that behave differently from standard data types. Understanding these values extemdash `null`, `undefined`, and `NaN` extemdash is crucial for avoiding common pitfalls and effectively managing data.

Null and Undefined:

- `undefined` is a primitive value automatically assigned to variables that have just been declared or to function parameters for which no arguments are provided. It signifies that the variable has been declared but not yet assigned a value.

- `null` is an intentional absence of any object value. It is commonly used to indicate that a variable should have no value.

Consider the following example to illustrate the distinct roles of `undefined` and `null`:

```
let x;
console.log(x); // Output: undefined

function exampleFunc(y) {
  console.log(y);
}
exampleFunc(); // Output: undefined

let z = null;
console.log(z); // Output: null
```

Here, the variable `x` is declared but not assigned, producing `undefined`. Similarly, calling `exampleFunc` without arguments results in `y` being `undefined`. Meanwhile, `z` is explicitly assigned the value `null`.

One of the common confusions arises when comparing `null` and `undefined`:

```
console.log(null == undefined); // Output: true
console.log(null === undefined); // Output: false
```

The loose equality (==) comparison shows that `null` and `undefined` are considered equal, whereas the strict equality (===) indicates they are not strictly equal because they are of different types.

NaN (Not-a-Number):

`NaN` is a special numeric value representing a quantitive value that is not a valid number. Operations resulting in undefined or unrepresentable numerical results yield `NaN`. Common instances leading to `NaN` include parsing errors or invalid arithmetic operations.

Examples of `NaN` occurrence are as follows:

```
console.log(parseInt("abc")); // Output: NaN
console.log(0 / 0); // Output: NaN
console.log(Math.sqrt(-1)); // Output: NaN
console.log(undefined + 1); // Output: NaN
```

The `parseInt` function returns `NaN` when it cannot parse a string as a number. Division by zero, taking the square root of a negative number, and performing arithmetic with `undefined` also result in `NaN`.

A notable property of `NaN` is that it is not equal to itself:

```
console.log(NaN == NaN); // Output: false
console.log(NaN === NaN); // Output: false
```

To test whether a value is `NaN`, the `Number.isNaN` method or the global `isNaN` function should be used, taking care to note that the global `isNaN` function has different behavior:

```
console.log(Number.isNaN(NaN)); // Output: true
console.log(Number.isNaN("NaN")); // Output: false

console.log(isNaN(NaN)); // Output: true
console.log(isNaN("NaN")); // Output: true
```

The `Number.isNaN` method is a more robust way to check for `NaN` as it does not coerce the argument to a number, unlike the global `isNaN` function.

Understanding how these special values work and how they differ ensures that developers can manage data effectively while avoiding unexpected behavior in their JavaScript programs. Each value has its specific application contexts, and recognizing them provides the foundation for managing control flows and error handling in scripts.

Chapter 3

Operators and Expressions

This chapter explores the various operators and expressions used in JavaScript to manipulate data and perform computations. It covers arithmetic, assignment, string, comparison, logical, and bitwise operators, as well as the ternary operator. The chapter also explains operator precedence, associativity, and the evaluation of expressions. Additionally, it introduces the concept of short-circuit evaluation, which can optimize code execution and decision-making. Understanding these concepts is essential for writing efficient and effective JavaScript code.

3.1 Introduction to Operators

In JavaScript, operators are special symbols used to perform operations on operands. These operands can be variables, constants, or literals. Operators allow for the manipulation of data, the evaluation of certain conditions, and the performance of calculations. Understanding the variety of operators in JavaScript is essential for the development of robust and efficient code.

JavaScript operators can be classified into multiple categories: arithmetic, assignment, string, comparison, logical, bitwise, and ternary. Each category encompasses different operations and has distinct functionalities. Operators are fundamental in building expressions that compute values and control the flow of the program.

Arithmetic operators are the most basic type of operators, enabling arithmetic computations. This category includes addition (+), subtraction (-), multiplication (*), division (/), modulus (%), increment (++), and decrement (–). Arithmetic operators are utilized to perform common mathematical operations.

```
// Examples of arithmetic operators
let x = 10;
let y = 5;

let addition = x + y; // Addition: 10 + 5 = 15
let subtraction = x - y; // Subtraction: 10 - 5 = 5
let multiplication = x * y; // Multiplication: 10 * 5 = 50
let division = x / y; // Division: 10 / 5 = 2
let modulus = x % y; // Modulus: 10 % 5 = 0

x++; // Increment: x becomes 11
y--; // Decrement: y becomes 4
```

Assignment operators are used to assign values to variables. The simplest assignment operator is the equal sign (=), which assigns the value on its right to the variable on its left. There are also compound assignment operators that combine arithmetic operations with assignment, such as +=, -=, *=, /=, and %=, which perform the arithmetic operation and then assign the result to the variable.

```
// Examples of assignment operators
let z = 10; // Simple assignment: z is assigned 10

z += 5; // Addition assignment: z is now 15 (10 + 5)
z -= 3; // Subtraction assignment: z is now 12 (15 - 3)
z *= 2; // Multiplication assignment: z is now 24 (12 * 2)
z /= 6; // Division assignment: z is now 4 (24 / 6)
z %= 3; // Modulus assignment: z is now 1 (4 % 3)
```

String operators primarily include the concatenation operator (+), which combines two strings into one. In JavaScript, the '+' operator can be used between strings to join them together, facilitating the construction of complex strings from simpler ones.

```
// Example of string concatenation
let str1 = "Hello";
let str2 = "World";

let greeting = str1 + " " + str2; // Concatenation: "Hello World"
```

Comparison operators are used to compare two values and determine their equality or relational order. These operators return a Boolean value: true or false. Common comparison operators include:

equal to (==), not equal to (!=), strict equal to (===), strict not equal to (!==), greater than (>), less than (<), greater than or equal to (>=), and less than or equal to (<=).

```
// Examples of comparison operators
let a = 10;
let b = 20;

console.log(a == b); // Equal to: false
console.log(a != b); // Not equal to: true
console.log(a === 10); // Strict equal to: true
console.log(a !== 10); // Strict not equal to: false
console.log(a > b); // Greater than: false
console.log(a < b); // Less than: true
console.log(a >= 10); // Greater than or equal to: true
console.log(a <= 9); // Less than or equal to: false
```

Logical operators are used to combine or invert Boolean values. The three main logical operators in JavaScript are: logical AND (&&), logical OR (||), and logical NOT (!). These operators are essential for constructing complex conditional statements and controlling the logical flow of a program.

```
// Examples of logical operators
let truthy = true;
let falsy = false;

console.log(truthy && falsy); // Logical AND: false
console.log(truthy || falsy); // Logical OR: true
console.log(!truthy); // Logical NOT: false
```

Bitwise operators perform operations on the binary representations of numbers. These include bitwise AND (&), OR (|), XOR (∧), NOT ( ), and bit shifts (<<, >>, >>>). Bitwise operators are often used for low-level programming tasks, such as manipulating individual bits in a data structure.

```
// Examples of bitwise operators
let m = 5; // Binary: 0101
let n = 3; // Binary: 0011

console.log(m & n); // Bitwise AND: 1 (Binary: 0001)
console.log(m | n); // Bitwise OR: 7 (Binary: 0111)
console.log(m ^ n); // Bitwise XOR: 6 (Binary: 0110)
console.log(~m); // Bitwise NOT: -6 (Binary: ...11111010 due to two's complement)
console.log(m << 1); // Left shift: 10 (Binary: 1010)
console.log(m >> 1); // Right shift: 2 (Binary: 0010)
```

The ternary operator (?:) is a shorthand for simple if-else statements. It takes three operands: a condition, a value if the condition is true, and a value if the condition is false. This operator provides a concise syntax to assign values conditionally.

```
// Example of ternary operator
let age = 18;
let canVote = (age >= 18) ? "Yes" : "No"; // Conditional assignment: "Yes"
```

Operators are evaluated based on a set of rules known as **operator precedence** and **associativity**. Precedence determines the order in which operations are performed in expressions with multiple operators. For instance, multiplication and division have higher precedence than addition and subtraction, so they are performed first. Associativity defines the direction in which operators with the same precedence level are processed, typically left-to-right or right-to-left.

```
// Example of operator precedence
let result = 2 + 3 * 5; // Multiplication is performed first, result is 17

// Example of operator associativity
let a = b = c = 10; // Assignment operators are right-associative, all variables
    are set to 10
```

Mastering operators and their usage in JavaScript expressions enables the creation of sophisticated and efficient programs. Each operator type serves a specific purpose and integrates unique functionalities, enhancing the language's capabilities in data manipulation, computation, and decision-making processes.

3.2 Arithmetic Operators

Arithmetic operators in JavaScript are employed to perform mathematical computations. The fundamental arithmetic operators include addition (+), subtraction (-), multiplication (*), division (/), modulus (%), increment (++), and decrement (–). These operators are integral in manipulating numerical data and constructing expressions that involve mathematical logic. Below, we will delve into each operator, providing examples and explaining their behavior.

Addition (+): The addition operator performs the arithmetic sum of two operands. It concatenates strings when used with string operands but retains its arithmetic functionality with numbers.

```
// Example of addition with numbers
let a = 5;
let b = 10;
let sum = a + b; // sum will be 15

// Example of addition with strings
let str1 = "Hello, ";
let str2 = "world!";
```

```
let greeting = str1 + str2; // greeting will be "Hello, world!"
```

Subtraction (-): The subtraction operator computes the difference between two operands.

```
// Example of subtraction
let c = 20;
let d = 8;
let difference = c - d; // difference will be 12
```

Multiplication (*): The multiplication operator calculates the product of two operands.

```
// Example of multiplication
let e = 6;
let f = 7;
let product = e * f; // product will be 42
```

Division (/): The division operator divides the first operand by the second operand. The result is a floating-point number unless both operands are integers and the result is exact.

```
// Example of division
let g = 20;
let h = 4;
let quotient = g / h; // quotient will be 5

let i = 22;
let j = 7;
let result = i / j; // result will be approximately 3.142857142857143
```

Modulus (%): The modulus operator returns the remainder of the division of the first operand by the second operand.

```
// Example of modulus
let k = 10;
let l = 3;
let remainder = k % l; // remainder will be 1
```

Increment (++): The increment operator increases the value of its operand by one. It can be used as a prefix (++var) or postfix (var++).

```
// Example of increment
let m = 5;
m++; // m will be 6 (postfix increment)

let n = 8;
++n; // n will be 9 (prefix increment)
```

Decrement (–): The decrement operator decreases the value of its operand by one. Similar to increment, it can be used as a prefix (–var) or postfix (var–).

```
// Example of decrement
let o = 5;
o--; // o will be 4 (postfix decrement)

let p = 8;
--p; // p will be 7 (prefix decrement)
```

When working with these operators, one should consider operator precedence and associativity rules that govern the order of operations within expressions. Arithmetic operators typically follow the conventional precedence where multiplication, division, and modulus are evaluated before addition and subtraction. For example:

```
let q = 5 + 3 * 2; // q will be 11 because multiplication is executed before
    addition
let r = (5 + 3) * 2; // r will be 16 because parentheses alter the natural
    precedence
```

In complex expressions, explicitly defining evaluation order with parentheses ensures clear intent and avoids errors due to unexpected operator precedence. Constructing expressions judiciously with a solid understanding of these operators fosters the development of efficient and predictable JavaScript code.

3.3 Assignment Operators

Assignment operators in JavaScript are fundamental to the process of storing values within variables. The basic assignment operator is the equal sign =, which assigns the value on its right to the variable on its left. Beyond the basic assignment, there are compound assignment operators that perform an operation on a variable and then assign the result back to that variable.

The syntax for the basic assignment is straightforward:

```
let x = 10;
```

In this example, `x` is assigned the value `10`.

Compound Assignment Operators

Compound assignment operators combine arithmetic or bitwise operations with assignment, providing a shorthand notation. The following table lists all compound assignment operators available in JavaScript:

Operator	Description	Equivalent Operation
+=	Addition assignment	a += b → a = a + b
-=	Subtraction assignment	a -= b → a = a - b
*=	Multiplication assignment	a *= b → a = a * b
/=	Division assignment	a /= b → a = a / b
%=	Remainder assignment	a %= b → a = a % b
&=	Bitwise AND assignment	a &= b → a = a & b
|=	Bitwise OR assignment	a |= b → a = a | b
^=	Bitwise XOR assignment	a ^= b → a = a ^b
<<=	Left shift assignment	a <<= b → a = a << b
>>=	Right shift assignment	a >>= b → a = a >> b
>>>=	Unsigned right shift assignment	a >>>= b → a = a >>> b

Examples and Use Cases

Consider the following examples which illustrate the use of the compound assignment operators:

```
let a = 5;
let b = 2;

// Addition assignment
a += b; // equivalent to a = a + b
console.log(a); // output: 7

// Subtraction assignment
a -= b; // equivalent to a = a - b
console.log(a); // output: 5

// Multiplication assignment
a *= b; // equivalent to a = a * b
console.log(a); // output: 10

// Division assignment
a /= b; // equivalent to a = a / b
console.log(a); // output: 5

// Remainder assignment
a %= b; // equivalent to a = a \% b
console.log(a); // output: 1
```

These operators help in making the code more concise and are especially useful in iterative operations commonly found in loops.

Practical Application in Loops

Assignment operators are particularly beneficial in cases where a variable needs to be updated iteratively. Consider a scenario of computing the factorial of a number using a loop:

```
function factorial(n) {
  let result = 1;
  for (let i = 1; i <= n; i++) {
    result *= i; // equivalent to result = result * i
  }
  return result;
}

console.log(factorial(5)); // output: 120
```

In this example, `result *= i` simplifies the cumulative product calculation inside the loop.

Bitwise Assignment Operators

Bitwise assignment operators combine bitwise operations and assignment. These are used less frequently but are useful in scenarios involving low-level data manipulation, such as graphics programming or implementing bit masks.

```
let x = 12; // binary: 1100
let y = 5; // binary: 0101

// Bitwise AND assignment
x &= y; // equivalent to x = x & y
console.log(x); // output: 4 (binary: 0100)

// Bitwise OR assignment
x |= y; // equivalent to x = x | y
console.log(x); // output: 5 (binary: 0101)

// Bitwise XOR assignment
x ^= y; // equivalent to x = x ^ y
console.log(x); // output: 0 (binary: 0000)

// Left shift assignment
x <<= 1; // equivalent to x = x << 1
console.log(x); // output: 0

// Right shift assignment
x >>= 1; // equivalent to x = x >> 1
console.log(x); // output: 0

// Unsigned right shift assignment
x >>>= 1; // equivalent to x = x >>> 1
console.log(x); // output: 0
```

Understanding and efficiently using assignment operators in JavaScript is key to writing optimized code by reducing redundancy and improving readability.

3.4 String Operators

String operators in JavaScript are fundamental for manipulating and evaluating string data. These operators enable you to concatenate strings, compare them, and perform various transformations and searches. Understanding how to effectively use string operators is crucial for tasks ranging from simple string concatenations to complex pattern matching.

The primary string operator is the concatenation operator, represented by the plus symbol (+). This operator merges two or more strings into one. For example:

```
let greeting = "Hello, " + "world!";
console.log(greeting); // Outputs: Hello, world!
```

This operation takes two string operands, `"Hello, "` and `"world!"`, and produces a single concatenated string.

In addition to the standard concatenation using the + operator, JavaScript also supports the concatenation assignment operator (+=). This operator appends the right-hand string operand to the left-hand string operand and assigns the result to the left-hand variable. Consider the following example:

```
let message = "The quick brown fox";
message += " jumps over the lazy dog.";
console.log(message); // Outputs: The quick brown fox jumps over the
    lazy dog.
```

Here, `message += " jumps over the lazy dog.";` effectively modifies the `message` variable by appending the new string to its existing content.

String comparison in JavaScript can be performed using the comparison operators discussed earlier, such as ===, !==, <, >, <=, and >=. These operators allow for lexicographical evaluation of strings based on Unicode values. For example:

```
let str1 = "apple";
let str2 = "banana";

console.log(str1 === str2); // Outputs: false
console.log(str1 < str2); // Outputs: true
```

In this snippet, `str1 < str2` evaluates to true because "apple" precedes "banana" lexicographically.

Furthermore, JavaScript provides several methods for manipulating strings, which function effectively as operators. Some of the most commonly used methods include `.concat()`, `.slice()`, `.substring()`, `.substr()`, and `.replace()`.

```
let text = "JavaScript";
let newText = text.concat(" is versatile.");
console.log(newText); // Outputs: JavaScript is versatile.

let slicedText = text.slice(0, 4);
console.log(slicedText); // Outputs: Java

let substringText = text.substring(4, 10);
console.log(substringText); // Outputs: Script

let replacedText = text.replace("Java", "Type");
console.log(replacedText); // Outputs: TypeScript
```

In this example, `.concat()` combines the strings "JavaScript" and " is versatile." into one string. `.slice()` extracts a section of the string from index 0 to 4, resulting in "Java". `.substring()` retrieves characters from index 4 to 10, yielding "Script". Lastly, `.replace()` substitutes "Java" with "Type", producing "TypeScript".

Another useful method is `.split()`, which divides a string into an array based on a specified delimiter.

```
let csv = "apple,banana,cherry";
let fruits = csv.split(",");
console.log(fruits); // Outputs: ["apple", "banana", "cherry"]
```

This method is particularly useful for breaking down strings into manageable parts, which can then be processed individually.

Additionally, template literals (introduced in ES6) offer a more flexible way to concatenate strings and embed expressions. Template literals are enclosed by backticks (`) and allow for interpolation using the `$expression` syntax.

```
let name = "John";
let age = 30;
let intro = `My name is \${name} and I am \${age} years old.`;
console.log(intro); // Outputs: My name is John and I am 30 years old.
```

Template literals enhance readability and maintainability by seamlessly embedding variables and expressions within strings.

Understanding string operators and methods is essential for effective string manipulation in JavaScript. These functionalities enhance the ability to handle text with precision, offering tools for a wide range of operations, from basic concatenation to complex pattern processing.

3.5 Comparison Operators

Comparison operators in JavaScript are used to compare two values and return a boolean result, true or false, based on whether the comparison is true or false. These operators are essential for making decisions in the code, guiding the program flow through conditional statements such as `if`, `else if`, and `switch` structures. Understanding how each comparison operator behaves with different types of operands is crucial for accurate and logical code execution.

JavaScript provides several types of comparison operators:

- == (equal to)
- === (strictly equal to)
- != (not equal to)
- !== (strictly not equal to)
- > (greater than)
- >= (greater than or equal to)
- < (less than)
- <= (less than or equal to)

Each of these operators can be used with various data types, including numbers, strings, and objects. Below are detailed explanations and examples showcasing the usage and nuances of each comparison operator.

== (Equal to) checks if the values of two operands are equal, performing type coercion if necessary. This means that before making the comparison, JavaScript converts the operands to the same type.

```
// Example of '=='
console.log(5 == '5'); // Output: true
```

```
true
```

In this example, the number `5` is compared to the string `'5'`. Due to type coercion, the string is converted to a number, and since they are equal, the result is `true`.

=== (Strictly equal to) checks if the values and the types of two operands are equal. No type coercion is performed, making it a more predictable and safer comparison.

```
// Example of '==='
console.log(5 === '5'); // Output: false
```

```
false
```

Here, since the number `5` and the string `'5'` are of different types, the result is `false`, highlighting the importance of using strict equality for type-safe comparisons.

!= (Not equal to) checks if the values of two operands are not equal, performing type coercion if necessary.

```
// Example of '!='
console.log(5 != '5'); // Output: false
```

```
false
```

In this instance, the number `5` and the string `'5'` are considered equal after type coercion, so the result is `false`.

!== (Strictly not equal to) checks if the values and types of two operands are not equal. No type coercion is performed.

```
// Example of '!=='
console.log(5 !== '5'); // Output: true
```

```
true
```

Since the types of `5` and `'5'` differ, the result is `true`, demonstrating that they are not strictly equal.

> (Greater than) checks if the value on the left operand is greater than the value on the right operand.

```
// Example of '>'
console.log(10 > 5); // Output: true
```

```
true
```

Here, `10` is indeed greater than `5`, so the comparison returns `true`.

>= (Greater than or equal to) checks if the value on the left operand is

greater than or equal to the value on the right operand.

```
// Example of '>='
console.log(10 >= 10); // Output: true
```

```
true
```

This operator returns `true` because `10` is equal to `10`.

< (Less than) checks if the value on the left operand is less than the value on the right operand.

```
// Example of '<'
console.log(5 < 10); // Output: true
```

```
true
```

Since `5` is less than `10`, the result is `true`.

<= (Less than or equal to) checks if the value on the left operand is less than or equal to the value on the right operand.

```
// Example of '<='
console.log(5 <= 5); // Output: true
```

```
true
```

Here, the operator returns `true` because `5` is equal to `5`.

These comparison operators also work with strings, comparing their Unicode values.

```
// Example with strings
console.log('apple' > 'banana'); // Output: false
```

```
false
```

In Unicode, the comparison proceeds character by character, and since `'a'` is less than `'b'`, the overall result is `false`.

Comparison operators can also be used in more complex expressions and conditions.

```
// Example with complex conditions
let age = 20;
let hasLicense = true;

if (age >= 18 && hasLicense) {
    console.log('You can drive.');
} else {
    console.log('You cannot drive.');
}
// Output: 'You can drive.'
```

```
You can drive.
```

In this example, multiple comparisons are combined using logical operators to create a compound condition, demonstrating how comparison operators are integral to control flow in JavaScript.

3.6 Logical Operators

Logical operators are fundamental components in JavaScript that are used to perform logical operations, typically involving Boolean values. These operators can also work with expressions that evaluate to non-Boolean values, utilizing JavaScript's type conversion and short-circuiting features. The logical operators include AND ('&&'), OR ('||'), and NOT ('¡). Each of these is essential for constructing complex decision-making expressions and enhancing code control flow.

The AND operator ('&&') returns 'true' if and only if both operands are 'true'. Otherwise, it returns 'false'. The OR operator ('||'), on the other hand, returns 'true' if at least one of the operands is 'true'. If both operands are 'false', then it returns 'false'. The NOT operator ('¡), which is a unary operator, inverts the value of its operand: if the operand is 'true', the result is 'false', and vice versa.

Consider the following simple examples that utilize these operators:

```
let x = true;
let y = false;

console.log(x && y); // Output: false
console.log(x || y); // Output: true
console.log(!x); // Output: false
console.log(!y); // Output: true
```

These outputs can be derived by evaluating each logical expression:

```
false
true
false
true
```

Type Conversion in Logical Operations

JavaScript's logical operators can work with non-Boolean operands due to implicit type conversion. This feature exploits JavaScript's ability to coerce operands to Boolean values during evaluation.

Consider the '&&' and '||' operators used with non-Boolean values:

```
let a = 0;
let b = 1;

console.log(a && b); // Output: 0
console.log(a || b); // Output: 1
console.log(b || a); // Output: 1
```

The outputs of these operations are determined as follows:

```
0
1
1
```

- For 'a && b', since 'a' is '0' (falsy), it returns 'a'.
- For 'a || b', since 'a' is falsy, it returns 'b'.
- For 'b || a', since 'b' is '1' (truthy), it returns 'b'.

Short-Circuit Evaluation

JavaScript utilizes short-circuit evaluation with logical operators. In '&&' operations, if the first operand evaluates to 'false', the second operand is not evaluated because the result is already 'false'. Similarly, in '||' operations, if the first operand evaluates to 'true', the second operand is not evaluated since the result is determined to be 'true'.

Consider the following:

```
let str = "";
let num = 10;

str && console.log("This will not be printed");
num || console.log("This will not be printed");
```

No output is produced by these lines because:

- In 'str && console.log("This will not be printed")', 'str' is an empty string (falsy), so 'console.log' is not executed.
- In 'num || console.log("This will not be printed")', 'num' is '10' (truthy), so the 'console.log' statement is not executed.

Combining Logical Operators

Logical operators can be combined to form complex logical expressions for intricate decision-making processes. The precedence of logical operators must be considered when combining them. The NOT operator ('¡) has the highest precedence, followed by the AND operator ('&&'), and then the OR operator ('||').

For instance:

```
let x = true;
let y = false;
let z = true;

let result = x && !y || z;
console.log(result); // Output: true
```

Here, the expression evaluates as:

```
true
```

The NOT operator applies first ('!y' becomes 'true'), then the AND operator evaluates ('x && true' yields 'true'), and lastly the OR operator ('true || z') determines the final result.

Logical operators are indispensable in JavaScript for managing flow control, conditional evaluations, and succinctly expressing complex logic. Understanding their behavior with type conversions and short-circuit evaluations allows developers to write more efficient and readable code.

3.7 Bitwise Operators

Bitwise operators perform operations on binary representations of integers. These operators allow manipulation at the most granular level, directly at the bit level, which is often essential for tasks that require optimization or interfacing with low-level systems such as hardware interfaces or network protocols.

JavaScript supports several bitwise operators, including AND (&), OR (|), XOR (^), NOT (~), Left Shift («), Sign-Propagating Right Shift (»), and Zero-Fill Right Shift (»>). Each operator treats its operands as a sequence of 32 bits (binary digits), rather than numbers. This section explores each of these operators in detail.

The bitwise operators include:

- **AND (&)**: This operator performs a bitwise AND operation, where each bit in the result is 1 if the corresponding bits of both operands are 1, otherwise it is 0.
- **OR (|)**: This operator performs a bitwise OR operation, where each bit in the result is 1 if at least one of the corresponding bits of the operands is 1, otherwise it is 0.
- **XOR (^)**: This operator performs a bitwise XOR (exclusive OR) operation, where each bit in the result is 1 if the corresponding bits of the operands are different, otherwise it is 0.
- **NOT (~)**: This operator performs a bitwise NOT operation, which inverts all bits of its operand. Every 0 becomes 1 and every 1 becomes 0.
- **Left Shift («)**: This operator shifts the bits of its first operand to the left by the number of positions specified by the second operand.
- **Sign-Propagating Right Shift (»)**: This operator shifts the bits of its first operand to the right. The leftmost bits are filled based on the sign bit (i.e., the sign bit is propagated).
- **Zero-Fill Right Shift (»>)**: This operator shifts the bits of its first operand to the right. The leftmost bits are always filled with zeros, regardless of the sign.

Let us look at each operator with JavaScript code examples.

```
let a = 5; // 5: 00000000000000000000000000000101
let b = 3; // 3: 00000000000000000000000000000011
let result = a & b; // And operation: 00000000000000000000000000000001
console.log(result); // 1
```

Listing 3.1: Bitwise AND (&)

In this example, ‘5‘ in binary is ‘00000000000000000000000000000101‘, and ‘3‘ is ‘00000000000000000000000000000011‘. The bitwise AND operation results in ‘00000000000000000000000000000001‘, which is ‘1‘ in decimal.

```
let a = 5; // 5: 00000000000000000000000000000101
let b = 3; // 3: 00000000000000000000000000000011
let result = a | b; // Or operation: 00000000000000000000000000000111
console.log(result); // 7
```

Listing 3.2: Bitwise OR (|)

Here, the bitwise OR operation between '5' ('00000000000000000000000000000101') and '3' ('00000000000000000000000000000011') results in '00000000000000000000000000000111', which is '7' in decimal.

```
let a = 5; // 5: 00000000000000000000000000000101
let b = 3; // 3: 00000000000000000000000000000011
let result = a ^ b; // XOR operation: 00000000000000000000000000000110
console.log(result); // 6
```

Listing 3.3: Bitwise XOR (^)

For the XOR operation, the result is '00000000000000000000000000000110', which is '6' in decimal.

```
let a = 5; // 5: 00000000000000000000000000000101
let result = ~a; // NOT operation: 11111111111111111111111111111010
console.log(result); // -6
```

Listing 3.4: Bitwise NOT (~)

The bitwise NOT operation inverts all the bits. For '5', the inverted bits are '11111111111111111111111111111010', which interprets as '-6' in JavaScript due to the two's complement representation of negative numbers.

```
let a = 5; // 5: 00000000000000000000000000000101
let result = a << 1; // Left shift: 00000000000000000000000000001010
console.log(result); // 10
```

Listing 3.5: Left Shift («)

In this example, left-shifting '5' by one position moves all its bits one place to the left, resulting in '10' ('00000000000000000000000000001010').

```
let a = -5; // -5: 11111111111111111111111111111011
let result = a >> 1; // Right shift: 11111111111111111111111111111101
console.log(result); // -3
```

Listing 3.6: Sign-Propagating Right Shift (»)

For negative numbers, the sign-propagating right shift fills the leftmost bits with the sign bit, resulting in '-3' ('11111111111111111111111111111101').

```
let a = -5; // -5: 11111111111111111111111111111011
let result = a >>> 1; // Zero-Fill Right Shift:
    01111111111111111111111111111101
console.log(result); // 2147483645
```

Listing 3.7: Zero-Fill Right Shift (»>)

In a zero-fill right shift, the leftmost bits are filled with zeros, providing a result of '2147483645' ('01111111111111111111111111111101').

Understanding and utilizing bitwise operators effectively necessitates a solid grasp on binary number manipulation. These operators can be used in various scenarios, including but not limited to, performance optimizations, data compression techniques, and cryptographic algorithms. Such capabilities are pillars for advanced computing tasks.

3.8 Ternary Operator

The ternary operator, also known as the conditional operator, is a succinct mechanism for evaluating expressions in JavaScript that results in one of two values based on a given condition. The syntax for the ternary operator is as follows:

```
// syntax: condition ? expressionIfTrue : expressionIfFalse;
```

This operator is particularly useful for simplifying certain 'if-else' statements, thereby making the code more readable and concise. The ternary operator consists of three parts: the condition, the expression to evaluate if the condition is true, and the expression to evaluate if the condition is false.

Consider the following example using an 'if-else' statement:

```
let age = 18;
let canVote;

if (age >= 18) {
   canVote = 'Yes';
} else {
   canVote = 'No';
}
```

This logic can be succinctly expressed using the ternary operator as:

```
let age = 18;
let canVote = (age >= 18) ? 'Yes' : 'No';
```

In this example, the condition 'age >= 18' is evaluated: - If the condition is true, the expression following the '¿ operator ("Yes") is executed. - If the condition is false, the expression following the ':' operator ("No") is executed.

To illustrate further usage, consider a situation where a numeric value is to be incremented if positive and decremented if negative:

```
let num = 42;
num = (num > 0) ? num + 1 : num - 1;
```

In this scenario, if ‘num‘ is greater than 0, it will be incremented by 1. If ‘num‘ is less than or equal to 0, it will be decremented by 1.

It is important to note that ternary operators can be nested, though this practice should be approached with caution as it can reduce code readability. Here is an example of nested ternary operators:

```
let mark = 75;
let grade = (mark >= 90) ? 'A' :
            (mark >= 80) ? 'B' :
            (mark >= 70) ? 'C' :
            (mark >= 60) ? 'D' : 'F';
```

In the nested ternary operator example, the value of ‘grade‘ is determined based on the range in which the ‘mark‘ falls. Although this example demonstrates the utility of nested ternary operators, it should be used judiciously to maintain code clarity.

Variable assignment is not the only use case for the ternary operator; it can also be applied in return statements or complex expressions. For instance:

```
function getResult(isPassed) {
   return isPassed ? 'Passed' : 'Failed';
}
```

This function evaluates ‘isPassed‘ and returns either 'Passed' or 'Failed' based on the condition.

When using the ternary operator, it's crucial to consider operator precedence to avoid unexpected results. The ternary operator has a lower precedence than most of the arithmetic and logical operators but higher than assignment operators.

To elaborate on its precedence with respect to other operators, consider the expression:

```
let number = 10;
let outcome = (number + 5 > 10) ? number * 2 : number / 2;
```

Here, the arithmetic operations ‘number + 5‘, ‘number * 2‘, and ‘number / 2‘ are evaluated before the ternary operation. Thus, the above expression becomes:

```
outcome = 15 > 10 ? 20 : 5
```

Given that '15 > 10' is true, 'outcome' will be '20'. Understanding the precedence is pivotal for crafting correct and efficient conditional expressions.

Lastly, while the ternary operator is an elegant way to condense branching logic, developers must be vigilant to ensure it does not compromise code comprehensibility. Clear and maintainable code is always preferable over overly complex one-liners.

3.9 Operator Precedence and Associativity

In JavaScript, operator precedence and associativity rules dictate the order in which parts of an expression are evaluated. Understanding these rules is crucial for writing accurate and predictable code. Errors and unexpected behaviors often result from a misunderstanding of how JavaScript interprets complex expressions.

Operator precedence determines the priority of operators in an expression with multiple operators. By default, expressions are evaluated from left to right. However, operators with higher precedence are evaluated before those with lower precedence. Consider the following expression:

```
let result = 2 + 3 * 4;
```

Despite the left-to-right default evaluation, the multiplication operator '*' has higher precedence than the addition operator '+'. Thus, the expression is interpreted as follows:

```
let result = 2 + (3 * 4); // Evaluates to 2 + 12
// result is 14
```

Associativity, on the other hand, determines the direction in which expressions with operators of the same precedence level are evaluated. Operators can be either left-associative or right-associative. Most operators in JavaScript are left-associative, meaning they are processed from left to right. For instance, the subtraction operator '-' is left-associative, as demonstrated below:

```
let result = 10 - 3 - 2;
// This is evaluated as (10 - 3) - 2
// result is 5
```

Conversely, the assignment operator '=' is right-associative. Thus, expressions involving assignments are processed from right to left:

```
let a, b, c;
a = b = c = 5;
// This is evaluated as a = (b = (c = 5))
// a, b, and c are all assigned the value 5
```

Here is a concise list of some common operators arranged by their precedence levels in descending order:

- Member Access: `object.property`
- Function Call: `myFunction()`
- Increment/Decrement: ++, --
- Logical NOT: !
- Multiplication/Division/Modulus: *, /, %
- Addition/Subtraction: +, -
- Bitwise Shift: <<, >>, >>>
- Comparison: <, <=, >, >=
- Equality: ==, !=, ===, !==
- Bitwise AND: &
- Bitwise XOR: ^
- Bitwise OR: |
- Logical AND: &&
- Logical OR: ||
- Conditional (ternary) Operator: ? :
- Assignment: =, +=, -=, *=, /=, %=, <<=, >>=, >>>=, &=, ^=, |=

To better illustrate how precedence and associativity work in tandem, consider the following expression:

```
let x = 3 + 4 * 2 / ( 1 - 5 ) ** 2 ** 3;
```

The expression above involves multiple operators with varying precedence levels. According to the precedence rules, the operator with the highest precedence should execute first. The ** (exponentiation) operator has the highest precedence, followed by parentheses (), then multiplication * and division /, and finally addition +.

Additionally, the associativity of operators must be taken into account:

1. Parentheses: `1 - 5` evaluates to `-4`.
2. Exponentiation: `2 ** 3` evaluates to `8`, then `-4 ** 8` evaluates within parentheses.
3. Multiplication/Division: `4 * 2` evaluates to `8`.
4. Division: `8 / -4 ** 8` evaluates next.
5. Addition: `3 + (result of 4 * 2 / ( 1 - 5 ) ** 2 ** 3)` as the final step.

A step-by-step evaluation would thus yield:

```
// 1 - 5 evaluates to -4
(1 - 5)

// 2 ** 3 evaluates to 8
// -4 ** 8 evaluates based on the result
// Combining the above, 3 + (4 * 2) results in the final value.
```

Improper understanding of these rules can lead to logic errors in code, making it essential to use parentheses for clear and intended precedence in complex expressions. This eliminates any ambiguity and ensures that expressions are evaluated in the correct order while enhancing code readability.

3.10 Expressions in JavaScript

An expression is any valid unit of code that resolves to a value. In JavaScript, expressions form the building blocks of the language and can be composed of variables, operators, and function calls. There are various types of expressions in JavaScript which include arithmetic expressions, string expressions, logical expressions, and more.

An expression can be as simple as a single value or variable, such as:

```
// Simple expression
let x = 5;
```

This example assigns the value ‘5‘ to the variable ‘x‘, forming a basic expression that resolves to the value ‘5‘.

Complex Expressions:

JavaScript expressions can also be more complex, involving multiple operators and operands. For instance:

```
// Complex expression
let y = (3 + x) * 2;
```

This example includes addition and multiplication operators. The expression within the parentheses ‘(3 + x)‘ is evaluated first due to the precedence rules, after which the result is multiplied by ‘2‘.

Function Call Expressions:

Function calls are a common type of expression in JavaScript. When a function is invoked, whatever it returns constitutes the value of the function call expression:

```
// Function call expression
function add(a, b) {
    return a + b;
}
let z = add(x, y);
```

Here, ‘add(x, y)‘ is an expression that calls the ‘add‘ function with ‘x‘ and ‘y‘ as arguments. The return value of the function, which is the sum of ‘x‘ and ‘y‘, becomes the value of the expression.

Object and Array Expressions:

JavaScript allows for expressions that create objects and arrays:

```
// Object and array expressions
let obj = { name: "Alice", age: 30 };
let arr = [1, 2, 3, 4];
```

In these cases, the expressions { name: ”Alice”, age: 30 } and

$$1, 2, 3, 4$$

result in an object and an array, respectively.

Logical Expressions:

Logical expressions use logical operators such as ‘&&‘ (AND), ‘||‘ (OR), and ‘¡ (NOT):

```
// Logical expressions
let isActive = true;
let isAdult = false;
let result = isActive && isAdult;
```

The expression ‘isActive && isAdult‘ evaluates to ‘false‘ because both must be ‘true‘ for the AND operation to resolve to ‘true‘.

String Expressions:

String expressions involve string literals and string operators. One of the most common string operations is concatenation using the ‘+‘ operator:

```
// String expressions
let greeting = "Hello";
let target = "World";
let message = greeting + " " + target + "!";
```

This concatenation results in the string "Hello World!".

Conditional (Ternary) Expressions:

The ternary operator provides a compact syntax for performing conditional operations:

```
// Ternary expressions
let age = 18;
let canVote = (age >= 18) ? "Yes" : "No";
```

This ternary expression evaluates ‘(age >= 18)‘. If the condition is true, ‘canVote‘ is set to "Yes", otherwise it is set to "No".

Expression Evaluation:

JavaScript evaluates expressions based on the precedence and associativity of operators. Operators with higher precedence are evaluated before operators with lower precedence. Associativity determines the order in which operators of the same precedence are processed. Most arithmetic operations have left-to-right associativity, while assignment operators have right-to-left associativity.

For example:

```
// Expression evaluation
let result = 10 + 5 * 2; // result is 20, not 30
```

Due to precedence rules, multiplication is performed before addition. Thus, ‘5 * 2‘ is computed first, yielding ‘10‘, which is then added to ‘10‘ resulting in ‘20‘.

JavaScript expressions also support short-circuit evaluation which will be detailed in the next section. Understanding how JavaScript evaluates expressions is crucial for writing predictable and efficient code.

3.11 Evaluating and Executing Expressions

In JavaScript, evaluating and executing expressions is fundamental to the language's operation. Expressions in JavaScript are combinations of variables, operators, and values that yield a result. The JavaScript engine processes these expressions to produce a value, which can then be utilized within the program. This section will delve into the intricacies of how JavaScript handles evaluation and execution of different types of expressions.

Primary Expressions:

Primary expressions are the most basic expressions in JavaScript and include constants, literals, and variables. These are often the building blocks for more complex expressions.

```
// Examples of primary expressions
42;
"Hello, World!";
true;
variableName;
```

In the above example, `42`, `"Hello, World!"`, `true`, and `variableName` are primary expressions. When evaluated, they return their inherent value.

Arithmetic Expressions:

Arithmetic expressions combine numerical values with arithmetic operators, allowing for mathematical computations. The JavaScript engine follows mathematical precedence rules to evaluate these expressions.

```
// Examples of arithmetic expressions
var sum = 3 + 5;
var product = 4 * 7;
var combined = (2 + 3) * (8 / 2);
```

Here, expressions such as `3 + 5` and `4 * 7` will be evaluated to produce the sum 8 and product 28, respectively. Parentheses can alter the precedence to ensure intended execution order, as shown with `(2 + 3) * (8 / 2)`.

Assignment Expressions:

Assignment expressions assign the result of an expression to a variable. The assignment operator = takes the value on the right and assigns it to the variable on the left.

```
// Examples of assignment expressions
var a = 10;
```

```
var b = a + 5;
a = b * 2;
```

In these examples, `a` is first assigned the value `10`, `b` is then assigned the value of `a + 5` (which is `15`), and finally `a` is updated to `b * 2`, yielding `30`.

String Expressions:

String expressions concatenate strings using the `+` operator. The evaluation yields a new string combining the operands.

```
// Examples of string expressions
var greeting = "Hello" + " " + "World!";
var customGreeting = greeting + " How are you today?";
```

In the above, `"Hello" + " " + "World!"` evaluates to `"Hello World!"`, which is then further concatenated with `"How are you today?"` to produce the string `"Hello World! How are you today?"`.

Logical Expressions:

Logical expressions involve boolean values and logical operators such as `&&` (AND), `||` (OR), and `!` (NOT). The result of these expressions depends on the logical relationship between operands.

```
// Examples of logical expressions
var isAdult = age >= 18 && hasID;
var canVote = isCitizen || hasVotingPermit;
var isNotMinor = !isMinor;
```

As shown, `age >= 18 && hasID` evaluates whether both conditions are true. If `age` is 18 or more and `hasID` is true, `isAdult` becomes true. Similarly, `isCitizen || hasVotingPermit` evaluates to true if either condition is true, and `!isMinor` returns the negation of `isMinor`.

Complex Expressions and Evaluation Order:

JavaScript evaluates complex expressions based on operator precedence and associativity. Operators with higher precedence are executed before those with lower precedence. Associativity determines the order when operators of the same precedence appear.

```
// Complex expression example
var result = 3 + 4 * 5 / 2 - 1;
```

In the expression `3 + 4 * 5 / 2 - 1`, the multiplication and division are resolved first (left-to-right due to their equal precedence), transforming it into `3 + 20 / 2 - 1` and then `3 + 10 - 1`. Afterward, the addition and subtraction are left (again resolved left-to-right), producing the final result 12.

Execution Flow:

The execution flow in JavaScript is sequential, meaning expressions are generally evaluated from top to bottom in the order they appear unless control structures alter the flow (such as loops or conditional statements).

```
// Examples illustrating execution flow
var x = 10;
x += 5; // Now, x is 15
if (x > 10) {
    x *= 2; // This executes because x is greater than 10, so x is now 30
}
```

Short-Circuit Evaluation:

Short-circuit evaluation in JavaScript refers to the process where an expression is only partially evaluated. In logical `&&` and `||` operations, if the result is determined by the first operand, the second operand is not evaluated.

```
// Example of short-circuit evaluation
var fullName = userName || "Guest"; // If userName is falsy, "Guest" is assigned
var proceed = isAuthenticated && hasAccess; // Only checks hasAccess if
    isAuthenticated is true
```

In the expression `userName || "Guest"`, if `userName` is a falsy value (e.g., `null`, `undefined`, `0`, `""`), `"Guest"` is chosen. For `isAuthenticated && hasAccess`, `hasAccess` is evaluated only if `isAuthenticated` is `true`. This behavior optimizes performance and prevents unnecessary computations.

Each of these evaluation processes underscores JavaScript's capability to handle expressions efficiently and effectively within its engine environment. Understanding these concepts equips developers with the knowledge to write more optimal and error-free code.

3.12 Short-Circuit Evaluation

Short-circuit evaluation is a feature of JavaScript that allows the programming language to make efficient decisions by minimizing the number of evaluations and computations needed. It primarily applies to logical AND ('&&') and logical OR ('||') operators. Understanding short-circuit evaluation is crucial for writing optimized, efficient, and sometimes even more readable code.

Short-circuit evaluation works as follows: when evaluating an expression involving logical operators, JavaScript stops processing as soon as the outcome is determined. This behavior reduces unnecessary computation and can prevent errors in certain scenarios, such as avoiding null or undefined dereference.

A logical AND ('&&') operation requires both operands to be true for the whole expression to be true. If the first operand is false, there is no need to evaluate the second operand since the whole expression will inevitably be false.

Consider the following example:

```
let a = false;
let b = true;

if (a && b) {
    console.log("Both are true");
} else {
    console.log("At least one is false");
}
```

The expression 'a && b' is evaluated. Since 'a' is false, JavaScript stops the evaluation and concludes that the whole expression is false without checking the value of 'b'. The output will be:

```
At least one is false
```

In contrast, a logical OR ('||') operation requires only one operand to be true for the whole expression to be true. If the first operand is true, there is no need to evaluate the second operand since the whole expression is guaranteed to be true.

Consider the following example:

```
let a = true;
let b = false;

if (a || b) {
    console.log("At least one is true");
} else {
    console.log("Both are false");
}
```

The expression 'a || b' is evaluated. Since 'a' is true, JavaScript stops the evaluation and concludes that the whole expression is true without checking the value of 'b'. The output will be:

```
At least one is true
```

This behavior can also be utilized to assign default values. For example, if a variable may be null or undefined, you can use short-circuit evaluation to assign a default value:

```
let input;
let value = input || "Default Value";
console.log(value);
```

Here, 'input' is 'undefined', so the expression evaluates to the string "Default Value":

```
Default Value
```

Short-circuit evaluation can also leverage functions. Consider the scenario where a function should execute only if a certain condition is true:

```
function logMessage() {
    console.log("Function executed.");
}

let executeFunction = false;

executeFunction && logMessage();
```

The function 'logMessage()' will not execute because the variable 'executeFunction' is 'false'. Therefore, the expression 'executeFunction && logMessage()' short-circuits and skips the function execution. There will be no output.

Conversely, if you set 'executeFunction' to 'true':

```
let executeFunction = true;

executeFunction && logMessage();
```

The output will be:

```
Function executed.
```

Another practical application is in preventing null pointer exceptions:

```
let obj = null;

if (obj && obj.property) {
    console.log(obj.property);
}
```

In this example, 'obj' is 'null', so 'obj && obj.property' short-circuits and the condition evaluates to 'false', thus preventing an attempt to access 'property' on a null object and avoiding a runtime error.

Using short-circuit evaluation, JavaScript ensures efficient operations and logical decisions while fostering concise and robust code.

Chapter 4

Control Structures

This chapter examines the control structures that govern the flow of a JavaScript program. It covers conditional statements such as if, else if, and else, along with the switch statement. Various looping constructs, including while, do...while, for, for...in, and for...of, are discussed in detail. The chapter also addresses control flow interruptions using break and continue statements, error handling with try, catch, and finally, as well as throwing custom errors. Key concepts like the conditional (ternary) operator and block and lexical scope are also explained, providing a thorough understanding of how to control program logic and flow.

4.1 Introduction to Control Structures

In JavaScript, control structures are essential language constructs that determine the flow of execution of a program. These structures enable a program to make decisions, repeat operations, and manage exceptional situations effectively. Mastering control structures is fundamental for developing efficient, readable, and maintainable code.

The primary categories of control structures in JavaScript include conditional statements, looping constructs, and control flow interruptions, each serving distinct purposes in program execution.

Conditional Statements allow a program to execute different code blocks based on certain conditions or logical expressions. The key conditional statements in JavaScript are `if`, `else if`, `else`, and `switch`.

These statements facilitate decision-making by evaluating expressions and executing code only when specific conditions are met.

`if` Statement: The `if` statement evaluates a Boolean expression and executes the associated code block if the expression evaluates to `true`.

```
if (condition) {
    // Execute this code block if the condition is true
}
```

`else if` Statement: The `else if` statement follows an `if` statement and provides an additional condition to test if the primary condition is not met.

```
if (condition1) {
    // Execute this code block if condition1 is true
} else if (condition2) {
    // Execute this code block if condition1 is false and condition2 is
        true
}
```

`else` Statement: The `else` statement acts as a fallback, executing a code block if none of the preceding `if` or `else if` conditions are `true`.

```
if (condition1) {
    // Execute this code block if condition1 is true
} else if (condition2) {
    // Execute this code block if condition1 is false and condition2 is
        true
} else {
    // Execute this code block if neither condition1 nor condition2 is
        true
}
```

`switch` Statement: The `switch` statement performs a series of comparisons against different cases and executes the corresponding code block when a match is found.

```
switch (expression) {
    case value1:
        // Execute this code block if expression equals value1
        break;
    case value2:
        // Execute this code block if expression equals value2
        break;
    default:
        // Execute this code block if expression does not match any case
}
```

Looping Constructs enable a program to repeat code execution based on specified conditions. The main loop constructs in JavaScript are `while`, `do...while`, `for`, `for...in`, and `for...of`.

`while` Loop: The `while` loop repeats code execution as long as the provided condition remains `true`.

```
while (condition) {
    // Execute this code block while the condition is true
}
```

`do...while` Loop: The `do...while` loop executes the code block at least once and then repeats it as long as the specified condition holds true.

```
do {
    // Execute this code block at least once
} while (condition);
```

`for` Loop: The `for` loop provides a compact form for specifying iteration by defining the initialization, condition, and increment/decrement in a single statement.

```
for (initialization; condition; increment) {
    // Execute this code block while the condition is true
}
```

`for...in` Loop: The `for...in` loop iterates over the enumerable properties of an object, executing the code block for each property.

```
for (property in object) {
    // Execute this code block for each property in the object
}
```

`for...of` Loop: The `for...of` loop iterates over iterable objects, such as arrays and strings, executing the code block for each element.

```
for (element of iterable) {
    // Execute this code block for each element in the iterable
}
```

Control Flow Interruptions manage the flow by prematurely terminating or continuing loops and handling errors. Key control flow interruptions include `break`, `continue`, `try`, `catch`, `finally`, and `throw`.

`break` Statement: The `break` statement terminates the closest enclosing loop or `switch` statement.

```
for (let i = 0; i < 10; i++) {
    if (i === 5) {
```

```
        break; // Exit the loop when i equals 5
    }
    console.log(i);
}
```

`continue` Statement: The `continue` statement skips the current iteration of the closest enclosing loop and proceeds to the next iteration.

```
for (let i = 0; i < 10; i++) {
    if (i % 2 === 0) {
        continue; // Skip even numbers
    }
    console.log(i); // Output: 1, 3, 5, 7, 9
}
```

`try...catch...finally` Block: These statements handle exceptions, allowing you to define a block of code to attempt (try), a handler for errors (catch), and a block to execute regardless of whether an error occurred (finally).

```
try {
    // Code that may throw an error
} catch (error) {
    // Code to handle the error
} finally {
    // Code that will always execute
}
```

The `throw` Statement: The `throw` statement allows you to create your own exceptions.

```
if (conditionNotMet) {
    throw new Error('Condition was not met');
}
```

Understanding and utilizing these control structures effectively enables the creation of complex and efficient programs, providing a robust means to control program logic and flow.

4.2 Conditional Statements: if, else if, else

In JavaScript, conditional statements control the flow of the program based on certain conditions. The primary conditional statements are `if`, `else if`, and `else`. These statements evaluate Boolean expressions and execute code blocks accordingly, allowing the program to make decisions and respond dynamically to different situations.

The basic syntax of an `if` statement is:

```
// Basic if statement
if (condition) {
    // Code to execute if condition is true
}
```

The `condition` is a Boolean expression, meaning it evaluates to either `true` or `false`. If the `condition` evaluates to `true`, the code inside the braces is executed. If the condition evaluates to `false`, the code inside the braces is skipped.

Consider the following example:

```
let temperature = 30;

if (temperature > 20) {
    console.log('It is warm outside.');
}
```

In this example, the `if` condition (`temperature > 20`) evaluates to `true` since `temperature` is 30. Therefore, the message `'It is warm outside.'` is logged to the console.

To handle multiple conditions, the `else if` statement comes into play. An `else if` statement follows an `if` or another `else if` statement and provides an additional condition to test if the previous `if` or `else if` conditions were false.

The syntax for an `else if` statement is:

```
// if and else if statements
if (condition1) {
    // Code to execute if condition1 is true
} else if (condition2) {
    // Code to execute if condition2 is true and condition1 is false
}
```

The `else if` statement is only evaluated if the preceding `if` statement's condition evaluates to `false`.

Consider the following example:

```
let temperature = 15;

if (temperature > 20) {
    console.log('It is warm outside.');
} else if (temperature > 10) {
    console.log('It is cool outside.');
}
```

In this case, the `if` condition (`temperature > 20`) evaluates to `false` since `temperature` is 15. However, the `else if` condition (`temperature > 10`) evaluates to `true`, so the message `'It is cool outside.'` is logged to the console.

The `else` statement provides a default block of code that runs if all preceding `if` and `else if` conditions are false. This ensures that there is an executable block when no conditions are met.

The syntax for an `else` statement is:

```
// if, else if, and else statements
if (condition1) {
    // Code to execute if condition1 is true
} else if (condition2) {
    // Code to execute if condition2 is true and condition1 is false
} else {
    // Code to execute if all preceding conditions are false
}
```

Here is an example that uses `if`, `else if`, and `else`:

```
let temperature = 5;

if (temperature > 20) {
    console.log('It is warm outside.');
} else if (temperature > 10) {
    console.log('It is cool outside.');
} else {
    console.log('It is cold outside.');
}
```

In this case, both the `if` condition (`temperature > 20`) and the `else if` condition (`temperature > 10`) evaluate to `false` since `temperature` is 5. Thus, the `else` block is executed, and the message `'It is cold outside.'` is logged to the console.

It is worth noting that the conditions inside `if`, `else if`, and `else` blocks can be any valid JavaScript expressions that return a Boolean value. For example, functions, comparisons, or Boolean variables can serve as conditions.

Moreover, it is important to use strict equality (===) or inequality (!==) operators when comparing values within `if` statements to avoid unintended type coercion, which may lead to logical errors:

```
let value = '10';

if (value === 10) {
    console.log('The value is exactly 10.');
} else {
    console.log('The value is not exactly 10.');
}
```

In this example, the `if` condition (`value === 10`) evaluates to `false` since `value` is a string `'10'` and not a number `10`. Thus, the message `'The value is not exactly 10.'` is logged to the console. Using strict equality helps ensure that both the type and value are considered in the comparison.

By understanding and properly utilizing `if`, `else if`, and `else` statements, developers can create efficient, understandable, and maintainable logic within their JavaScript programs. These conditional constructs are fundamental to making decisions and controlling the flow of execution based on varying runtime conditions.

4.3 Switch Statement

The `switch` statement in JavaScript provides a powerful and concise mechanism for executing different blocks of code based on the value of an expression. It acts as an alternative to using multiple `if` statements when you need to compare a single value against many possible matches. This section elucidates the syntax, usage, and best practices for implementing a `switch` statement, ensuring clarity and efficiency in your code.

The general syntax of the `switch` statement is as follows:

```
switch (expression) {
  case value1:
    // code block to be executed if expression === value1
    break;
  case value2:
    // code block to be executed if expression === value2
    break;
  ...
  default:
    // code block to be executed if expression does not match any case
}
```

Here the `expression` is evaluated once. The value of the `expression` is then compared with the values of each `case`. If a match is found, the associated block of code is executed. The `break` statement ensures that the code execution stops and exits the `switch` after the matched case. Without a `break` statement, the code execution falls through to the next case.

The `default` keyword specifies the default block of code that executes if no `case` matches the `expression`. It's analogous to the `else` clause in an `if-else` construct.

For better understanding, consider the following example where a `switch` statement is used to perform different actions based on the day of the week:

```
let day = new Date().getDay();

switch (day) {
  case 0:
    console.log("Today is Sunday");
    break;
  case 1:
    console.log("Today is Monday");
    break;
  case 2:
    console.log("Today is Tuesday");
    break;
  case 3:
    console.log("Today is Wednesday");
    break;
  case 4:
    console.log("Today is Thursday");
    break;
  case 5:
    console.log("Today is Friday");
    break;
  case 6:
    console.log("Today is Saturday");
    break;
  default:
    console.log("Invalid day");
}
```

In this example, the `getDay()` method of the `Date` object returns an integer representing the day of the week (0 for Sunday, 1 for Monday, and so on). The `switch` statement evaluates this integer and prints the corresponding day. If the day value falls outside the range 0 to 6, it prints "Invalid day".

Notably, the `break` statement plays a crucial role here. Omitting `break` results in a "fall through," where the switch statement continues to execute subsequent case blocks even if a match has been found. This behavior can lead to unexpected results, as illustrated in the following example:

```
let fruit = "Apple";

switch (fruit) {
  case "Apple":
```

```
    console.log("Fruit is Apple");
  case "Banana":
    console.log("Fruit is Banana");
  case "Mango":
    console.log("Fruit is Mango");
  default:
    console.log("Unknown fruit");
}
```

```
Output:
Fruit is Apple
Fruit is Banana
Fruit is Mango
Unknown fruit
```

As seen in the output, because there are no `break` statements after each case, all subsequent cases execute after the matching case.

To handle multiple conditions that should perform the same action, `switch` cases can be stacked without break statements between them:

```
let color = "red";

switch (color) {
  case "red":
  case "blue":
  case "green":
    console.log("Color is a primary color");
    break;
  case "yellow":
  case "purple":
  case "orange":
    console.log("Color is a secondary color");
    break;
  default:
    console.log("Unknown color");
}
```

```
Output:
Color is a primary color
```

In the provided example, cases "red", "blue", and "green" execute the same block of code because they stack up without intervening break statements, and similarly for secondary colors.

JavaScript's `switch` statement strictly compares the value and the type (=== operator) of the expression and the case values. As a result, subtle nuances such as type coercion, prevalent in ==, do not come into play. Here is an example highlighting strict comparison:

```
let number = '10';

switch (number) {
```

```
  case 10:
    console.log("Number is 10");
    break;
  case '10':
    console.log("Number is '10'");
    break;
  default:
    console.log("No match found");
}
```

```
Output:
Number is '10'
```

The `switch` statement compares `number` to the case values. The first case `10` (number) does not match `'10'` (string), so it skips to the next case where `number` matches `'10'`.

The `switch` statement, while similar to multiple `if-else` conditions, provides cleaner and more readable code when handling a single expression with numerous potential values. Correct use of `break` and default cases ensures accurate and efficient code execution. Proper understanding and careful implementation are essential to leverage the full potential of the `switch` statement in JavaScript programming.

4.4 Loops: while and do...while

JavaScript provides the `while` and `do...while` loops to handle scenarios where preconditions or postconditions determine the repetition of specific code blocks. These loops ensure that a segment of code executes as long as a particular condition remains true.

while Loop

The `while` loop is a control flow statement that allows code to be executed repeatedly based on a given Boolean condition. The condition is evaluated before executing the loop's body. If the condition is true, the code block inside the loop is executed. This process repeats until the condition evaluates to false.

The syntax for a `while` loop is as follows:

```
// while loop syntax
while (condition) {
    // code block to be executed
    // update the condition to avoid infinite loops
}
```

Consider the following example where we use a `while` loop to print numbers from 1 to 5:

```
// Example: Using a while loop to print numbers from 1 to 5
let num = 1;
while (num <= 5) {
    console.log(num);
    num++;
}
```

```
1
2
3
4
5
```

In this example, the variable `num` is initialized to 1. The condition `num <= 5` is evaluated before the loop body executes. As long as the condition remains true, `console.log(num);` is executed, and `num` is incremented by 1. When `num` exceeds 5, the condition becomes false, and the loop terminates.

Special care must be taken to ensure that the loop condition will eventually become false; otherwise, the loop will result in an infinite loop, which can crash the program or the host environment. Always ensure the loop body includes an operation that alters the condition.

do...while Loop

The `do...while` loop is similar to the `while` loop, but with a fundamental difference: it executes the loop body at least once before checking the condition. The condition is evaluated after the execution of the loop's body.

The syntax for a `do...while` loop is:

```
// do...while loop syntax
do {
    // code block to be executed
    // update the condition to avoid infinite loops
} while (condition);
```

Consider the following example, where we use a `do...while` loop to print numbers from 1 to 5:

```
// Example: Using a do...while loop to print numbers from 1 to 5
let num = 1;
do {
    console.log(num);
    num++;
} while (num <= 5);
```

```
1
2
3
4
5
```

In this example, the body of the loop executes first, printing the current value of `num`. After execution, `num` is incremented by 1. The condition `num <= 5` is evaluated, and as long as it remains true, the loop repeats. Even if `num` were initially greater than 5, the body of the loop would execute at least once because the condition is checked after the first iteration.

To illustrate the difference between `while` and `do...while`, consider the following example with an initial condition that is false:

```
// Example: Comparing while and do...while with initial false condition
let num1 = 6;
let num2 = 6;

while (num1 <= 5) {
    console.log("This will not be printed:", num1);
    num1++;
}

do {
    console.log("This will be printed once:", num2);
    num2++;
} while (num2 <= 5);
```

```
This will be printed once: 6
```

In this case, the `while` loop skips execution because `num1 <= 5` is false initially. On the other hand, the `do...while` loop executes once despite the condition `num2 <= 5` being false, showing the clear distinction between these two looping constructs.

Understanding the differences between `while` and `do...while` loops is critical for deciding which loop to use based on the necessity of prior condition checking.

4.5 Loops: for and for...in

Loops in JavaScript are fundamental constructs for executing a block of code repeatedly, based on a specified condition. Among the various looping mechanisms, the `for` loop and the `for...in` loop serve distinct but significant roles in iterating over collections. This section delves into the syntax, semantics, and common use cases of these loops, enhancing your ability to manipulate control flow effectively.

The `for` loop is an entry-controlled loop, which evaluates the condition before executing the block of code. Its syntax can be broken down into three parts: initialization, condition, and incrementdecrement. The loop executes as long as the condition remains true.

```
for (let i = 0; i < 10; i++) {
    console.log(i);
}
```

Listing 4.1: Basic `for` Loop Example

In this example, the loop runs ten times, outputting numbers 0 through 9. Breaking down the components:

- `let i = 0;` initializes the counter `i` to 0.
- `i < 10;` is the condition evaluated before each iteration.
- `i++` increments `i` by 1 after each iteration.

The `for` loop offers flexibility in the initialization step. It can initialize multiple variables or even propagate values from outside the loop:

```
let start = 2;
for (let i = start, j = start * start; i < 10; i++, j = j + i) {
    console.log(`i: ${i}, j: ${j}`);
}
```

Listing 4.2: Advanced `for` Loop Initialization

Here:

- `let i = start, j = start * start;` initializes two counters `i` and `j`.
- The update expression `j = j + i` recalculates `j` based on `i`.

In contrast, the `for...in` loop is designed for iterating over the enumerable properties of an object. It is often utilized when the goal is to examine object properties or traverse keys in an array.

```
const object = { a: 1, b: 2, c: 3 };
for (let key in object) {
    console.log(`${key}: ${object[key]}`);
}
```

Listing 4.3: `for...in` Loop Example

The `for...in` loop:

- Iterates through each property key in the object.
- The variable `key` is assigned the property names of `object`.
- `object[key]` accesses the value associated with the property key.

It is important to note that the `for...in` loop iterates over inherited properties as well, which distinguishes it from more restrictive iteration methods:

```
function Parent() {
   this.a = 1;
}
Parent.prototype.b = 2;
const child = new Parent();
for (let key in child) {
   console.log(`${key}: ${child[key]}`);
}
```

Listing 4.4: `for...in` with Inherited Properties

In this example, the properties `a` and `b` are both listed during iteration, indicating the `for...in` loop's ability to enumerate prototype chain properties.

For array iteration, a `for` loop might be preferred to avoid non-index properties:

```
const arr = [10, 20, 30];
for (let i = 0; i < arr.length; i++) {
   console.log(`Element at index ${i}: ${arr[i]}`);
}
```

Listing 4.5: Array Iteration with `for` Loop

The use of `for` loops ensures index-based traversal, directly accessing array elements without unexpected interference from enumerable properties.

In understanding the distinctions and specific applications of these loops, one achieves greater control and precision in navigating JavaScript's data structures.

4.6 Loops: for...of

The `for...of` loop is a modern construct introduced in ECMAScript 2015 (also known as ES6). It provides a simpler and more readable way to iterate over iterable objects including arrays, strings, maps, sets, and other collections. Unlike the `for...in` loop which iterates over the enumerable properties of an object, the `for...of` loop iterates over the values of an iterable object.

The syntax for the `for...of` loop is straightforward:

```
// Syntax of the for...of loop
for (variable of iterable) {
    // code block to be executed
}
```

Here, `variable` is a variable that stores the value of the current iteration and `iterable` is an object that has iterable properties. Each time the `for...of` loop iterates, it assigns the next value from the iterable to `variable`, until it has iterated over all values.

Consider an example where we iterate over an array of numbers:

```
let numbers = [1, 2, 3, 4, 5];

for (let number of numbers) {
    console.log(number);
}
```

The output of the above JavaScript code will be:

```
1
2
3
4
5
```

In this example, each element of the `numbers` array is logged to the console on a new line.

The `for...of` loop can also be used to iterate over strings. When applied to a string, it iterates over each character:

```
let message = "Hello";

for (let character of message) {
    console.log(character);
}
```

The output will be:

```
H
e
l
l
o
```

This makes it a convenient way to loop through each character in a string without needing to manually access each character by its index.

Moreover, `for...of` can be used with other iterable objects such as `Map` and `Set`. For example:

```
let mySet = new Set([1, 2, 3]);

for (let value of mySet) {
   console.log(value);
}
```

This results in:

```
1
2
3
```

And similarly with `Map`:

```
let myMap = new Map([
   ['key1', 'value1'],
   ['key2', 'value2'],
   ['key3', 'value3']
]);

for (let entry of myMap) {
   console.log(entry);
}
```

This outputs the key-value pairs as arrays:

```
[ 'key1', 'value1' ]
[ 'key2', 'value2' ]
[ 'key3', 'value3' ]
```

To iterate over just the keys or values of a `Map`, the `for...of` loop can be used with the `keys()` or `values()` methods respectively:

```
// Iterating over keys
for (let key of myMap.keys()) {
   console.log(key);
}

// Iterating over values
for (let value of myMap.values()) {
   console.log(value);
}
```

The first loop will produce:

```
key1
key2
key3
```

And the second loop will produce:

```
value1
value2
value3
```

Finally, it is worth noting that the `for...of` loop can be combined with the `yield` keyword to iterate over custom iterable objects defined by generator functions:

```
function* generatorFunction() {
    yield 1;
    yield 2;
    yield 3;
}

let iterator = generatorFunction();

for (let value of iterator) {
    console.log(value);
}
```

The output will be:

```
1
2
3
```

This example demonstrates iterating over values produced by a generator function, which can create sequences of values lazily, i.e., one at a time as they are needed, rather than all at once.

The `for...of` loop simplifies iteration over iterable objects, making the code more readable and concise, an important aspect of writing maintainable and efficient JavaScript.

4.7 Control Flow Interruptions: break and continue

Control flow interruptions in JavaScript are crucial for managing the execution flow within loops and conditional statements. The two primary statements used for these interruptions are `break` and `continue`. Both can significantly alter the flow of execution, providing fine-grained control over how loops operate. Understanding their proper use is essential for writing efficient and readable code.

The `break` statement is used to terminate the execution of a loop or a switch statement prematurely. When a `break` statement is encountered, the control is immediately transferred out of the enclosing loop or switch structure. This can be particularly useful when a condition is met, and there's no need to perform further iterations or checks.

Let's consider a simple example demonstrating the use of the `break` statement in a `for` loop:

```
for (let i = 0; i < 10; i++) {
    if (i === 5) {
        break; // Exit the loop when i equals 5
    }
    console.log(i);
}
```

Listing 4.6: Using break in a for loop

```
0
1
2
3
4
```

In this example, the loop starts and iterates from 0 to 9. However, when the loop variable `i` equals 5, the `break` statement is executed, causing the loop to terminate immediately. As a result, the console only logs the numbers from 0 to 4.

The `break` statement is also often used within `switch` statements to terminate a particular case and prevent the execution of subsequent cases:

```
let fruit = 'apple';

switch (fruit) {
    case 'apple':
        console.log('Apple is selected.');
        break;
    case 'banana':
        console.log('Banana is selected.');
        break;
    default:
        console.log('No fruit is selected.');
}
```

Listing 4.7: Using break in a switch statement

```
Apple is selected.
```

In the `switch` statement above, when the `fruit` variable matches 'apple', the corresponding `case` is executed, and the message `Apple is selected.` is printed. The `break` statement then exits the `switch` block, preventing the execution of subsequent cases.

On the other hand, the `continue` statement is used to skip the current iteration of a loop and proceed to the next iteration immediately. It does not terminate the loop but simply bypasses the remaining code within the current loop iteration.

Here is an example demonstrating the use of the `continue` statement within a `for` loop:

```
for (let i = 0; i < 10; i++) {
    if (i % 2 === 0) {
        continue; // Skip the rest of the loop when i is even
    }
    console.log(i);
}
```

Listing 4.8: Using continue in a for loop

```
1
3
5
7
9
```

In this example, the loop iterates through numbers from 0 to 9. However, whenever the loop variable `i` is an even number, the `continue` statement is executed, which skips the console logging and proceeds to the next iteration. Consequently, the console logs only the odd numbers from 1 to 9.

The use of `break` and `continue` enhances the control flow within loops, making it possible to avoid unnecessary computations and handle specific conditions more efficiently. Consider a scenario where we want to find the first multiple of 3 and 5 in a given range:

```
let found = false;

for (let i = 1; i <= 100; i++) {
    if (i % 3 === 0 && i % 5 === 0) {
        console.log(`Found: ${i}`);
        found = true;
        break; // Exit the loop once the first multiple is found
    }
}
if (!found) {
    console.log('No multiple of 3 and 5 found in the range.');
}
```

Listing 4.9: Using break to find the first multiple of 3 and 5

```
Found: 15
```

In this code example, the loop checks each number from 1 to 100 to see if it is a multiple of both 3 and 5. As soon as it finds such a number, it logs the number and uses `break` to exit the loop immediately. The `found` flag prevents the need for further checks, making the code more efficient.

Contrarily, `continue` can be utilized to filter out unwanted values and perform operations on the remaining ones. Here is an example of using `continue` to log numbers that are not divisible by 3:

```
for (let i = 1; i <= 20; i++) {
    if (i % 3 === 0) {
        continue; // Skip multiples of 3
    }
    console.log(i);
}
```

Listing 4.10: Using continue to filter out multiples of 3

```
1
2
4
5
7
8
10
11
13
14
16
17
19
20
```

The loop iterates from 1 to 20, and when the current number `i` is divisible by 3, the `continue` statement is executed, skipping the console logging for those numbers. The console then logs all numbers except multiples of 3.

Integrating both `break` and `continue` statements in complex loops and conditional structures can lead to more readable and efficient code. By utilizing these statements strategically, one can avoid excessive calculations and manage control flow more effectively. This is particularly important in real-world scenarios where loops might involve large datasets or computationally expensive operations.

4.8 Error Handling: try, catch, finally

JavaScript provides robust mechanisms for error handling using the `try`, `catch`, and `finally` statements. These constructs enable developers to manage exceptions, ensuring that the application can handle unexpected conditions without crashing.

The `try` statement allows you to define a block of code to be tested for errors during execution. The `catch` statement lets you handle the error, and the `finally` statement contains code that will run, regardless of the outcome of the try-catch block. This mechanism is crucial for maintaining the integrity and availability of applications, especially in environments requiring high reliability.

```
try {
  // Block of code to try
  let result = riskyOperation();
  console.log(result);
} catch (error) {
  // Block of code to handle errors
  console.error('An error occurred:', error.message);
} finally {
  // Block of code to be executed regardless of the try / catch result
  console.log('Execution completed.');
}
```

In the example above, the `riskyOperation()` function call is wrapped within a `try` block, which allows you to attempt executing it. If an error occurs during execution, control is passed to the `catch` block, where the error is handled. The `finally` block will execute irrespective of the error's occurrence, allowing for any necessary cleanup actions.

Detailed Breakdown

- **The `try` Statement:** The `try` block surrounds the code that might throw an exception. This block seeks to execute without an error, allowing the program to continue running as expected.

```
try {
  // Code that may throw an error
  let data = fetchDataFromAPI();
  process(data);
}
```

- **The `catch` Statement:** If an error occurs in the `try` block, the `catch` block is executed. The `catch` block can take an error object as a parameter, which provides information about the error.

```
catch (error) {
  console.error('Error fetching data:', error.message);
  // Additional error handling logic
}
```

The error object could contain properties such as:

```
name: The error type (e.g., 'ReferenceError', 'TypeError').
message: A human-readable description of the error.
stack: The stack trace at the point the error was thrown (non-standard, but widely supported).
```

- **The `finally` Statement:** The `finally` block is optional and will execute after the `try` and `catch` blocks have finished, regardless of whether an exception was thrown or caught.

```
finally {
  console.log('Cleaning up resources.');
  // Code to clean up or release resources
}
```

Nested `try-catch-finally` Blocks

```
try {
  try {
    let result = complexOperation();
    console.log(result);
  } catch (operationError) {
    console.error('Operation error:', operationError.message);
  } finally {
    console.log('Completed complexOperation.');
  }
} catch (generalError) {
  console.error('General error:', generalError.message);
} finally {
  console.log('Nested try-catch-finally block completed.');
}
```

Handling Specific Error Types

Handling specific error types allows more granular control over the application flow. You can check the error type using the `instanceof` operator within the `catch` block.

```
try {
  riskyFunction();
```

```
} catch (error) {
  if (error instanceof TypeError) {
    console.error('Type Error encountered:', error.message);
  } else if (error instanceof ReferenceError) {
    console.error('Reference Error encountered:', error.message);
  } else {
    console.error('Unexpected error:', error.message);
  }
} finally {
  console.log('Error handling process completed.');
}
```

Best Practices for Error Handling

- **Catch only what you can handle:** Avoid broad catch-all error handling. This practice makes debugging harder and can obscure the root cause of issues.
- **Log meaningful errors:** Ensure your error messages are descriptive and provide enough context to understand the issue.
- **Clean up resources:** Use the `finally` block for cleanup activities, such as closing files or network connections.
- **Fail gracefully:** Ensure your application can recover or degrade gracefully if an error occurs.

Proper error handling is vital for creating resilient and user-friendly applications. Understanding and implementing `try`, `catch`, and `finally` blocks correctly will help ensure that your code is robust and can handle unexpected situations efficiently.

4.9 Throwing Custom Errors

In JavaScript, error handling is a critical aspect that ensures robust and reliable application behavior. When pre-defined error types such as 'TypeError', 'SyntaxError', or 'ReferenceError' do not fully capture a specific issue, developers can define and throw custom errors. Throwing custom errors enhances the clarity and precision of error reporting and handling, which is essential during debugging and logging processes.

To throw a custom error, you typically make use of the 'throw' statement in conjunction with the 'Error' constructor or extend the 'Error' class to create more specific error types. The following sections delve into the syntax, usage, and best practices for throwing custom errors.

```
throw new Error('Custom error message');
```

Listing 4.11: Syntax of Throwing Custom Errors

The ‘Error‘ constructor creates an error object with a ‘message‘ property providing a human-readable description of the error. The ‘throw‘ statement then raises this error, which can be caught using ‘try...catch‘.

Example usage:

```
try {
   function processInput(input) {
      if (typeof input !== 'string') {
         throw new Error('Invalid input: Expected a string.');
      }
      // Further processing of input
   }

   processInput(42); // This will throw an error
} catch (error) {
   console.error(error.message); // Output: Invalid input: Expected a
       string.
}
```

Listing 4.12: Throwing and Catching a Custom Error

When defining more specific custom error types, extending the ‘Error‘ class is a recommended approach. This allows for the creation of custom error classes that provide additional context through properties and methods. Below is a detailed example of creating and using a custom error class.

```
class ValidationError extends Error {
   constructor(message) {
      super(message); // Call the constructor of the parent class (Error
          )
      this.name = 'ValidationError'; // Assign a name property
   }
}

function validateUser(user) {
   if (!user.name) {
      throw new ValidationError('Missing name in user object.');
   }
   if (!user.email) {
      throw new ValidationError('Missing email in user object.');
   }
   // Further validation logic
```

```
}

try {
   validateUser({ email: 'user@example.com' }); // Missing name will
       throw a ValidationError
} catch (error) {
   if (error instanceof ValidationError) {
      console.error(`Validation failed: ${error.message}`);
   } else {
      console.error('An unexpected error occurred.');
   }
}
```

Listing 4.13: Creating a Custom Error Class

In the above example, 'ValidationError' is a custom error class that inheres from the built-in 'Error' class. By overriding the constructor, we can ensure that the 'ValidationError' instances have a meaningful name, making it easier to distinguish them from other errors. Within the 'try...catch' block, it's also possible to employ 'instanceof' to handle different error types selectively.

Extending the 'Error' class can also involve adding additional properties. For instance, one might add an 'errorCode' to provide further context useful for debugging and logging purposes.

```
class DatabaseError extends Error {
   constructor(message, errorCode) {
      super(message);
      this.name = 'DatabaseError';
      this.errorCode = errorCode;
   }
}

function connectToDatabase() {
   // Hypothetical connection logic
   let success = false; // Simulate a failure
   if (!success) {
      throw new DatabaseError('Failed to connect to the database.',
          5001);
   }
}

try {
   connectToDatabase();
} catch (error) {
   if (error instanceof DatabaseError) {
      console.error(`Database error occurred: ${error.message} (Code: ${
          error.errorCode})`);
   } else {
      console.error('An unexpected error occurred.');
```

```
    }
}
```

Listing 4.14: Custom Error Class with Additional Properties

By creating 'DatabaseError', we encode more specific information about the error condition, enabling more precise error handling.

When extending the 'Error' class, developers should adhere to best practices: - Always call the 'super' constructor to ensure the error message and other properties are correctly initialized. - Define a meaningful 'name' property for the error class. - Optionally, include additional descriptive properties that convey more context about the error.

Custom errors, when correctly implemented, provide a structured and informative system for error reporting and handling. This rigor allows for more maintainable and debuggable code, essential for developing scalable and dependable JavaScript applications.

4.10 Conditional (Ternary) Operator

The conditional (ternary) operator is a succinct mechanism for making conditional decisions in JavaScript. It serves as a condensed form of the `if... else` statement, allowing for simple conditional assignments and expressions within a single line. The syntax for the ternary operator is as follows:

```
condition ? expr1 : expr2
```

In this structure: - `condition`: An expression that evaluates to `true` or `false`. - `expr1`: The expression that is evaluated if `condition` is `true`. - `expr2`: The expression that is evaluated if `condition` is `false`.

Practical Usage

Consider a simple example where we evaluate whether a number is odd or even:

```
let number = 4;
let result = (number % 2 === 0) ? "even" : "odd";
console.log(result);
```

The above code will output:

```
even
```

Here, the expression `(number % 2 === 0)` acts as the `condition`. If true, `"even"` is assigned to the variable `result`; otherwise, `"odd"` is assigned.

Nesting Ternary Operators

It is possible to nest ternary operators within each other for multiple conditions. However, readability may suffer, and such practices should be used judiciously. Consider the following nested ternary operator example:

```
let a = 3, b = 5;
let max = (a > b) ? a : ((a === b) ? "equal" : b);
console.log(max);
```

Here, the first ternary operator checks if `a` is greater than `b`. If true, `a` is returned. If false, another ternary operator checks if `a` equals `b`, returning `"equal"` if true or `b` if false. The code succinctly demonstrates the compactness that ternary operations can achieve, albeit with potential readability concerns.

Best Practices and Caveats

While the ternary operator offers syntactic brevity, it may often yield less readable code, especially for complex conditions. It is suitable for simple decisions but should be avoided for more complex logic where standard `if... else` constructs provide better clarity. Here are some best practices and considerations:

1. **Single-line simplicity**: Prefer ternary operators for straightforward, single-line decisions. 2. **Avoid deep nesting**: Refrain from deeply nesting ternary operators to maintain better readability and maintainability. 3. **Consider readability**: Evaluate the trade-off between code brevity and readability. When in doubt, choose the construct that improves code clarity.

Examples

Let us explore some more examples that illustrate the practical application of the ternary operator.

Example 1: Assigning default values

```
let userName = userInput ? userInput : "Guest";
console.log(userName);
```

In this example, `userName` is assigned `userInput` if it is truthy; otherwise, it defaults to `"Guest"`. This pattern is useful for handling optional user input.

Example 2: Simplifying `if... else if... else` chains

```
let age = 20;
let category = (age < 13) ? "child" : (age < 20) ? "teenager" : "adult";
console.log(category);
```

Here, the ternary operator replaces a chain of `if... else if... else` statements, classifying a person's age into "child", "teenager", or "adult". It enhances readability for straightforward, multi-branch conditions.

Application in Functions

The ternary operator also finds usage in functions, where it can simplify return statements for conditional logic.

```
function checkEligibility(age) {
    return (age \geq 18) ? "Eligible" : "Not eligible";
}
console.log(checkEligibility(21));
```

This function `checkEligibility` uses a ternary operator to return eligibility status based on the `age` parameter, exemplifying how ternary operators can streamline function bodies.

The conditional (ternary) operator is a powerful tool in JavaScript for concise conditional evaluations. Its correct use enhances code brevity while maintaining clarity, provided it is not overused or improperly nested. Mastery of the ternary operator broadens a developer's toolkit for writing efficient and readable JavaScript code.

4.11 Understanding Block Scope and Lexical Scope

In JavaScript, understanding scoping mechanisms is pivotal for effective coding and debugging. Block scope and lexical scope are the two scopes that dictate the accessibility of variables within different parts of a program.

Block scope is a scope defined by a block, which is a set of statements enclosed in curly brackets { }. Variables declared with `let` and `const` are block-scoped.

```
{
    let x = 10;
    const y = 20;
    console.log(x); // 10
    console.log(y); // 20
}
console.log(x); // ReferenceError: x is not defined
console.log(y); // ReferenceError: y is not defined
```

In the above example, `x` and `y` are inaccessible outside the block defined by the curly braces, demonstrating block scope. Variables declared with `var` do not have block scope. Instead, they are function-scoped.

```
{
    var z = 30;
    console.log(z); // 30
}
console.log(z); // 30
```

Despite being declared within a block, `z` is accessible outside of it, highlighting the difference between `var` and `let`/`const`.

Lexical scope, also known as static scope, is determined at the time of writing the code, not at runtime. It refers to the ability of a function to access variables from its parent lexical context.

```
let a = 100;

function outerFunction() {
    let b = 200;

    function innerFunction() {
        let c = 300;
        console.log(a); // 100
        console.log(b); // 200
        console.log(c); // 300
    }

    innerFunction();
```

```
    console.log(a); // 100
    console.log(b); // 200
    console.log(c); // ReferenceError: c is not defined
}

outerFunction();
console.log(a); // 100
console.log(b); // ReferenceError: b is not defined
console.log(c); // ReferenceError: c is not defined
```

In this example, `innerFunction` can access the variables `a` and `b` because they belong to its containing environment. However, variables declared in `innerFunction` are not accessible outside of it due to lexical scope.

Nested functions form closures which preserve the lexical environment in which they are created.

```
function createCounter() {
    let count = 0;

    return function() {
        count++;
        return count;
    }
}

const counter = createCounter();
console.log(counter()); // 1
console.log(counter()); // 2
```

Here, the `createCounter` function returns another function which forms a closure over the `count` variable. Each call to `counter()` increments and returns the preserved `count` variable.

Variables declared in the global scope (outside any function or block) remain accessible throughout the entire program, unless shadowed by another variable of the same name in a local scope.

```
let globalVar = 'I am global';

function checkScope() {
    let localVar = 'I am local';
    console.log(globalVar); // I am global
    console.log(localVar); // I am local

    if(true) {
        let blockVar = 'I am block scoped';
        console.log(blockVar); // I am block scoped
    }

    console.log(blockVar); // ReferenceError: blockVar is not defined
}

checkScope();
console.log(globalVar); // I am global
```

```
console.log(localVar); // ReferenceError: localVar is not defined
```

This example illustrates how variables are accessible within their respective scopes and the errors encountered when trying to access them outside of their scope. Block-scoped variables ‘blockVar‘ are inaccessible outside the block in which they are defined. Similarly, function-scoped variables ‘localVar‘ and lexically scoped variables ‘globalVar‘ and ‘localVar‘ respect their boundaries.

Understanding these scoping rules is essential for writing clean, efficient, and error-free code in JavaScript. Proper scoping ensures that variables are only accessible where needed and helps prevent potential bugs due to unexpected modifications of variables.

Chapter 5

Functions and Scope

This chapter provides an in-depth look at functions and scope in JavaScript. It covers different ways to define functions, including function declarations, expressions, and arrow functions. Topics such as parameters, arguments, default parameters, and the use of the return statement are examined. The chapter also explains closures, Immediately Invoked Function Expressions (IIFE), and higher-order functions. Additionally, it explores various types of scope—global, local, and block—and the implications of scope on variable accessibility and function hoisting. Understanding these concepts is crucial for writing modular, reusable, and well-structured code.

5.1 Introduction to Functions

Functions are one of the fundamental building blocks in JavaScript. They encapsulate code that can be reused, making programs more modular and maintainable. A function can be defined once and executed multiple times, reducing code duplication and enhancing readability.

In JavaScript, functions are objects. This means they have properties and methods, can be assigned to variables, passed as arguments, and returned from other functions. To understand the flexibility and power of functions, it is necessary to appreciate their syntax and behavior in JavaScript.

The most common way to define a function is through a *function declaration*. This traditional method uses the `function` keyword, followed by the function name, a list of parameters enclosed in parentheses, and the function body enclosed in curly braces. Here's an example of a simple function that calculates the sum of two numbers:

```
function add(a, b) {
    return a + b;
}
```

In this example, `add` is the function name, and `a` and `b` are parameters. The function returns the sum of the two parameters. This function can be called later in the code by using its name followed by parentheses and passing the required arguments:

```
let result = add(5, 3);
console.log(result);  // Output: 8
```

Functions can also be defined using *function expressions*. This involves declaring a function, but instead of giving it a name, the function is anonymous and assigned to a variable. For instance:

```
const multiply = function(a, b) {
    return a * b;
};
```

Here, the function has no name, and it is assigned to the variable `multiply`. This function can be invoked using the variable name:

```
let product = multiply(4, 2);
console.log(product);  // Output: 8
```

The introduction of ES6 brought the *arrow function*, a concise way to define functions using the => syntax. Arrow functions are particularly useful for simple functions and provide a shorter syntax compared to traditional function expressions. An equivalent `add` function using arrow syntax would look like this:

```
const add = (a, b) => {
    return a + b;
};
```

For functions with a single return statement, you can omit the curly braces and the `return` keyword:

```
const add = (a, b) => a + b;
```

Arrow functions differ from traditional functions in a crucial way: they do not have their own `this` context. The `this` value inside an arrow function is inherited from the enclosing lexical context, making them particularly suitable for use in scenarios where you require the `this` context of the surrounding code.

Function parameters allow functions to accept inputs. When calling a function, the values passed are known as arguments. JavaScript functions are versatile in how they handle parameters and arguments. They do not enforce a strict rule on the number of arguments passed, meaning you can call a function with fewer or more arguments than the defined parameters. Missing arguments are set to `undefined`:

```
function greet(name) {
    console.log(`Hello, ${name}!`);
}

greet();  // Output: Hello, undefined!
```

Conversely, if more arguments are supplied than the number of parameters, the extra arguments are ignored. This behavior offers great flexibility but requires careful handling to avoid logical errors in your code:

```
greet('Alice', 'Bob');  // Output: Hello, Alice!
```

Functions can also have *default parameters*, where default values are specified if no arguments or `undefined` are passed. Consider the following example:

```
function greet(name = 'Guest') {
   console.log(`Hello, ${name}!`);
}

greet(); // Output: Hello, Guest!
greet('Alice'); // Output: Hello, Alice!
```

By setting `name` to 'Guest', the function outputs a default greeting when no argument is supplied.

Understanding these foundational aspects of functions prepares us to dive deeper into concepts like closures, higher-order functions, and scope, which are critical for mastering JavaScript's advanced functionalities. Functions are not just callable pieces of code; they play a pivotal role in creating more complex, efficient, and manageable programs by fostering code reuse and modular design.

5.2 Function Declarations

A function declaration in JavaScript consists of the function keyword followed by the name of the function, a list of parameters enclosed in parentheses, and a block of statements enclosed in curly braces. This is one of the most commonly used methods for defining a function and is also the basis of understanding more complex functions and scope behaviors in JavaScript.

The syntax for a function declaration is as follows:

```
function functionName(parameter1, parameter2, ...) {
   // function body
   // statements
}
```

A simple example of a function declaration to add two numbers is:

```
function add(a, b) {
   return a + b;
}
```

In this example, the function `add` takes two parameters `a` and `b`. When called, it returns the sum of these parameters. Function declarations are hoisted to the top of their scope, meaning that they can be called before they are defined in the code.

```
console.log(sum(5, 3)); // Outputs: 8

function sum(a, b) {
   return a + b;
}
```

This output reflects the behavior of function hoisting in JavaScript, where the function `sum` is available before its actual declaration due to hoisting.

When using function declarations, it is important to understand scope and how it affects the visibility of variables and functions. A function declared within another function has local scope, meaning it can only be accessed within that containing function or nested functions, not from outside.

```
function outerFunction() {
   function innerFunction() {
      console.log("Hello from Inner Function");
   }
   innerFunction();
}

outerFunction(); // Outputs: Hello from Inner Function
// innerFunction(); // Uncaught ReferenceError: innerFunction is not
   defined
```

Here, the `innerFunction` is only accessible within the `outerFunction`. Trying to call the `innerFunction` from outside its containing function results in a reference error.

Function declarations can also handle default parameters, where if an argument is not provided, the function uses the default value provided in the declaration.

```
function greet(name = 'Guest') {
  return `Hello, ${name}`;
}

console.log(greet()); // Outputs: Hello, Guest
console.log(greet('John')); // Outputs: Hello, John
```

In this example, the function `greet` uses the default parameter `Guest` if no argument is passed. Default parameters are useful for ensuring that functions behave correctly even when not all arguments are supplied.

Moreover, nested functions within function declarations have access to the outer function's scope, which leads to the concept of closures. Closures will be extensively discussed in the section on closures and lexical environments, but it is valuable to recognize that function declarations play a foundational part in their formation.

Function declarations are also applicable in creating reusable modules of code. Functions declared can be invoked multiple times with different arguments to produce desired results, illustrating the significance of understanding the structure and implications of function declarations in JavaScript.

Integrating these properties of function declarations into your programming practices facilitates the creation of more modular, readable, and maintainable code, which is a fundamental aspect of modern JavaScript development practices.

5.3 Function Expressions

In JavaScript, functions can be defined using expressions, which allows functions to be assigned to variables, passed as arguments, or returned from other functions. This approach provides flexibility in coding and enables the creation of anonymous functions and higher-order functions. Understanding function expressions is crucial for writing dynamic and modular code segments.

A function expression defines a function and can be stored in a variable. This results in the function having a reference name, which can then be used to invoke the function. The syntax for a function expression is as follows:

```
const myFunction = function (parameter1, parameter2) {
    // function body
    return parameter1 + parameter2;
};
```

In this example, `myFunction` is a variable that stores a function which takes two parameters, `parameter1` and `parameter2`, and returns their sum. Unlike function declarations, function expressions do not have a hoisting feature; they are not moved to the top of their scope at runtime.

```
// Attempt to call before initialization results in an error
try {
  console.log(myFunction(2, 3));
} catch (e) {
  console.log(e);
}

// Properly declared function expression
const myFunction = function (parameter1, parameter2) {
    return parameter1 + parameter2;
};

// Valid call after declaration
console.log(myFunction(2, 3));
```

```
ReferenceError: Cannot access 'myFunction' before initialization
5
```

Function expressions can also be anonymous, meaning they do not have a name. These are particularly useful in scenarios involving callbacks, as they provide a concise way to define inline functions.

```
const numbers = [1, 2, 3, 4, 5];

// Using an anonymous function as a callback
const squares = numbers.map(function (num) {
    return num * num;
});

console.log(squares);
```

```
[1, 4, 9, 16, 25]
```

Function expressions can also be named, providing additional benefits such as better debugging and self-referencing. Named function expressions are similar to anonymous function expressions, but they include a name after the `function` keyword. This name is local only to the function's scope and cannot be accessed outside of it.

```
const factorial = function fact(n) {
    if (n <= 1) {
        return 1;
    }
    return n * fact(n - 1); // self-reference using the name 'fact'
};

console.log(factorial(5));
```

```
120
```

A critical aspect of function expressions is their interaction with scope and higher-order functions. Function expressions enable the creation of closures, which capture the lexical environment of the function at the time it is declared. This concept is elaborated in the chapter section on closures.

```
function makeCounter() {
    let count = 0; // count is a free variable captured by the closure

    return function () {
        count += 1;
        return count;
    };
}

const counter = makeCounter(); // counter is a function that has access
    to 'count'
console.log(counter());
console.log(counter());
```

```
1
2
```

In this example, `makeCounter` returns a function expression that forms a closure over the `count` variable. Each invocation of `counter()` increments and retains the state of `count`, demonstrating how function expressions can create powerful abstractions and stateful functions.

By understanding and utilizing function expressions, developers can write more versatile and modular code in JavaScript. The capability to create anonymous functions, named functions, and leverage closures makes function expressions an indispensable feature in modern JavaScript programming.

5.4 Arrow Functions

Arrow functions, introduced in ECMAScript 6 (ES6), offer a succinct way to write functions in JavaScript. Arrow functions differ syntactically and behaviorally from traditional function expressions, with one of the primary differences being their handling of the `this` keyword, which we will explore in detail.

Arrow functions use a shorter syntax and do not have their own `this`, `arguments`, `super`, or `new.target` bindings. These functions are best suited for non-method functions and are particularly useful when working with higher-order functions, as they streamline the code, making it more readable and maintainable.

The basic syntax of an arrow function is:

```
// Traditional Function Expression
var multiply = function(a, b) {
    return a * b;
};

// Arrow Function Expression
var multiply = (a, b) => a * b;
```

If there is only one parameter, the parentheses surrounding the parameter list can be omitted:

```
var square = x => x * x;
```

When the body contains multiple statements, curly braces are required, and an explicit `return` statement must be used to return a value:

```
var sum = (a, b) => {
    let result = a + b;
    return result;
};
```

Arrow functions do not have their own `this` context; instead, they inherit `this` from the enclosing function, which makes them particularly suitable for certain use cases, such as within methods in classes or when dealing with callbacks where binding `this` manually could be cumbersome.

```
function Person() {
    this.age = 0;

    setInterval(() => {
        this.age++; // `this` properly refers to the instance
    }, 1000);
}
```

```
var p = new Person();
```

In a traditional function, `this` would be undefined inside the `setInterval` callback unless explicitly bound.

To illustrate further, compare the following examples using traditional functions and arrow functions:

```
// Traditional Function Example
function Counter() {
    this.count = 0;
    setInterval(function() {
        this.count++; // this is undefined here
    }, 1000);
}

// Correcting with bind()
function Counter() {
    this.count = 0;
    setInterval(function() {
        this.count++; // this now refers to the Counter instance
    }.bind(this), 1000);
}

// Using Arrow Function
function Counter() {
    this.count = 0;
    setInterval(() => {
        this.count++; // this refers to the Counter instance
    }, 1000);
}
```

Arrow functions cannot be used as constructors and will throw an error if the `new` keyword is used with them:

```
TypeError: Arrow function cannot be used as a constructor
```

Another significant limitation is that arrow functions do not have an `arguments` object. To access arguments in arrow functions or to implement variadic functions, the rest parameters syntax must be used:

```
// Traditional Function with arguments object
function traditionalSum() {
    let sum = 0;
    for (let i = 0; i < arguments.length; i++) {
        sum += arguments[i];
    }
    return sum;
}

// Arrow Function with rest parameters
var arrowSum = (...numbers) => {
    return numbers.reduce((acc, curr) => acc + curr, 0);
};
```

Arrow functions streamline the syntax for writing concise functions and are particularly effective for cases where the `this` context needs to be inherited from the enclosing scope. They are well-suited for functional programming paradigms, including the use of higher-order functions, as demonstrated in the following example of array manipulation:

```
let numbers = [1, 2, 3, 4, 5];
let squares = numbers.map(n => n * n);
```

This section has provided an in-depth examination of arrow functions, highlighting their syntax, context for `this`, and practical applications. Readers are encouraged to apply arrow functions in appropriate contexts to leverage their advantages in modern JavaScript development.

5.5 Parameters and Arguments

In JavaScript, functions are defined with parameters, which act as placeholders for the values that are passed into the function when it is called. These values are referred to as arguments. Parameters and arguments play a critical role in the dynamic and flexible nature of JavaScript functions, allowing functions to be reused and to operate on a variety of inputs.

Parameters are specified in the function declaration or function expression within parentheses, separated by commas. When the function is called, the arguments provided must match the parameters in order (positionally). Here is an example demonstrating the use of parameters and arguments:

```
function sum(a, b) {
   return a + b;
}
let result = sum(3, 7); // Arguments 3 and 7 are passed to parameters a and b
console.log(result); // Output: 10
```

Default Parameters

JavaScript allows for default parameter values, which are used if no argument or an `undefined` value is passed. This feature provides flexibility and prevents errors due to missing arguments.

```
function greet(name = 'Guest') {
   console.log("Hello, " + name);
}
greet(); // Output: Hello, Guest
greet('Alice'); // Output: Hello, Alice
```

When a default parameter is used, if the function call omits the corresponding argument, the default value is utilized, ensuring the function operates smoothly.

Rest Parameters

Rest parameters allow a function to accept an indefinite number of arguments as an array. This is particularly useful when the number of parameters is not known beforehand or when you want to handle multiple arguments collectively.

```
function multiply(multiplier, ...numbers) {
    return numbers.map(num => num * multiplier);
}
let result = multiply(2, 1, 2, 3, 4); // Arguments 1, 2, 3, and 4 are captured into
     an array
console.log(result); // Output: [2, 4, 6, 8]
```

In this example, the rest parameter `...numbers` collects all additional arguments into an array, allowing `numbers.map()` to iterate over them and apply the `multiplier`.

Argument Object

Functions in JavaScript have access to an array-like object named `arguments` containing all the arguments passed to the function. This object allows functions to be called with more parameters than those explicitly defined.

```
function findMax() {
    let max = -Infinity;
    for (let i = 0; i < arguments.length; i++) {
        if (arguments[i] > max) {
            max = arguments[i];
        }
    }
    return max;
}
let max = findMax(1, 5, 3, 9, 2); // Arguments 1, 5, 3, 9, and 2 are in arguments
     object
console.log(max); // Output: 9
```

Parameter Destructuring

JavaScript supports parameter destructuring, which allows for extracting values from objects or arrays passed as arguments. This feature can lead to more readable and concise code.

```
function displayUser({name, age}) {
    console.log("Name: " + name);
    console.log("Age: " + age);
}
let user = {name: 'John', age: 30};
displayUser(user); // Output: Name: John Age: 30
```

In the example above, the function `displayUser` destructures the `user` object argument to directly access the `name` and `age` properties.

Parameter Scope

Parameters have a function-level scope, meaning they can be accessed and modified within the function body. Any changes to the parameters are local modifications and do not affect the arguments passed by the caller, provided the arguments are primitive values. For objects, changes to their properties will reflect outside the function due to the reference nature of objects.

```
function modifyValue(x) {
    x = 5; // This modification is local to the function scope
}
let value = 10;
modifyValue(value);
console.log(value); // Output: 10

function modifyObject(obj) {
    obj.name = 'Alice'; // This modification reflects outside the function
}
let person = {name: 'John'};
modifyObject(person);
console.log(person.name); // Output: Alice
```

Understanding the distinction between passing by value (for primitive types) and passing by reference (for objects) is crucial in predicting function behavior and debugging.

Overloading in JavaScript

JavaScript does not support function overloading in the traditional sense, unlike some other languages. This means functions cannot be defined with the same name but with different parameter lists. However, similar behavior can be achieved using conditional logic and the `arguments` object.

```
function add(a, b, c) {
    if (typeof c !== 'undefined') {
```

```
        return a + b + c;
    } else {
        return a + b;
    }
}
console.log(add(1, 2)); // Output: 3
console.log(add(1, 2, 3)); // Output: 6
```

By checking the number and types of arguments, you can simulate multiple function signatures, allowing flexible function implementations.

Through these various features—default parameters, rest parameters, the `arguments` object, destructuring, and function scope—JavaScript offers a robust and flexible mechanism for managing function inputs, enhancing the language's capability to handle complex and varied coding requirements.

5.6 Default Parameters

Default parameters were introduced in ECMAScript 6 (ES6) and have since become a fundamental tool for JavaScript developers. They provide a way to initialize function parameters with default values if no argument is passed or if the argument is `undefined`. This feature greatly enhances function flexibility and robustness by reducing the need for manual checks and assignments in the function body.

To define default parameters, assign a value to the parameter in the function signature, which will be used only if no argument is provided for that parameter. If an argument is supplied, the provided argument takes precedence over the default value.

The following example demonstrates basic usage of default parameters:

```
function greet(name = 'Guest') {
    console.log(`Hello, ${name}!`);
}

greet(); // Output: Hello, Guest!
greet('John'); // Output: Hello, John!
```

In the `greet` function, the parameter `name` is assigned a default value of 'Guest'. When the function is called without any argument, the default value is used. If an argument (e.g., 'John') is supplied, the default value is overridden.

Combining Default Parameters with Other Parameters

Default parameters can coexist with regular parameters and can be placed anywhere in the parameter list. However, it is a good practice to place default parameters at the end to maintain clear and predictable behavior.

```
function order(item, quantity = 1) {
  console.log(`Ordered ${quantity} ${item}(s)`);
}

order('apple'); // Output: Ordered 1 apple(s)
order('banana', 3); // Output: Ordered 3 banana(s)
```

In this function, `quantity` is a default parameter while `item` is a regular parameter. When the function is invoked with only one argument ('apple'), `quantity` defaults to 1.

Complex Default Values

Default parameters can be expressions, including function calls and complex operations. This behavior allows for dynamic and flexible default values.

```
function randomlyAssignId(id = Math.floor(Math.random() * 1000)) {
  console.log(`Assigned ID: ${id}`);
}

randomlyAssignId(); // Output: Assigned ID: 435 (random value)
randomlyAssignId(27); // Output: Assigned ID: 27
```

In this example, the `id` parameter is assigned a random integer between 0 and 999 if no argument is specified. The use of `Math.floor(Math.random() * 1000)` illustrates how default parameters can leverage JavaScript's extensive built-in methods.

Dealing with `undefined`

Only when an argument is explicitly `undefined` does the default parameter take effect. Passing any other `falsy` value (e.g., `null`, `0`, `false`, `''`) will not trigger the default value.

```
function logValue(value = 10) {
  console.log(value);
}

logValue(undefined); // Output: 10 (default value)
logValue(null); // Output: null
```

```
logValue(0); // Output: 0
logValue(''); // Output:
```

In the function `logValue`, default value assignment occurs only when the argument is `undefined`. This behavior is crucial to consider when designing functions intended to handle a variety of input values.

Interplay with the Rest Parameter

Default parameters can be used in conjunction with the rest parameter, allowing for even more versatile function definitions. The rest parameter aggregates all remaining arguments into an array and must always be the last parameter in the function signature.

```
function addValues(a, b = 2, ...others) {
    let sum = a + b;
    for (let value of others) {
        sum += value;
    }
    return sum;
}

console.log(addValues(1)); // Output: 3 (1 + 2)
console.log(addValues(1, 3)); // Output: 4 (1 + 3)
console.log(addValues(1, 3, 4, 5, 6)); // Output: 19 (1 + 3 + 4 + 5 + 6)
```

In this example, `b` is a default parameter, while `...others` is a rest parameter. The rest parameter groups additional arguments into an array, enabling the function to process an arbitrary number of arguments.

Performance Considerations

While default parameters provide significant benefits regarding readability and error-handling, developers should be mindful of their performance implications. Default values are evaluated at call time, which can lead to performance overhead if the default value computation is complex or resource-intensive.

For instance, consider the following example where a complex default value is computed only when necessary:

```
function createComplexObject(config = expensiveComputation()) {
    // Function body
}

function expensiveComputation() {
    // Simulates a resource-intensive task
    return new Array(1000000).fill(0).map((_, i) => i * 2);
}
```

```
const start = performance.now();
createComplexObject(undefined); // Pass undefined to trigger default parameter
const end = performance.now();

console.log(`Execution time: ${end - start} ms`); // Output: Execution time: <some
    time> ms
```

In the example, the `expensiveComputation` function generates a large array, simulating a time-consuming operation. When `createComplexObject` is called with `undefined`, the default value triggers the costly computation, which contributes to overall execution time.

Best Practices

1. **Order Parameters Intuitively**: Place required parameters before optional ones with default values to avoid potential confusion. 2. **Use Default Parameters Judiciously**: Reserve default parameters for cases that genuinely benefit from them, particularly when an argument is often omitted. 3. **Avoid Side Effects**: Ensure that default parameters are expressions without side effects, preserving the predictability and reliability of function calls. 4. **Consider Readability and Maintenance**: Strive for clarity and simplicity when defining default parameters to facilitate ease of understanding and maintenance.

By leveraging default parameters, developers can design functions that handle missing arguments gracefully, leading to more robust and maintainable code.

5.7 Rest Parameters

Rest parameters allow functions to accept an indefinite number of arguments as an array, enabling a more flexible and concise way to handle function inputs. This is particularly useful for functions that need to operate on a variable number of arguments or when additional parameters should be captured without explicitly specifying each one.

To declare rest parameters in JavaScript, the ellipsis syntax (`...`) is used before the parameter name. This parameter must be the last one in the function's parameter list, as it collects all remaining arguments passed to the function into a single array. The inability to precede rest parameters with other parameters is due to JavaScript's argument parsing mechanism, which channels all trailing arguments into the rest parameter when encountered.

Consider the following example to illustrate the usage of rest parameters:

```
function sum(...numbers) {
   return numbers.reduce((acc, curr) => acc + curr, 0);
}

console.log(sum(1, 2, 3)); // Outputs: 6
console.log(sum(1, 2, 3, 4, 5)); // Outputs: 15
```

In this example, the function s̀umt̀akes a varying number of arguments. The rest parameter ǹumbersàggregates these arguments into an array. The r̀educem̀ethod is then utilized to compute the sum of all elements within this array. It is also important to note the initial value of 0̀in the r̀educem̀ethod to manage the accumulation process effectively.

Rest parameters are particularly advantageous when creating functions that need to handle scenarios such as gathering and manipulating extraneous inputs or forwarding arguments to other functions. By capturing an arbitrary number of arguments in a structured way, rest parameters eliminate the need to reference the special àrgumentsòbject, providing a more modern and intuitive approach.

For instance, a function tailored to concatenate multiple strings can leverage rest parameters as follows:

```
function concatenate(separator, ...strings) {
   return strings.join(separator);
}

console.log(concatenate(', ', 'apple', 'banana', 'cherry')); // Outputs:
     "apple, banana, cherry"
console.log(concatenate(' - ', 'red', 'blue', 'green')); // Outputs: "
     red - blue - green"
```

In this implementation, the first argument s̀eparators̀pecifies the delimiter to be used between concatenated strings. The rest parameter s̀tringsc̀ollects all subsequent arguments for joining. This pattern ensures that the function's usability remains straightforward while maintaining flexibility.

When integrating rest parameters in conjunction with other parameters, programmers must adhere to positional constraints. Rest parameters effectively handle trailing arguments but cannot be interspersed with regular parameters. The parameter list should be structured such that rest parameters always appear at the end:

```
function description(title, ...details) {
   console.log(`Title: ${title}`);
   console.log(`Details: ${details.join(', ')}`);
}

description('Meeting Agenda', 'Discuss project milestones', 'Budget
    review', 'Q&A session');
```

In the above code, descriptiontakes a fixed titleparameter followed by an indefinite number of details. The console output confirms correct aggregation of the remaining arguments:

```
Title: Meeting Agenda
Details: Discuss project milestones, Budget review, Q&A session
```

By incorporating rest parameters efficiently, developers can design versatile functions capable of handling diverse input sets, fostering modularity and adaptability in code structure. This feature, combined with other modern JavaScript capabilities, underscores the language's evolution toward accommodating expressive and concise programming paradigms.

5.8 The return Statement

The `return` statement in JavaScript is an essential feature for controlling the output of functions and manipulating the program's execution flow. It serves the dual purpose of terminating a function's execution and optionally returning a value to the location where the function was called. This section delves into the syntax, behavior, and nuances of the `return` statement, providing a comprehensive understanding essential for effective JavaScript programming.

The general syntax of the `return` statement is:

```
return [expression];
```

When a function encounters a `return` statement, the following occurs:

- The function stops executing.
- The value specified by the `expression` is returned to the function caller. If no `expression` is provided, `undefined` is returned.

To illustrate, consider a function that calculates the sum of two numbers:

```
function addNumbers(a, b) {
    return a + b;
}
```

In this example, the `return` statement calculates the sum of `a` and `b` and returns the result. When we call `addNumbers(5, 10)`, the function returns 15.

A key aspect of the `return` statement is its ability to halt the function's execution. Any code following a `return` statement within the same function is unreachable and, therefore, not executed. For example:

```
function exampleFunction() {
    console.log('This message is logged.');
    return; // Function execution stops here
    console.log('This message is NOT logged.');
}
```

Executing `exampleFunction()` will only log 'This message is logged.' to the console. The second `console.log` statement will not execute because the function terminates upon reaching the `return` statement.

When considering whether to include an `expression` with the `return` statement, it's important to examine the use case. Functions can be designed to provide outputs or simply perform actions. For instance:

```
function sayHello() {
    return 'Hello, World!';
}
```

Calling `sayHello()` returns the string 'Hello, World!'. Conversely, functions that perform tasks without needing to return values might look like this:

```
function printHello() {
    console.log('Hello, World!');
}
```

Here, `printHello()` performs an action but does not return a value.

Conditional Return Statements

It is common to use `return` within conditional structures to terminate a function and optionally return a value when certain conditions are met. This can streamline code and enhance readability. Consider a function that checks if a number is even:

```
function isEven(number) {
    if (number % 2 === 0) {
        return true;
    }
    return false;
}
```

Here, the function immediately returns `true` if the number is even, otherwise it returns `false`. This approach ensures that the function exits early when the condition is satisfied, avoiding unnecessary code execution.

Returning Objects and Functions

The `return` statement is not limited to primitive values; it can also return complex data types, such as objects and functions. This capability is particularly useful in functional programming and when designing modular systems.

For example, to return an object:

```
function createUser(name, age) {
    return {
        name: name,
        age: age
    };
}
```

Calling `createUser('Alice', 30)` returns an object `{ name: 'Alice', age: 30 }`.

Returning functions allows for higher-order functions, which will be covered in a subsequent section:

```
function createMultiplier(multiplier) {
    return function(number) {
        return number * multiplier;
    };
}
```

Here, `createMultiplier` returns a new function that multiplies its input by a specified multiplier. Calling `let double = createMultiplier(2)` results in `double(5)` returning 10.

Understanding the versatile role of the `return` statement enables developers to write clear, efficient, modular, and maintainable code. Through judicious use of `return`, functions can be designed explicitly to provide outputs, perform actions, or encapsulate complex behaviors within callable units, enhancing the overall robustness and readability of JavaScript programs.

5.9 Closures and Lexical Environment

Closures are a fundamental concept in JavaScript, acting as a powerful feature that allows for the creation of more expressive and modular code. A closure is formed when a function is defined inside another function and accesses variables from its parent function's scope. This capability relies on the lexical environment model.

When you define a function inside another function, the inner function has access to the following:

- Its own local variables.
- Variables declared in its parent's scope.
- Global variables.

To illustrate closures, consider the following example:

```
function outerFunction(outerVariable) {
    return function innerFunction(innerVariable) {
        console.log('Outer Variable: ' + outerVariable);
        console.log('Inner Variable: ' + innerVariable);
    };
}

const newFunction = outerFunction('outside');
newFunction('inside');
```

The output of this code is:

```
Outer Variable: outside
Inner Variable: inside
```

In this example, 'innerFunction' is a closure. It captures the variable 'outerVariable' from 'outerFunction''s scope and retains access to it even after 'outerFunction' has completed execution. This is possible because the lexical environment associated with 'outerFunction' is preserved in memory due to 'innerFunction' maintaining a reference to it.

Lexical Environment

A lexical environment is a data structure that holds identifier-variable mappings. Lexical scoping means that functions are executed using the scope chain that was in effect when they were defined, not the scope chain that is in effect when they are executed.

Every time a function is invoked, a new execution context is created. This execution context consists of two parts: the environment record and the outer environment reference.

- **Environment Record**: This part of the execution context contains the local variables, functions, and arguments defined within the context.
- **Outer Environment Reference**: This is a reference to the lexical environment of the parent context, allowing the function to access variables from its parent scope.

Consider another example to delve deeper into how closures utilize lexical environments:

```
function createCounter() {
    let count = 0;
    return function increaseCounter() {
        count++;
        return count;
    };
}

const counter = createCounter();
console.log(counter()); // Output: 1
console.log(counter()); // Output: 2
console.log(counter()); // Output: 3
```

The 'createCounter' function returns the 'increaseCounter' function, which forms a closure. The variable 'count' is encapsulated within the 'createCounter' function's lexical environment. Each call to 'counter' increments and returns the updated count. The value of 'count' persists between function calls because it is preserved in the closure's lexical environment.

Practical Use Cases of Closures

Closures are incredibly useful in various programming scenarios such as data privacy and partial application of functions. Here, we explore some practical applications.

Data Privacy

Closures help in implementing private variables. By encapsulating variables inside a function, we can prevent them from being accessed directly from the outside. This encapsulation is a way to create "private" variables in JavaScript.

```
function Person(name) {
   let privateName = name;
   return {
      getName: function() {
         return privateName;
      },
      setName: function(newName) {
         privateName = newName;
      }
   };
}

const person1 = Person('Alice');
console.log(person1.getName()); // Output: Alice
person1.setName('Bob');
console.log(person1.getName()); // Output: Bob
```

In this example, 'privateName' is not accessible outside of the 'Person' function scope, ensuring that it can only be modified or accessed through the 'getName' and 'setName' methods provided by the returned object.

Partial Application

Partial application refers to the process of fixing a number of arguments to a function, producing another function of smaller arity. Closures facilitate the creation of partially applied functions.

```
function multiply(a) {
   return function(b) {
      return a * b;
   };
}

const double = multiply(2);
console.log(double(5)); // Output: 10
console.log(double(10)); // Output: 20
```

Here, ‘double‘ is a partially applied function created by fixing the first argument of ‘multiply‘ to ‘2‘. This is achieved through the closure formed by the inner function which captures and utilizes the argument ‘a‘ from its enclosing function.

Closures, by leveraging the lexical environment model, provide a powerful mechanism for managing state and creating modular and maintainable code. Understanding and correctly using closures is fundamental to mastering JavaScript.

5.10 Immediately Invoked Function Expressions (IIFE)

Immediately Invoked Function Expressions, abbreviated as IIFE (pronounced ïffy)̈, are a fundamental concept in JavaScript that involve creating and executing functions simultaneously. This technique is particularly useful for controlling variable scope and ensuring that variables do not interfere with one another within the broader scope of the application.

An IIFE is a function that is defined and invoked in the same expression. The basic syntax of an IIFE is as follows:

```
// An example of an IIFE
(function() {
    // Code to be executed immediately
})();
```

The function definition is wrapped within parentheses ‘()‘, which converts the function declaration into a function expression. This is crucial because only expressions can be invoked immediately. The final pair of parentheses ‘()‘ at the end of the function definition executes the function instantaneously.

Consider a practical example where IIFEs can be effectively utilized:

```
var result = (function() {
    var name = "John Doe";
    return name;
})();
console.log(result); // Outputs: John Doe
console.log(name); // ReferenceError: name is not defined
```

In this example, the variable ‘name‘ is defined inside the IIFE and is not accessible outside of it. Instead, the value of 'name' is returned by the IIFE and assigned to the variable 'result'. This ensures that 'name' is confined to the scope of the IIFE and does not pollute the global namespace.

IIFEs can also take parameters, adding an additional layer of customization and flexibility:

```
var result = (function(name) {
    return `Hello, ${name}!`;
})("Jane Doe");
console.log(result); // Outputs: Hello, Jane Doe!
```

In this instance, the IIFE accepts an argument 'name', which can be used within its scope. This pattern is beneficial for initializing configurations or performing setup tasks that require specific inputs.

IIFEs are particularly beneficial in situations where you need to encapsulate code to avoid variable collisions. This encapsulation enforces strong encapsulation principles, leading to fewer unintended side-effects:

```
(function() {
    var counter = 0;
    var incrementCounter = function() {
        counter++;
        console.log(counter);
    };

    incrementCounter(); // Outputs: 1
    incrementCounter(); // Outputs: 2
})();
console.log(counter); // ReferenceError: counter is not defined
```

Here, the 'counter' variable and 'incrementCounter' function are encapsulated within the IIFE, ensuring that they are not accessible from the global scope, which prevents global namespace pollution.

One of the classic use cases of IIFE is in the context of module pattern implementation, allowing the declaration of private and public members:

```
var module = (function() {
    var privateVariable = "I am private";

    var privateMethod = function() {
        console.log(privateVariable);
    };

    return {
```

```
    publicMethod: function() {
        privateMethod();
    }
  };
})();

module.publicMethod(); // Outputs: I am private
module.privateMethod(); // TypeError: module.privateMethod is not a
    function
```

In the module pattern, the IIFE creates a module where 'privateVariable' and 'privateMethod' are private, but 'publicMethod' is exposed and can interact with the private members. This pattern is instrumental for creating a clean, modular code base that avoids direct manipulation of internal states and ensures better management of complex code.

IIFEs are essential for achieving function-level modularization and encapsulation in JavaScript, providing a robust mechanism for immediate code execution and namespace management. Their ability to confine scopes and prevent global leakage enables developers to write cleaner, more maintainable code.

5.11 Understanding Scope: Global, Local, and Block Scope

In JavaScript, the concept of scope defines the accessibility and lifetime of variables and functions within a code block. To ensure a comprehensive understanding, it is vital to explore three primary types of scope: global, local, and block scope.

Variables declared outside any function or block have global scope and are accessible from anywhere in the code. Global scope persists for the duration of the program's execution, which makes it particularly powerful but also potentially dangerous due to the risk of name conflicts and unintended side effects.

```
var globalVar = 'I am global';

function displayGlobalVar() {
    console.log(globalVar);
}

displayGlobalVar(); // Output: I am global
```

In the above example, `globalVar` is declared in the global scope, making it accessible within the `displayGlobalVar` function and throughout the entire script.

Local scope pertains to variables declared within a function. These variables are only accessible within the function they are declared in and cease to exist once the function execution is complete. This encapsulation protects against external interference and mitigates the risk of variable conflicts.

```
function showLocalVar() {
    var localVar = 'I am local';
    console.log(localVar);
}

showLocalVar(); // Output: I am local
console.log(localVar); // ReferenceError: localVar is not defined
```

Here, `localVar` resides in the local scope of the `showLocalVar` function and remains inaccessible outside of it, illustrated by the ReferenceError when attempting to log `localVar` externally.

ES6 introduced the `let` and `const` keywords, reinforcing the concept of block scope. Block scope is defined by curly braces {}, typically in constructs such as loops and `if` statements. Variables declared with `let` or `const` are confined within the block they are declared, promoting tighter control over variable lifecycle compared to `var`.

```
if (true) {
    let blockScopedVar = 'I am block scoped';
    console.log(blockScopedVar); // Output: I am block scoped
}
console.log(blockScopedVar); // ReferenceError: blockScopedVar is not
    defined
```

In this scenario, `blockScopedVar` is declared within the `if` block, limiting its visibility and lifespan to within the block. Using `var`, the variable would have global or function scope, depending on whether it was inside a function or not.

```
if (true) {
    var functionScopedVar = 'I am function scoped';
    console.log(functionScopedVar); // Output: I am function scoped
}
console.log(functionScopedVar); // Output: I am function scoped
```

Although the variable is confined to a block, using `var` makes it accessible outside the block if not nested within a function. It is worth noting that employing block-scoped variables enhances code modularization and minimizes unintentional modifications.

The `this` keyword's behavior is closely related to scope. In global context, `this` refers to the global object (`window` in browsers). Within a function, it depends on how the function is invoked, potentially leading to convoluted behaviors unless clearly understood and controlled.

```
console.log(this); // Output: Window object

function displayThis() {
   console.log(this); // Output: Window object
}

displayThis();

const obj = {
   value: 'I am within an object',
   showValue: function() {
      console.log(this.value);
   }
};

obj.showValue(); // Output: I am within an object
```

The carefully controlled namespace and variable lifespan conferred by block scope, alongside specialized local scope within functions, foster clearer, more maintainable codebases. This distinction reduces the risk of unexpected behaviors, forming a foundation for mastering JavaScript's intricacies.

5.12 The 'this' Keyword in Functions

The `this` keyword is an essential aspect of working with functions in JavaScript, playing a vital role in defining the execution context of a function. Understanding `this` is crucial for mastering object-oriented JavaScript and ensuring that functions behave as expected in various contexts.

In JavaScript, `this` is a dynamically scoped keyword, meaning its value is determined not by the lexical scope (where `this` is written) but by the context in which the function is invoked. The behavior of `this` changes based on the execution context.

```
console.log(this); // In a browser, this refers to the global window
    object
```

Listing 5.1: Basic 'this' in Global Context

In the global execution context, `this` references the global object, which is `window` in browsers and `global` in Node.js. However, this is modified within functions and objects.

Method Invocation

When a function is invoked as a property of an object, `this` references the object that owns the method.

```
const obj = {
  name: 'JavaScript Book',
  getName: function() {
    return this.name;
  }
};

console.log(obj.getName()); // 'JavaScript Book'
```

Listing 5.2: `this` in Method Invocation

In the above example, `this.name` inside `getName` refers to the `name` property of the object `obj`.

Function Invocation

When a function is invoked independently without reference to an object, `this` defaults to the global object (in non-strict mode).

```
function show() {
  console.log(this);
}

show(); // In a browser, this refers to the global window object
```

Listing 5.3: `this` in Function Invocation

In strict mode (`use strict`), `this` in a standalone function call is `undefined`.

```
'use strict';
function show() {
  console.log(this);
}

show(); // undefined
```

Listing 5.4: `this` in Function Invocation with Strict Mode

Arrow Functions

Arrow functions have a lexical scope for `this`, meaning they inherit `this` from the parent scope at the time of their creation. This behavior is different from traditional functions.

```
const parent = {
  name: 'Parent Object',
  getName: function() {
    const arrow = () => {
      console.log(this.name);
    };
    arrow();
  }
};

parent.getName(); // 'Parent Object'
```

Listing 5.5: `this` in Arrow Functions

In the example, the arrow function `arrow` inherits `this` from the `getName` method of the `parent` object.

Explicit Binding

In JavaScript, functions can explicitly bind `this` using `call`, `apply`, and `bind` methods.

```
function greet() {
  console.log(this.name);
}

const obj = { name: 'JavaScript Book' };

greet.call(obj); // 'JavaScript Book'
greet.apply(obj); // 'JavaScript Book'
const boundGreet = greet.bind(obj);
boundGreet(); // 'JavaScript Book'
```

Listing 5.6: Explicit Binding with `call`, `apply`, and `bind`

`call` and `apply` invoke the function immediately with `this` set to the specified object, `obj`. The `bind` method creates a new function with `this` bound to `obj`, which can be invoked later.

Constructor Invocation

When a function is used as a constructor with the `new` keyword, `this` refers to the new instance created by the constructor.

```
function Book(title) {
  this.title = title;
```

```
}

const myBook = new Book('JavaScript Deep Dive');
console.log(myBook.title); // 'JavaScript Deep Dive'
```

Listing 5.7: `this` in Constructor Invocation

The function `Book` acts as a constructor, and `this` within the constructor points to the newly created instance, `myBook`.

Understanding the nuances of the `this` keyword enables developers to write more predictable and maintainable code, leveraging object-oriented concepts in JavaScript effectively.

5.13 Higher-Order Functions

Higher-order functions are a fundamental concept in JavaScript and many other programming languages. A higher-order function is one that either takes one or more functions as arguments, returns a function as its result, or both. These functions offer numerous advantages, including improved modularity, code reusability, and the ability to create more abstract and generalized solutions to problems.

To define a higher-order function, one can leverage JavaScript's capability to handle functions as first-class citizens. This means functions can be assigned to variables, passed as arguments to other functions, and returned by other functions. Consider the following basic example:

```
function multiplyBy(factor) {
    return function(x) {
        return x * factor;
    };
}

const double = multiplyBy(2);
console.log(double(5)); // 10
```

In this example, 'multiplyBy' is a higher-order function because it returns another function. The inner function captures the 'factor' parameter from its lexical scope, demonstrating a closure. When 'double' is called with 5, it multiplies 5 by 2, yielding 10.

Higher-order functions are commonplace in JavaScript, especially when working with arrays. JavaScript provides several built-in higher-order functions such as 'map', 'filter', and 'reduce', which are methods of arrays.

The ‘map‘ function is used to transform an array by applying a given function to each element, returning a new array of transformed elements. Here is an example of how ‘map‘ operates:

```
const numbers = [1, 2, 3, 4, 5];
const squares = numbers.map(function(number) {
   return number * number;
});

console.log(squares); // [1, 4, 9, 16, 25]
```

In this case, ‘map‘ is a higher-order function that accepts a callback function to square each element in the ‘numbers‘ array. The result is a new array containing the squares of the original numbers.

The ‘filter‘ function creates a new array with all elements that pass a test implemented by the provided function. The test is a function that returns a boolean value. Consider the following use case:

```
const numbers = [1, 2, 3, 4, 5];
const evenNumbers = numbers.filter(function(number) {
   return number % 2 === 0;
});

console.log(evenNumbers); // [2,4]
```

The ‘filter‘ function iterates through ‘numbers‘, applying the callback to each element, and includes only those elements for which the callback returns ‘true‘.

The ‘reduce‘ function is particularly powerful as it applies a function against an accumulator and each element in the array to reduce it to a single value. Here is a demonstration of ‘reduce‘:

```
const numbers = [1, 2, 3, 4, 5];
const sum = numbers.reduce(function(accumulator, current) {
   return accumulator + current;
}, 0);

console.log(sum); // 15
```

In this example, the ‘reduce‘ function starts with an initial accumulator value of ‘0‘ and adds each number in the ‘numbers‘ array to this accumulator. The final result is the sum of the numbers.

An essential aspect of higher-order functions is their role in promoting functional programming patterns and immutability. When using functions like ‘map‘, ‘filter‘, and ‘reduce‘, original data structures remain unaltered, fostering a functional approach where functions do not produce side effects.

Higher-order functions can also be manually created for use in other contexts. Consider event handling where a function is executed in response to an event. A common scenario is debouncing, where you limit the rate at which a function can fire. This can be implemented using higher-order functions:

```
function debounce(func, wait) {
    let timeout;
    return function(...args) {
        clearTimeout(timeout);
        timeout = setTimeout(() => func.apply(this, args), wait);
    };
}

window.addEventListener('resize', debounce(function() {
    console.log('Resize event delayed');
}, 250));
```

In this example, ‘debounce‘ is a higher-order function that takes a function (‘func‘) and a delay time (‘wait‘). It returns a new function that delays the execution of ‘func‘ until after the specified ‘wait‘ time has elapsed since the last time it was invoked. This is useful for improving performance during frequent event triggers like window resizing.

Higher-order functions offer great flexibility and expressive power in JavaScript. By understanding and utilizing these constructs, developers can write more modular, readable, and maintainable code that adheres to functional programming principles. Further exploration and practice with higher-order functions will enhance one’s capability to create robust applications in JavaScript.

5.14 Function Hoisting

Function hoisting is a fundamental concept in JavaScript that impacts how functions are interpreted and executed. Hoisting is a behavior in JavaScript where function declarations are moved, or "hoisted," to the top of their containing scope during the compile phase, before the actual execution of the code. This means that functions declared using function declarations can be utilized before their definition within the code.

When a JavaScript engine processes the code, it splits the execution into two main phases: the compilation phase and the execution phase. During the compilation phase, the engine allocates memory for variables and functions, which results in function declarations getting hoisted. Consequently, these functions become accessible throughout their entire scope, allowing them to be invoked even before the place in the code where they are defined.

Consider the following example to illustrate function hoisting:

```
console.log(sayHello()); // Output: Hello, world!

function sayHello() {
   return "Hello, world!";
}
```

In this code snippet, the function ‘sayHello‘ is called before it is defined. Due to hoisting, the JavaScript engine moves the function declaration to the top of its scope during the compilation phase, allowing the function call to succeed and produce the output:

```
Hello, world!
```

It is important to note that only function declarations are hoisted; function expressions and arrow functions do not enjoy the same behavior. Here is an example contrasting function declarations with function expressions:

```
// Function call using a function expression
console.log(sayHi()); // Throws TypeError: sayHi is not a function

var sayHi = function() {
   return "Hi, world!";
};
```

In this case, attempting to call ‘sayHi‘ before its definition results in a ‘TypeError‘. Variable ‘sayHi‘ is hoisted to the top of its scope as an uninitialized variable (i.e., it is defined but not assigned any value), and thus it is not a function at the time of the call. The JavaScript runtime interprets ‘sayHi‘ as ‘undefined‘ and raises the error.

To further solidify the understanding of hoisting, consider another example involving nested scopes:

```
console.log(sayGoodbye()); // Output: Goodbye, world!

function outerFunction() {
   function sayGoodbye() {
      return "Goodbye, world!";
```

```
    }
    return sayGoodbye();
}

outerFunction();
```

In this scenario, the function ‘sayGoodbye‘ has been hoisted within its containing function ‘outerFunction‘, making it accessible for a call inside ‘outerFunction‘. Therefore, invoking ‘outerFunction‘ results in the output:

```
Goodbye, world!
```

Understanding the distinction between function declarations and expressions, and their hoisting behavior, is crucial for avoiding scope-related errors and writing reliable JavaScript code. This knowledge also plays a significant role in debugging, as unanticipated hoisting can lead to confusion and unexpected behaviors, especially in large codebases.

The logical next steps after comprehending function hoisting include learning about variable hoisting, which encompasses both ‘var‘-declared variables and those defined with ‘let‘ and ‘const‘, further refining one’s understanding of JavaScript scoping and execution contexts.

Chapter 6

Objects and Prototypes

This chapter delves into the fundamental concepts of objects and prototypes in JavaScript. It covers the creation and initialization of objects, accessing and modifying object properties, and defining object methods. The chapter explores the 'this' keyword, property descriptors, getters and setters, and working with arrays as objects. A detailed discussion on prototypes, prototype chain, and inheritance is included, along with the use of constructor functions, the 'new' operator, and Object.create(). The chapter also introduces ES6 classes, static methods, and properties, and clarifies object and prototype relationships, essential for mastering object-oriented programming in JavaScript.

6.1 Introduction to Objects

Objects are a cornerstone of JavaScript and provide a way to group related data and functionality. At their core, JavaScript objects facilitate the storage and retrieval of values using a simple key-value mapping. Each key is a string (or symbol) that corresponds to a value. These values can be of any data type, including other objects, functions, arrays, and primitives such as strings and numbers.

Defining Objects

The most common way to define an object is by using object literal notation. A set of comma-separated key-value pairs are enclosed within curly braces {}. Below is an example of an object representing a person:

```
const person = {
    name: 'Alice',
    age: 30,
    isStudent: false,
    greet: function() {
        console.log('Hello, my name is ' + this.name);
    }
};
```

In this example, the object `person` has four properties: `name`, `age`, `isStudent`, and `greet`. The keys are `name`, `age`, `isStudent`, and `greet`, while the corresponding values are `'Alice'`, 30, `false`, and a function that logs a greeting message.

Accessing Object Properties

Properties of an object can be accessed in two ways: dot notation and bracket notation. Dot notation is typically preferred for its simplicity and readability:

```
console.log(person.name); // Output: Alice
console.log(person.age); // Output: 30
```

Bracket notation is useful when the property name is dynamic or not a valid identifier:

```
console.log(person['name']); // Output: Alice
const key = 'age';
console.log(person[key]); // Output: 30
```

Modifying Object Properties

Properties can be added, updated, or deleted from an object dynamically:

```
person.age = 31; // Update existing property
person.height = 172; // Add new property
delete person.isStudent; // Remove property
```

After executing the above code, the `person` object will be modified as follows:

```
{
    name: 'Alice',
    age: 31,
    greet: [Function: greet],
    height: 172
}
```

Objects Are Passed by Reference

In JavaScript, objects are passed by reference. This means that when an object is assigned to another variable, both variables refer to the same object. Any changes made through one variable will be reflected in the other.

```
const anotherPerson = person;
anotherPerson.name = 'Bob';
console.log(person.name); // Output: Bob
```

Here, `person` and `anotherPerson` point to the same object in memory. Changing the `name` property through `anotherPerson` also affects `person`.

Methods as Object Properties

Methods are functions assigned to object properties, enabling objects to carry out actions:

```
person.greet(); // Output: Hello, my name is Alice
```

Within a method, the `this` keyword refers to the object from which the method was called. Understanding this is crucial for correctly utilizing methods in objects.

Built-in Object Methods

JavaScript provides several built-in methods to operate on objects. Some of the most commonly used methods include:

```
const keys = Object.keys(person); // ['name', 'age', 'greet', 'height']
const values = Object.values(person); // ['Alice', 31, [Function: greet], 172]
const entries = Object.entries(person); // [['name', 'Alice'], ['age', 31], ['greet
    ', [Function: greet]], ['height', 172]]
```

`Object.keys()` returns an array of an object's own property names, `Object.values()` returns an array of an object's own property values, and `Object.entries()` returns an array of an object's own property [key, value] pairs.

Exploring these foundational aspects of objects prepares us to delve deeper into the concepts of prototypes, inheritance, property descriptors, and more advanced object manipulation techniques. In the following sections, we will build on this understanding to explore JavaScript's powerful object-oriented capabilities.

6.2 Creating and Initializing Objects

In JavaScript, objects are a collection of properties, where each property is a key-value pair. Creating and initializing objects are fundamental practices in JavaScript programming, enabling developers to structure data and functions cohesively. There are multiple approaches to creating and initializing objects, each serving various needs and use cases. This section covers the core methods: object literals, the `Object` constructor, and the `create` method.

One of the most straightforward ways to create objects in JavaScript is using object literals. An object literal is a comma-separated list of key-value pairs encapsulated within curly braces. Here is an example:

```
let person = {
    firstName: "John",
    lastName: "Doe",
    age: 30,
    isEmployed: true
};
```

In the above code, `person` is an object with four properties: `firstName`, `lastName`, `age`, and `isEmployed`. Each property is defined by a key (a string) and a value, which can be of any data type, including objects and functions.

To access these properties, use either dot notation or bracket notation:

```
console.log(person.firstName); // Output: John
console.log(person['lastName']); // Output: Doe
```

Dot notation is more concise and readable, while bracket notation allows access to properties using variables or strings with special characters or spaces.

The `Object` constructor provides another method for creating objects. Initially, an empty object is created, and properties are added using dot notation or bracket notation:

```
let car = new Object();
car.make = "Toyota";
car.model = "Camry";
car.year = 2020;
car["color"] = "blue";
```

Although functionally equivalent to object literals, the `Object` constructor's primary advantage lies in its ability to create objects when the property names are dynamic or not predetermined.

Another powerful method for creating and initializing objects is `Object.create()`. This method creates a new object with the specified prototype object and properties. It allows for more fine-tuned control over an object's prototype chain and property descriptors. For example:

```
let personProto = {
    greet: function() {
        console.log("Hello, my name is " + this.firstName + " " + this.lastName);
    }
};

let person1 = Object.create(personProto, {
    firstName: { value: "Jane", enumerable: true },
    lastName: { value: "Smith", enumerable: true },
    age: { value: 28, enumerable: true },
    isEmployed: { value: false, enumerable: true }
});

person1.greet(); // Output: Hello, my name is Jane Smith
```

In this code snippet, `personProto` is an object functioning as a prototype, providing the `greet` method. The `person1` object is created using `Object.create()`, inheriting `greet` from `personProto` and initializing its properties with descriptive configurations.

JavaScript developers often use functions to create and initialize objects with shared structures and behaviors. Constructor functions serve this purpose effectively, especially in pre-ES6 codebases. Here is an example of a constructor function:

```
function Employee(firstName, lastName, position) {
    this.firstName = firstName;
    this.lastName = lastName;
    this.position = position;
    this.introduce = function() {
        console.log("Hi, I am " + this.firstName + " " + this.lastName + ", " + this.
            position);
    }
}

let emp1 = new Employee("Alice", "Johnson", "Developer");
emp1.introduce(); // Output: Hi, I am Alice Johnson, Developer
```

The `Employee` function acts as a template for creating `Employee` objects. When called with the `new` operator, it initializes a new object and assigns the properties defined within the function to `this`.

The advent of ES6 classes offers a more streamlined syntax for creating constructor functions and organizing methods. Classes are syntactic sugar over JavaScript's existing prototype-based inheritance model and do not introduce a new object-oriented inheritance paradigm:

```
class Animal {
    constructor(name, species) {
        this.name = name;
        this.species = species;
    }

    describe() {
        console.log(this.name + " is a " + this.species);
    }
}

let animal1 = new Animal("Buddy", "Dog");
animal1.describe(); // Output: Buddy is a Dog
```

The example demonstrates creating an `Animal` class with a constructor to initialize instances and a `describe` method to output an animal's description.

As JavaScript evolves, the foundational knowledge of creating and initializing objects using various methodologies empowers developers to write more flexible, reusable, and maintainable code. Whether using object literals for simplicity, `Object.create()` for prototypal inheritance, or ES6 classes for clarity, the approaches to object creation are diverse and context-specific.

6.3 Accessing and Modifying Object Properties

In JavaScript, interacting with object properties is fundamental and can be performed using two principal methods: dot notation and bracket notation. Understanding when and how to use each notation is critical for both efficiency and code readability. This section covers the various techniques and nuances involved in accessing and modifying object properties, providing a comprehensive understanding essential for effective JavaScript programming.

Accessing Properties

Dot Notation: This is the most straightforward method for accessing object properties. It uses the syntax `object.propertyName`. Consider the following example where we have an object representing a car:

```
let car = {
  make: 'Toyota',
  model: 'Camry',
```

```
  year: 2020
};

console.log(car.make); // Outputs: 'Toyota'
console.log(car.year); // Outputs: 2020
```

Bracket Notation: This method allows for more dynamic property access using the syntax `object['propertyName']`. One significant advantage of bracket notation is that the property name can be a variable. This capability is particularly useful when dealing with property names that are not valid identifiers or contain spaces or special characters.

```
let car = {
  make: 'Toyota',
  model: 'Camry',
  'production year': 2020
};

console.log(car['make']); // Outputs: 'Toyota'
console.log(car['production year']); // Outputs: 2020

let prop = 'model';
console.log(car[prop]); // Outputs: 'Camry'
```

Modifying Properties

Modifying object properties can similarly be performed through dot notation or bracket notation.

Dot Notation:

```
car.year = 2021;
console.log(car.year); // Outputs: 2021
```

Bracket Notation:

```
car['model'] = 'Corolla';
console.log(car['model']); // Outputs: 'Corolla'
```

In both cases, if a property does not exist, JavaScript will create it dynamically.

Adding New Properties

New properties can be added using the assignment operator (=) with either dot or bracket notation. This does not require the property to exist initially.

Dot Notation:

```
car.color = 'blue';
console.log(car.color); // Outputs: 'blue'
```

Bracket Notation:

```
car['owner'] = 'Alice';
console.log(car['owner']); // Outputs: 'Alice'
```

Deleting Properties

Deleting properties from an object can be done using the `delete` operator. This action does not affect the object's prototype.

```
delete car.year;
console.log(car.year); // Outputs: undefined
```

Property Descriptors

JavaScript allows for more detailed control over the behavior of object properties via property descriptors. These descriptors provide attributes that define properties' characteristics, including their enumerability, configurability, and writability. Using `Object.defineProperty()` or `Object.defineProperties()`, developers can modify these attributes.

```
Object.defineProperty(car, 'make', {
  value: 'Toyota',
  writable: false,
  enumerable: true,
  configurable: false
});

console.log(car.make); // Outputs: 'Toyota'
car.make = 'Honda'; // Ignored, as writable is false
console.log(car.make); // Outputs: 'Toyota'
```

Note: Attempting to delete a non-configurable property, or redefining its configurable attribute, will result in a TypeError in strict mode.

Enumerating Properties

There are multiple ways to iterate over object properties:

`for...in` loop:

```
for (let key in car) {
  if (car.hasOwnProperty(key)) {
    console.log(`${key}: ${car[key]}`);
  }
}
```

This loop includes enumerable properties from an object's prototype chain. To ensure the loop accesses only the object's own properties, it's advisable to use the `hasOwnProperty()` method.

`Object.keys()`:

```
let keys = Object.keys(car);
keys.forEach(key => {
  console.log(`${key}: ${car[key]}`);
});
```

This method returns an array of an object's own enumerable properties, making it ideal for direct iteration.

`Object.getOwnPropertyNames()`:

```
let keys = Object.getOwnPropertyNames(car);
keys.forEach(key => {
  console.log(`${key}: ${car[key]}`);
});
```

This method returns an array of all properties found directly in a given object, including non-enumerable properties.

Understanding these methods and their appropriate use cases is crucial for effective JavaScript development. Enumerating object properties provides flexibility and control which are vital for tasks ranging from simple data retrieval to complex manipulations within objects.

6.4 Object Methods

An object method in JavaScript is a function that is a property of an object. Methods enable objects to exhibit behaviors by executing code that operates on the object's properties or attributes.

Consider an example of an object representing a simple bank account. The account can execute operations such as deposit and withdrawal. Here is how you might define such an object and its associated methods in JavaScript:

```
let bankAccount = {
  balance: 0,
  deposit: function(amount) {
    this.balance += amount;
    return this.balance;
  },
  withdraw: function(amount) {
    if (amount > this.balance) {
      console.log('Insufficient funds');
      return false;
    }
    this.balance -= amount;
    return this.balance;
  },
  showBalance: function() {
    console.log(`Balance: $${this.balance}`);
    return this.balance;
  }
};
```

In this example, ‘bankAccount‘ is an object with a ‘balance‘ property and three methods: ‘deposit‘, ‘withdraw‘, and ‘showBalance‘. Each method is defined as a function that operates on the ‘balance‘ property of ‘bankAccount‘. Notice the usage of the ‘this‘ keyword within these methods, referencing the object to which the methods belong.

To invoke these methods on the ‘bankAccount‘ object:

```
bankAccount.deposit(100); // Adds 100 to the balance
bankAccount.showBalance(); // Displays 'Balance: $100'
bankAccount.withdraw(50); // Deducts 50 from the balance
bankAccount.showBalance(); // Displays 'Balance: $50'
bankAccount.withdraw(60); // Attempts to deduct 60, logs 'Insufficient
    funds'
```

Executing these commands results in:

```
Balance: $100
Balance: $50
Insufficient funds
```

Defining methods within an object provides a powerful way to encapsulate both data and functionality. This approach is crucial for object-oriented programming (OOP), as it enhances modularity and reusability.

Additionally, methods in JavaScript can also be defined using ES6's concise method syntax. This syntax simplifies the definition by eliminating the 'function' keyword:

```
let bankAccount = {
  balance: 0,
  deposit(amount) {
    this.balance += amount;
    return this.balance;
  },
  withdraw(amount) {
    if (amount > this.balance) {
      console.log('Insufficient funds');
      return false;
    }
    this.balance -= amount;
    return this.balance;
  },
  showBalance() {
    console.log(`Balance: $${this.balance}`);
    return this.balance;
  }
};
```

The concise method syntax offers enhanced readability and is generally preferred in modern JavaScript codebases.

Arrow Functions and Object Methods

Arrow functions, introduced in ES6, provide a shorter syntax for writing functions. However, their behavior regarding the 'this' keyword is different from regular functions. Arrow functions do not have their own 'this' context; they inherit 'this' from the parent scope at the time they are defined.

Using arrow functions to define methods in objects can lead to unexpected results. Consider the following example:

```
let bankAccount = {
  balance: 0,
  deposit: (amount) => {
    this.balance += amount;
    return this.balance;
  },
  showBalance: () => {
    console.log(`Balance: $${this.balance}`);
    return this.balance;
  }
};

bankAccount.deposit(100); // Unintended behavior
```

```
bankAccount.showBalance(); // Unintended behavior
```

Here, the 'deposit' and 'showBalance' methods are defined as arrow functions. Since arrow functions do not bind their own 'this', 'this.balance' does not refer to 'bankAccount.balance' but rather the global context. This results in incorrect behavior:

```
NaN
NaN
```

Therefore, arrow functions should generally be avoided when defining object methods to ensure that the 'this' keyword refers to the object instance itself.

Method Shorthand in ES6 Classes

In ES6, classes provide a more structured way of defining objects and their methods. Here's how the 'bankAccount' example might look using an ES6 class:

```
class BankAccount {
  constructor() {
    this.balance = 0;
  }

  deposit(amount) {
    this.balance += amount;
    return this.balance;
  }

  withdraw(amount) {
    if (amount > this.balance) {
      console.log('Insufficient funds');
      return false;
    }
    this.balance -= amount;
    return this.balance;
  }

  showBalance() {
    console.log(`Balance: $${this.balance}`);
    return this.balance;
  }
}

let account = new BankAccount();
account.deposit(100); // Adds 100 to the balance
account.showBalance(); // Displays 'Balance: $100'
account.withdraw(50); // Deducts 50 from the balance
account.showBalance(); // Displays 'Balance: $50'
account.withdraw(60); // Attempts to deduct 60, logs 'Insufficient funds
    '
```

Classes not only provide a clear and organized way to create objects but also facilitate inheritance and reuse within the object-oriented paradigm.

6.5 The 'this' Keyword in Objects

In JavaScript, the `this` keyword is a fundamental concept, especially when working with objects. Understanding how `this` works is crucial for manipulating object properties and methods efficiently. The behavior of `this` varies depending on the context in which it is used, and it is determined at the time a function is called, not when the function is defined.

The primary utility of `this` is to reference the object that is currently executing the code. This allows methods or other operations within an object to access or modify the object's properties dynamically.

Basic Usage in Object Methods

When a method is called on an object, `this` refers to the object from which the method was called. Here is an example to illustrate this:

```
const person = {
  firstName: 'Jane',
  lastName: 'Doe',
  fullName: function() {
    return `${this.firstName} ${this.lastName}`;
  }
};

console.log(person.fullName());
```

Listing 6.1: Basic usage of `this` in object methods

In the example above, the `fullName` method of the `person` object uses `this` to access `firstName` and `lastName` properties. When `fullName` is called as `person.fullName()`, `this` inside the method refers to the `person` object. The output of the code would be:

```
Jane Doe
```

Context Sensitivity of `this`

The value of `this` changes with the context in which a function is invoked. A function can be called in different ways: as a method, as a standalone function, as a constructor function, or using `call()`, `apply()`, or `bind()` methods.

When a function is called as a standalone function, `this` does not refer to the calling object; it refers to the global object in non-strict mode, or it is `undefined` in strict mode.

```
function showThis() {
   console.log(this);
}

showThis(); // In non-strict mode, it logs the global object (window in
    browsers)
          // In strict mode, it logs undefined
```

Listing 6.2: Standalone function invocation

If you use `strict mode` within the function, `this` will be `undefined` when the function is called in a standalone context:

```
"use strict";

function showThisStrict() {
   console.log(this); // Prints undefined
}

showThisStrict();
```

Listing 6.3: Strict mode standalone function

`this` in Arrow Functions

Arrow functions (=>) behave differently from regular functions when it comes to `this`. They do not have their own `this` context; instead, they inherit `this` from the surrounding lexical context at the time they are defined. This makes arrow functions particularly useful in certain situations, such as in nested functions or callbacks, where maintaining the intended `this` is necessary.

```
const person = {
   firstName: 'John',
   lastName: 'Smith',
   fullName: function() {
```

```
        const getInitials = () => `${this.firstName.charAt(0)}. ${this.
            lastName.charAt(0)}.`;
        return getInitials();
    }
};

console.log(person.fullName()); // Output: J. S.
```

Listing 6.4: `this` in arrow functions

In this example, the arrow function `getInitials` inherits `this` from the `fullName` method, which ultimately refers to the `person` object. Thus, it can access `firstName` and `lastName` properties correctly.

Using `bind()`, `call()`, and `apply()`

JavaScript provides methods like `bind()`, `call()`, and `apply()` to explicitly set the value of `this` in a function, overriding the default context.

- - `bind()` returns a new function with a specified `this` value.
- - `call()` invokes a function with a specified `this` value and arguments passed individually.
- - `apply()` is similar to `call()`, but arguments are passed as an array or array-like object.

Here is an example demonstrating their usage:

```
const person1 = { firstName: 'Alice', lastName: 'Jones' };
const person2 = { firstName: 'Bob', lastName: 'Brown' };

function greet(greeting) {
    console.log(`${greeting}, ${this.firstName} ${this.lastName}`);
}

// Using bind()
const greetAlice = greet.bind(person1);
greetAlice('Hello'); // Output: Hello, Alice Jones

// Using call()
greet.call(person2, 'Hi'); // Output: Hi, Bob Brown

// Using apply()
greet.apply(person1, ['Hey']); // Output: Hey, Alice Jones
```

In this example, using `bind()`, `call()`, and `apply()` methods allows specifying different objects for the `this` value within the `greet` function, illustrating the flexibility these methods provide in controlling function context.

Understanding how `this` operates in various contexts and learning to manipulate its value effectively is instrumental in mastering JavaScript and developing robust, context-aware object-oriented code.

6.6 Property Descriptors and Getters/Setters

Property descriptors provide a mechanism to configure various behaviors and attributes of object properties. When creating and modifying properties in JavaScript, it is crucial to understand what property descriptors are and how they can be used to define and customize the attributes of object properties.

A property descriptor is an object that describes a property on another object. It is returned by the `Object.getOwnPropertyDescriptor()` method and can be used with `Object.defineProperty()` to create or modify properties. Property descriptors can define characteristics such as whether a property is writable, enumerable, or configurable.

```
const obj = {
  prop1: 42
};

const descriptor = Object.getOwnPropertyDescriptor(obj, 'prop1');
console.log(descriptor);
```

```
{
  value: 42,
  writable: true,
  enumerable: true,
  configurable: true
}
```

The descriptor object has five key properties:

- `value`: The propertyś value.
- `writable`: Boolean indicating if the property value can be changed.
- `enumerable`: Boolean indicating if the property can be enumerated in a loop.

- `configurable`: Boolean indicating if the descriptor can be changed and if the property can be deleted.
- `get` and `set`: Getter and setter functions (covered later).

To define or modify a property using a descriptor, use `Object.defineProperty()`.

```
Object.defineProperty(obj, 'prop2', {
  value: 100,
  writable: false,
  enumerable: true,
  configurable: false
});

console.log(obj.prop2); // 100
obj.prop2 = 200; // Attempt to change: Fails silently in non-strict mode
console.log(obj.prop2); // 100
```

In this example, `prop2` is non-writable, hence attempting to modify it does not change its value. Additionally, with `configurable: false`, we can neither delete `prop2` nor modify its descriptor.

```
delete obj.prop2; // Fails because configurable is false
console.log(obj.prop2); // 100
```

Getters and setters are special methods that allow for dynamically computed property values and enable encapsulation. They are defined within property descriptors using `get` and `set` keywords.

```
const person = {
  firstName: "John",
  lastName: "Doe",
  get fullName() {
    return `${this.firstName} ${this.lastName}`;
  },
  set fullName(name) {
    [this.firstName, this.lastName] = name.split(' ');
  }
};

console.log(person.fullName); // "John Doe"
person.fullName = "Jane Smith";
console.log(person.firstName); // "Jane"
console.log(person.lastName); // "Smith"
```

In this example, `fullName` is a virtual property. The getter method retrieves the full name by combining `firstName` and `lastName`. The setter method splits the given name and updates both first and last names.

Thus, getters and setters provide a way to create computed properties and validate data before storing it.

You can also add getters and setters to properties using `Object.defineProperty()`.

```
const car = {};
Object.defineProperty(car, 'speed', {
  get() {
    return this._speed;
  },
  set(value) {
    if (value < 0) {
      throw new Error('Speed must be a positive value');
    }
    this._speed = value;
  }
});

car.speed = 50; // Sets speed to 50
console.log(car.speed); // 50
car.speed = -10; // Throws error "Speed must be a positive value"
```

In this example, we define a `speed` property with validation logic: the setter ensures that only positive values are accepted, throwing an error otherwise.

Getters and setters are not enumerated in loops by default. This behavior can be managed using property descriptors to ensure encapsulation while maintaining operational control over an objectś properties.

```
const point = { xValue: 5, yValue: 10 };

Object.defineProperty(point, 'x', {
  get() {
    return this.xValue;
  },
  set(value) {
    this.xValue = value;
  },
  enumerable: true,
  configurable: true
});
Object.defineProperty(point, 'y', {
  get() {
    return this.yValue;
  },
  set(value) {
    this.yValue = value;
  },
  enumerable: true,
  configurable: true
```

```
});

for (let key in point) {
  console.log(key); // Enumerates xValue and yValue but not x or y
}

console.log(Object.keys(point)); // Logs ["xValue", "yValue"]
```

This section demonstrates how property descriptors and getters/setters allow for fine-grained control over object properties in JavaScript, enabling developers to define, protect, and derive property values dynamically.

6.7 Working with Arrays as Objects

In JavaScript, arrays are objects with additional properties and methods designed to facilitate working with ordered collections of data. Arrays are special cases of objects where the keys are standard integers, ranging from 0 to n-1, and they come with several built-in methods to perform operations such as sorting, filtering, and iteration.

To elucidate the similarities and differences between arrays and objects, consider the structure of an array in JavaScript:

```
let array = [10, 20, 30];
console.log(typeof array); // "object"
```

The output clearly indicates that an array is, at its core, an object. Thus, we can perform object-like operations on arrays, such as adding properties and methods dynamically.

```
array.customProp = "This is a custom property";
console.log(array.customProp); // "This is a custom property"
```

Arrays utilize a prototype-based inheritance model. The internal prototype (__proto__) for arrays points to `Array.prototype`, which contains predefined methods useful for managing array elements. Let us delve into some commonly used methods:

```
// Adding elements to the array
array.push(40); // array is now [10, 20, 30, 40]

// Removing the last element
array.pop(); // array is now [10, 20, 30]

// Iterating over the array
array.forEach((element) => {
    console.log(element); // Outputs 10, 20, 30
```

```
});
```

The above methods push, pop, and forEach are defined on Array.prototype. This signifies that all array objects inherit these methods, exemplifying the concept of prototypes as discussed in previous sections.

The length property of an array is a special attribute that dynamically adjusts as elements are added or removed. For instance:

```
console.log(array.length); // 3

array.push(50);
console.log(array.length); // 4, after adding the element
```

Unlike typical object properties, directly manipulating the length property of an array alters its contents:

```
array.length = 2;
console.log(array); // [10, 20] - the array now contains only the first two
    elements
```

This automatic adaptation signifies that the length property is not merely an indicator of the number of elements but an integral part of the array's behavior.

JavaScript arrays are heterogeneously typed, meaning they can hold elements of varied types, such as numbers, strings, and objects simultaneously:

```
let mixedArray = [10, "text", { key: "value" }, [1, 2, 3]];
console.log(mixedArray);
// Output: [10, "text", { key: "value" }, [1, 2, 3]]
```

Though arrays are specialized objects, they do not include some object operations such as property enumeration via for-in loops, which is intentionally optimized for object properties rather than array elements. Instead, we utilize loops such as for, forEach, or methods like map:

```
// Using 'for' loop for iteration
for (let i = 0; i < mixedArray.length; i++) {
   console.log(mixedArray[i]);
}

// Using 'map' for transformation
let squaredArray = [1, 2, 3, 4].map((num) => num * num);
console.log(squaredArray); // [1, 4, 9, 16]
```

Although arrays provide many advanced methods, one must be cautious about their performance. Operations such as splice, shift, and unshift alter the original array and could lead to high computational times for large or complex arrays due to index recalculations.

To conclude, arrays in JavaScript hold the dual characteristics of objects, augmented with specialized methods for processing sequences. Being adept in leveraging these features while understanding their underlying mechanics forms a cornerstone of proficient JavaScript programming.

6.8 Introduction to Prototypes

In JavaScript, every object has a prototype, which is an attribute that allows for the sharing of properties and methods between objects. The prototype serves as a blueprint from which objects can inherit properties and behaviors, fostering efficient memory utilization and streamlined inheritance patterns. Unlike class-based languages where inheritance is typically handled through classes, JavaScript employs prototypes to achieve a similar purpose.

The prototype object is introduced using the special attribute __proto__ (or Object.getPrototypeOf() in ES5 and later). When an object is created, it automatically links to the prototype object of its constructor. Consequently, any property or method defined on the prototype of the constructor can be accessed by instances created from that constructor.

```
function Person(name, age) {
    this.name = name;
    this.age = age;
}

Person.prototype.greet = function() {
    console.log('Hello, my name is ' + this.name);
};

var alice = new Person('Alice', 30);
alice.greet(); // Output: Hello, my name is Alice
```

Listing 6.5: Creating an object with a prototype

In this code, the constructor function Person creates objects representing individuals with a name and an age. The greet method is defined on Person.prototype, making it available to all objects created using the Person constructor without bloating each instance with a new copy of the greet method.

The prototype chain is key to understanding how property lookups work in JavaScript. When attempting to access a property on an object, JavaScript first looks at the object itself. If the property does not exist on the object, the search moves up the prototype chain, checking the object's prototype, and continues iterating up the chain until the property is found or until `null` is reached.

```
var objectA = {
    propertyA: 'valueA'
};

var objectB = Object.create(objectA);
objectB.propertyB = 'valueB';

console.log(objectB.propertyA); // Output: valueA
console.log(objectB.propertyB); // Output: valueB
```

Listing 6.6: Prototype chain example

In the example above, `objectB` is created with `objectA` as its prototype. Accessing `propertyA` on `objectB` results in the lookup proceeding to `objectA`, where `propertyA` is found.

When defining constructors, it is crucial to understand that each function in JavaScript contains a distinct `prototype` property, which is an object that will be assigned as the prototype to all instances created by that constructor. This object has a `constructor` property that points back to the function itself.

```
function Animal(type) {
    this.type = type;
}

console.log(Animal.prototype.constructor === Animal); // Output: true
```

Listing 6.7: Constructor's prototype

Modifying the prototype of a constructor after objects have been instantiated does not alter the prototype link for the existing objects.

```
function Car(model) {
    this.model = model;
}

var tesla = new Car('Model S');
Car.prototype.honk = function() {
    console.log('Beep!');
};

tesla.honk(); // Output: Beep!
```

Listing 6.8: Modifying prototype after instantiation

In capturing more complex inheritance structures, prototypes allow developers to create a hierarchy of relationships between different object types, thereby enabling features such as method overriding and polymorphism.

Lastly, understanding and leveraging prototypes in JavaScript promotes better memory usage and performance. Prototypes ensure that each instance does not hold its copy of methods, facilitating a shared and efficient approach to method invocation and property access across object instances. To verify the formal prototype chain, the following method can be useful:

```
function tracePrototypeChain(obj) {
    let currentProto = obj;
    while (currentProto) {
        console.log(currentProto);
        currentProto = Object.getPrototypeOf(currentProto);
    }
}

tracePrototypeChain(tesla);
```

Listing 6.9: Verifying prototype chain

The careful management and understanding of prototypes underpin robust and efficient object-oriented programming in JavaScript, enabling both code reuse and object behavior extension.

6.9 Prototype Chain and Inheritance

In JavaScript, the prototype chain is a fundamental concept for understanding inheritance and the delegation of properties. To fully grasp the prototype chain, it's essential to understand that each JavaScript object can have a prototype object from which it inherits properties and methods. This chain of prototypes can be traversed, forming what is known as the prototype chain.

Overview of the Prototype Chain

Every JavaScript object has an internal property called `[[Prototype]]`, accessible via `__proto__` in some environments. The `[[Prototype]]` property can be set to another object, creating a chain of objects linked together. When a property or method is accessed on an object, JavaScript first checks the object itself. If the property is not found, it proceeds to look at the object's `[[Prototype]]`. This continues up the chain until the property is found or the end of the chain is reached, which is typically `null`.

```
function Person(name) {
    this.name = name;
}

Person.prototype.greet = function() {
    return `Hello, my name is ${this.name}`;
};

const alice = new Person('Alice');
console.log(alice.greet()); // Output: Hello, my name is Alice
```

Listing 6.10: Prototype Chain Example

In this example, the `alice` object does not have a `greet` method directly on it. Instead, JavaScript looks up the prototype chain and finds `greet` on `Person.prototype`.

Constructors and Prototypes

A prototype is just an object itself, which can have its prototype, creating nested layers of inheritance. For built-in objects such as arrays and functions, JavaScript uses constructors like `Array` and `Function`, which have their prototypes set up logically. For example:

```
const arr = [];
console.log(arr.\_\_proto\_\_ === Array.prototype); // Output: true
console.log(Array.prototype.\_\_proto\_\_ === Object.prototype); //
    Output: true
```

Listing 6.11: Constructor and Prototype

In this example, the `arr` array's prototype is `Array.prototype`, and `Array.prototype`'s prototype is `Object.prototype`. At the end of this chain is `null`.

Inheritance and the Prototype Chain

By utilizing the prototype chain, we can achieve inheritance. Inheritance allows an object to use properties and methods of another object. JavaScript traditionally implements inheritance through constructor functions and prototypes, and more recently through `class` syntax introduced in ES6.

```
function Animal(name) {
```

```
    this.name = name;
}

Animal.prototype.speak = function() {
    return `${this.name} makes a noise.`;
};

function Dog(name, breed) {
    Animal.call(this, name);
    this.breed = breed;
}

Dog.prototype = Object.create(Animal.prototype);
Dog.prototype.constructor = Dog;

Dog.prototype.speak = function() {
    return `${this.name} barks.`;
};

const fido = new Dog('Fido', 'Labrador');
console.log(fido.speak()); // Output: Fido barks.
```

Listing 6.12: Inheritance Using Constructor Functions

In this example, `Dog` inherits from `Animal`. The `Dog` prototype is set to an object created with `Animal.prototype` using `Object.create`, preserving the prototype chain so that `Dog` objects can access properties and methods defined on `Animal.prototype`.

Class Syntax and Inheritance

The class syntax introduced in ES6 provides a more intuitive and accessible way to achieve inheritance. Classes in JavaScript are syntactic sugar over the existing prototype-based inheritance.

```
class Animal {
    constructor(name) {
        this.name = name;
    }

    speak() {
        return `${this.name} makes a noise.`;
    }
}

class Dog extends Animal {
    constructor(name, breed) {
        super(name);
        this.breed = breed;
    }

    speak() {
```

```
        return `${this.name} barks.`;
    }
}

const buddy = new Dog('Buddy', 'Golden Retriever');
console.log(buddy.speak()); // Output: Buddy barks.
```

Listing 6.13: Class Syntax for Inheritance

In this example, the `Dog` class extends the `Animal` class, inheriting its properties and methods. The `super` keyword is used to call the parent class's constructor, ensuring that `name` is properly initialized.

Property Lookup and Shadowing

When JavaScript attempts to access a property on an object, it looks up the prototype chain if the property is not found on the object itself. If a property with the same name is defined on both the object and one of its prototypes, the property on the object shadows the one on the prototype.

```
const parent = {
    value: 42
};

const child = Object.create(parent);
child.value = 7;

console.log(child.value); // Output: 7
delete child.value;
console.log(child.value); // Output: 42
```

Listing 6.14: Property Shadowing

In this example, the `child` object initially shadows the `value` property from `parent`. After deleting `child.value`, the lookup continues to `parent` where `value` is 42.

This seamless operation of property delegation in the prototype chain is a cornerstone of JavaScript's inheritance model, vital for creating robust and maintainable applications.

6.10 Creating and Using Constructor Functions

A constructor function is a special type of function in JavaScript that is used to create and initialize objects. This type of function allows for the encapsulation of object creation logic in a reusable and organized way. When a function is used as a constructor, the resulting objects inherit properties and methods from the constructor's prototype.

A constructor function is distinguished from regular functions by the use of the 'new' keyword when calling the function. Let's investigate the syntax and mechanics of constructor functions in detail.

```
function Person(name, age) {
    this.name = name;
    this.age = age;
}
```

In this example, the 'Person' function serves as a constructor. It takes two parameters, 'name' and 'age', and assigns them to the properties 'name' and 'age' of the object being created, which is referenced by 'this'.

Objects can be created using the 'new' keyword:

```
let person1 = new Person('Alice', 30);
let person2 = new Person('Bob', 25);
```

Here, 'person1' and 'person2' are objects created by the 'Person' constructor function. They have individual 'name' and 'age' properties, as specified during their creation.

The 'new' keyword performs several operations:

- A new empty object is created.
- The prototype property of the constructor function is assigned to the new object's __proto__.
- The constructor function is executed with 'this' bound to the new object.
- If the constructor function doesn't explicitly return an object, the newly created object is returned.

We can extend the 'Person' constructor's functionality by adding methods to its prototype:

```
Person.prototype.greet = function() {
    console.log('Hello, my name is ' + this.name);
};
```

By modifying the prototype, all instances of 'Person' will have access to the 'greet' method:

```
person1.greet(); // Outputs: Hello, my name is Alice
person2.greet(); // Outputs: Hello, my name is Bob
```

Constructor functions can also encapsulate more complex behavior. Suppose we want to add a 'birthday' method that increments the person's age:

```
Person.prototype.birthday = function() {
    this.age++;
};
```

With this method, we can update a person's age directly:

```
person1.birthday();
console.log(person1.age); // Outputs: 31
```

JavaScript also provides built-in constructor functions, such as 'Array' and 'Date'. These constructors create specialized objects that come with additional properties and methods. For example, creating a new array using the 'Array' constructor:

```
let myArray = new Array('apple', 'banana', 'cherry');
console.log(myArray); // Outputs: ['apple', 'banana', 'cherry']
```

Custom constructors can employ advanced patterns, such as inheritance. Suppose we want to define a 'Student' constructor that inherits from 'Person':

```
function Student(name, age, grade) {
    Person.call(this, name, age); // Call the parent constructor
    this.grade = grade;
}
```

The 'Student' constructor uses 'Person.call(this, name, age)' to invoke the 'Person' constructor with the context ('this') of the 'Student' object. This ensures that 'name' and 'age' are properly assigned. Next, we set up the inheritance chain:

```
Student.prototype = Object.create(Person.prototype);
Student.prototype.constructor = Student;
```

With this setup, 'Student' instances inherit from 'Person.prototype':

```
Student.prototype.study = function() {
    console.log(this.name + ' is studying.');
};
```

Creating 'Student' objects and accessing inherited methods:

```
let student1 = new Student('Charlie', 20, 'A');
student1.greet(); // Outputs: Hello, my name is Charlie
student1.study(); // Outputs: Charlie is studying.
```

This demonstrates how constructor functions provide a powerful tool for creating and organizing objects, encapsulating initialization logic, and establishing prototypes for inheritance. The technique ensures code reusability and a clear structure, making it a staple in object-oriented JavaScript programming.

6.11 The 'new' Operator

The `new` operator in JavaScript is instrumental in constructing and initializing objects created by constructor functions. Understanding the `new` operator's mechanism enhances the clarity around object instantiation, prototype linkage, and inheritance.

To understand how the `new` operator functions, consider the following constructor function example:

```
function Person(name, age) {
  this.name = name;
  this.age = age;
}
```

Listing 6.15: Constructor Function Example

Using this constructor function, we can create new instances of `Person` by invoking the `new` operator as shown below:

```
const person1 = new Person('Alice', 30);
const person2 = new Person('Bob', 25);
```

Listing 6.16: Creating Instances Using 'new'

Upon execution, `person1` and `person2` are newly created objects with their properties set to the values passed to the `Person` constructor.

The `new` operator performs several critical steps to facilitate object creation:

- It creates a new, empty object.
- It sets the prototype of the newly created object to the constructor function's `prototype` property.
- It binds the `this` keyword to the newly created object within the constructor function.
- It executes the constructor function with the supplied arguments.
- It returns the newly created object, unless the constructor function explicitly returns a non-primitive value.

Consider the following code execution details for a deeper understanding:

```
const person1 = new Person('Alice', 30);
console.log(person1); // { name: 'Alice', age: 30 }
console.log(person1 instanceof Person); // true
console.log(Object.getPrototypeOf(person1) === Person.prototype); // true
```

In this context, `person1` is an instance of `Person`, highlighting that the `new` operator links `person1`'s prototype to `Person.prototype`.

To delve deeper, consider the algorithm for object creation with the `new` operator:

Input: Constructor function *Ctor*, parameters *params*
Output: Newly created object *obj* or explicitly returned object

begin
  obj $\leftarrow$ {} `// Step 1: Create new empty object;`
  obj.__proto__ $\leftarrow$ *Ctor*.prototype `// Step 2: Set prototype;`
  Ctor.call(*obj*, *params*...) `// Step 3: Bind this and execute constructor;`
  return *obj if Ctor does not explicitly return a non-primitive*
end

The `new` operator's internal algorithm ensures that the created object correctly inherits properties and methods from the constructor's prototype, facilitating classical inheritance patterns in JavaScript.

A key aspect of the `new` operator is its role in establishing prototype linkage. When an object is created using `new`, its __proto__ property points to the constructor's `prototype` object. The relationship helps to leverage shared methods defined on the prototype. For instance:

```
Person.prototype.greet = function() {
  console.log(`Hello, my name is ${this.name}.`);
};

const person3 = new Person('Charlie', 28);
person3.greet(); // Hello, my name is Charlie.
```

Listing 6.17: Defining Methods on Prototype

In the example above, the `greet` method is defined on `Person.prototype` and is available to all instances created with `new Person()`.

The `new` operator is essential for classical inheritance in pre-ES6 versions of JavaScript and for cases requiring explicit constructor function invocations. ES6 introduced class syntax as syntactic sugar over existing prototype-based inheritance. Nonetheless, the `new` operator remains foundational, as class instantiation uses it under the hood. Understanding the `new` operator helps in comprehending broader JavaScript inheritance and object creation mechanisms.

6.12 Object.create() and Object.assign()

JavaScript provides versatile methods for creating and manipulating objects, key among them being `Object.create()` and `Object.assign()`. These methods facilitate object creation and property cloning, extending the functionality available within the language and enhancing the capacity to build complex applications efficiently.

`Object.create()` allows the creation of a new object with a specified prototype object and properties. This method is instrumental in setting up prototypes for inheritance without needing constructor functions. The syntax is straightforward:

```
let newObject = Object.create(proto[, propertiesObject]);
```

Here, `proto` is the object which should be the prototype of the newly created object, and `propertiesObject` is an optional parameter allowing you to add properties to the new object, similarly to `Object.defineProperties()`.

Consider an example where we create an object with a person prototype:

```
const person = {
    isHuman: false,
    printIntroduction: function() {
        console.log(`My name is ${this.name}. Am I human? ${this.isHuman}`);
    }
};

const me = Object.create(person);

me.name = 'Matthew'; // Adding property
me.isHuman = true; // Modifying inherited property

me.printIntroduction();
// Output: My name is Matthew. Am I human? true
```

In this example, `me` is an object created with `person` as its prototype. It inherits the `isHuman` property and the `printIntroduction` method, which it can re-use and override if needed.

The optional `propertiesObject` parameter can be used to define additional properties on the new object with the detailed property descriptors:

```
const anotherPerson = Object.create(person, {
    name: {
        value: 'Alice',
        writable: true,
        configurable: true,
        enumerable: true
    },
    isHuman: {
        value: true,
        writable: false,
        configurable: true,
        enumerable: true
    }
});
```

In this case, `anotherPerson` is created with `person` as its prototype and assigns specific descriptors to `name` and `isHuman`, highlighting the flexibility of `Object.create()` to cater to different object creation scenarios.

`Object.assign()`, on the other hand, is used for copying values from one or more source objects to a target object. This method returns the modified target object and is often used for cloning or merging objects. The basic syntax is:

```
Object.assign(target, ...sources);
```

Here, `target` is the object to which properties are added, and `sources` are the source objects from which the properties are copied. Example usage:

```
const target = {
    a: 1,
    b: 2
};
const source = {
    b: 4,
    c: 5
};

const returnedTarget = Object.assign(target, source);

console.log(target); // Output: {a: 1, b: 4, c: 5}
console.log(returnedTarget); // Output: {a: 1, b: 4, c: 5}
```

In this example, the properties from `source` overwrite those in `target`, demonstrating how `Object.assign()` performs a shallow copy of properties. This is also useful in implementing mixins, merging properties from multiple objects:

```
const mixin = {
    greet: function() {
        console.log(`Hello, ${this.name}`);
    }
};

const personCopy = Object.assign({}, person, mixin);

personCopy.name = 'John';
personCopy.greet(); // Output: Hello, John
```

This practice shows how `Object.assign()` can combine functionalities from various objects into a single object, enhancing code reuse and composability.

It is crucial to note that `Object.assign()` performs only a shallow clone. If the source object contains nested objects, references to these nested objects are copied, not the objects themselves. Consider this example:

```
const nestedSource = {
    level1: {
        level2: {
            prop: 'value'
        }
    }
};
const nestedTarget = {};
Object.assign(nestedTarget, nestedSource);

// Modifying the original object's nested property
nestedSource.level1.level2.prop = 'newValue';

console.log(nestedTarget.level1.level2.prop); // Output: newValue
```

Here, both `nestedSource` and `nestedTarget` point to the same nested object, highlighting `Object.assign()`'s limitation for deep cloning.

Algorithm 1: Object.assign() Pseudo-code

Input: target object, source objects
Output: merged target object
1 for each source object do; for each key in source object do;
target[key] $\leftarrow$ source[key]; return target;

For deep cloning, utility libraries such as Lodash provide methods like `cloneDeep`, or one might employ more sophisticated strategies such as recursive cloning or using `JSON.parse(JSON.stringify())` for simple, serializable data structures.

Both `Object.create()` and `Object.assign()` are pivotal for effective object-oriented programming in JavaScript. Leveraging these methods enhances the flexibility and efficiency of object manipulation and prototype management in your applications.

6.13 The Class Syntax in ES6

JavaScript ES6 introduced a new syntax for creating and working with objects and inheritance: the `class` syntax. Although JavaScript still remains a prototype-based language, the `class` syntax offers a more familiar, classical object-oriented approach, making it easier for developers coming from languages like Java or C++.

`class` declarations simplify the syntax and introduce a highly readable format:

```
class Person {
    constructor(name, age) {
        this.name = name;
        this.age = age;
    }

    greet() {
        return `Hello, my name is ${this.name} and I am ${this.age} years
             old.`;
    }
}
```

In the example above, the `class` keyword is used to declare a class named `Person`. The `constructor` method is a special method used for creating and initializing objects created by the class. There is only one special method with the name `constructor` in a class. If a `constructor` method is not explicitly defined, a default constructor is used.

The method `greet` declares a function that can be called on instances of `Person`. These methods are added to the prototype of the class, not directly to the instance, which is a key concept in JavaScript's prototype-based inheritance system.

To create an instance of `Person`, the `new` operator is used:

```
const person1 = new Person('John', 30);
console.log(person1.greet());
```

The output will be:

```
Hello, my name is John and I am 30 years old.
```

`class` declarations can also include getters and setters that allow for the encapsulation and controlled access to the object's properties:

```
class Rectangle {
    constructor(width, height) {
        this.width = width;
        this.height = height;
    }

    get area() {
        return this.width * this.height;
    }

    set width(value) {
        if (value <= 0) {
            throw new Error('Width must be a positive number');
        }
        this\_width = value;
    }

    get width() {
        return this\_width;
    }

    set height(value) {
        if (value <= 0) {
            throw new Error('Height must be a positive number');
        }
        this\_height = value;
    }

    get height() {
        return this\_height;
    }
}
```

In this example, properties `width` and `height` use getter and setter methods to control their values. Notice how underscore-prefixed properties (e.g., `_width`) are used internally to store the actual data, a common convention to avoid conflicts with the getter and setter accessors.

To extend another class, the `extends` keyword is used, and the `super` keyword calls the parent class's constructor and methods:

```
class Square extends Rectangle {
    constructor(side) {
        super(side, side);
    }
}
```

In the example above, `Square` inherits from `Rectangle`, meaning instances of `Square` have all methods and properties of `Rectangle`. The `super` keyword is used to call the constructor of the parent class.

Static methods, denoted with the `static` keyword, are called directly on the class itself, not on instances:

```
class MathUtil {
    static add(a, b) {
        return a + b;
    }
}

console.log(MathUtil.add(5, 7));
```

The output will be:

```
12
```

Understanding the `class` syntax requires recognizing that it is essentially syntactic sugar over JavaScript's existing prototype-based inheritance model. This means behind the scenes, the classes are still functioning within the prototype system. For instance, methods are still added to the class's prototype and instances still reference their class's prototype for method resolution.

The following example illustrates a complete usage of class inheritance, method override, and the use of static methods:

```
class Animal {
    constructor(name) {
        this.name = name;
    }

    speak() {
        return `${this.name} makes a noise.`;
```

```
    }

    static info() {
        return 'Animals are multicellular eukaryotic organisms.';
    }
}

class Dog extends Animal {
    constructor(name, breed) {
        super(name);
        this.breed = breed;
    }

    speak() {
        return `${this.name} barks.`;
    }

    static identify() {
        return 'Dogs belong to the Canidae family.';
    }
}

const d = new Dog('Rex', 'German Shepherd');
console.log(d.speak());
console.log(Dog.identify());
console.log(Animal.info());
```

The expected output is:

```
Rex barks.
Dogs belong to the Canidae family.
Animals are multicellular eukaryotic organisms.
```

In summary, the ES6 `class` syntax introduces a more structured and familiar approach to object-oriented programming in JavaScript, while providing syntactic clarity and making inheritance and encapsulation mechanisms more straightforward. This syntactic enhancement significantly aids in the readability and maintainability of JavaScript code.

6.14 Static Methods and Properties

Static methods and properties in JavaScript provide a way to define functions and properties that are accessible on the class itself rather than on instances of the class. This section delves into the utility and implementation of static methods and properties, illustrating their importance in encapsulating functionality that does not pertain to instance-specific data.

In JavaScript, class definitions can include methods and properties marked with the `static` keyword. These static members are called on the class itself, not on objects instantiated from that class. To define static methods and properties, we precede the method or property name with the `static` keyword within the class definition.

```
class MathUtils {
    static add(a, b) {
        return a + b;
    }
}
```

Listing 6.18: Example of a Static Method

In the above example, the `MathUtils` class includes a static method called `add`, which can be invoked directly on the class:

```
MathUtils.add(5, 3); // Outputs: 8
```

This invocation directly on the class demonstrates the essence of static methods: they provide behavior related to the class as a whole, instead of behavior related to instances of the class.

Static properties function similarly. They are defined with the `static` keyword and are accessed on the class itself. Consider the following example:

```
class Config {
    static apiKey = "12345-ABCDE";
}
```

Listing 6.19: Example of a Static Property

Here, `Config` includes a static property `apiKey`. You can reference this property directly on the class:

```
console.log(Config.apiKey); // Outputs: 12345-ABCDE
```

Static methods and properties are especially useful when you have utility functions or global constants that do not require the overhead of creating class instances. This approach adheres to the principle of organizing code in a more modular and hierarchical manner.

Algorithm 2: Utility class with static methods in JavaScript

```
class MathOps
    Data: none
    Result: Class with utility methods
    static add(a, b) return a + b
    static subtract(a, b) return a - b
Usage:
result1 := MathOps.add(10, 5)
result2 := MathOps.subtract(10, 5)
```

Static methods and properties are inherently part of the class, not the instances generated by the class. Attempting to access static methods or properties from an instance will result in an error. Consider the following code:

```
let mathInstance = new MathUtils();
mathInstance.add(5, 3); // Error: mathInstance.add is not a function
```

Listing 6.20: Instance Access Attempt

The error highlights that the method add exists purely on the constructor, not on the object instantiated from that constructor. This distinctive behavior emphasizes the design choice behind static members: they belong conceptually and semantically to the class encapsulation.

Furthermore, static methods can be employed within the class definition itself, effectively using them to modularize internal class logic without exposing these utilities as instance methods. Below is an example demonstrating this concept:

```
class Validator {
    static isNumber(value) {
        return typeof value === 'number';
    }

    static validateNumber(value) {
        if (!Validator.isNumber(value)) {
            throw new TypeError('Value must be a number');
        }
    }

    constructor(age) {
        Validator.validateNumber(age);
        this.age = age;
    }
}
```

Listing 6.21: Internal Class Usage of Static Methods

In the `Validator` class, the constructor utilizes the static method `validateNumber` to ensure the `age` property is correctly assigned. By keeping the validation logic within static methods, we maintain a clear separation of concerns, and enhance code reusability and readability.

This disciplined use of static methods and properties reinforces a structured approach to class design in JavaScript, emphasizing that the class themselves can be functional entities, not just blueprints for objects.

6.15 Understanding Object and Prototype Relationships

Understanding the relationship between objects and prototypes is fundamental to mastering JavaScript's object-oriented programming. This section breaks down the intricacies of this relationship by examining how JavaScript links objects through prototypes and by illustrating the prototype chain.

JavaScript uses a feature known as *[*

$$Prototype$$

] to extend the functionality of objects. Every object in JavaScript has an implicit reference to another object known as its prototype, denoted as *[*

$$Prototype$$

]. This prototype can also have its own prototype, forming what is called the *prototype chain*. The chain ends when an object reaches *null* as its prototype.

Object relationships are established through different syntaxes. One common approach is to use constructor functions with the `new` operator.

```
function Animal(name) {
    this.name = name;
}

Animal.prototype.speak = function() {
    console.log(this.name + ' makes a noise.');
```

```
};

const dog = new Animal('Dog');
dog.speak(); // Output: Dog makes a noise.
```

Listing 6.22: Creating an Object using a Constructor

The above code demonstrates that the object `dog` not only inherits properties directly assigned within the constructor function such as `name` but also methods from `Animal.prototype`, like `speak()`.

Furthermore, the `Object.create()` method allows for the creation of a new object, using an existing object as the prototype.

```
const animalMethods = {
    speak: function() {
        console.log(this.name + ' makes a noise.');
    }
};

const cat = Object.create(animalMethods);
cat.name = 'Cat';
cat.speak(); // Output: Cat makes a noise.
```

Listing 6.23: Using Object.create() to Set Prototype

In the above example, the *animalMethods* object acts as a prototype for *cat*, and thus *cat* inherits the `speak` method.

The prototype chain allows properties and methods to be resolved dynamically. When an object accesses a property, JavaScript first checks if the property exists on the object itself. If it does not, the search continues up the prototype chain until the property is found or the chain ends.

Examining prototypes in a real-world context:

```
function Car(model) {
    this.model = model;
}

Car.prototype.drive = function() {
    console.log(this.model + ' is driving.');
};

const myCar = new Car('Toyota');
myCar.drive(); // Output: Toyota is driving.

console.log(myCar.\_\_proto\_\_ === Car.prototype); // Output: true
```

Listing 6.24: Prototype Chain

The line `console.log(myCar.__proto__ === Car.prototype);` verifies that *myCar.__proto__* (or `Object.getPrototypeOf(myCar)`) indeed points to `Car.prototype`.

In ES6, the introduction of `class` syntax simplifies prototype-based inheritance yet operates under the same principle.

```
class Person {
    constructor(name) {
        this.name = name;
    }

    greet() {
        console.log(this.name + ' says hello.');
    }
}

const john = new Person('John');
john.greet(); // Output: John says hello.
```

Listing 6.25: Using ES6 Class Syntax

Despite the streamlined syntax, the *Person* class creates a constructor function and defines methods on `Person.prototype`. Consequently, *john* inherits the `greet` method from `Person.prototype`.

A more advanced aspect of prototype relationships includes understanding the `Function.prototype` and `Object.prototype`. Every function is itself an object and thus has a prototype. By default, functions derive from `Function.prototype` while non-function objects derive from `Object.prototype`.

```
console.log(Object.getPrototypeOf(Object) === Function.prototype); //
    true
console.log(Object.getPrototypeOf(Function) === Function.prototype); //
    true
console.log(Object.getPrototypeOf(Object.prototype) === null); // true
```

Listing 6.26: Object and Function Prototypes

These examples illustrate the foundational role prototypes play in JavaScript's inheritance model. Consequently, a deep understanding of object and prototype relationships enables the developer to leverage the full power of JavaScript in creating complex, scalable applications.

Chapter 7

The Document Object Model (DOM)

This chapter introduces the Document Object Model (DOM), focusing on its importance in web development. It covers the structure of the DOM tree and various methods to select, traverse, and manipulate DOM elements. Readers will learn how to create, append, remove, and replace elements, modify attributes, and work with CSS classes and styles. The chapter also details handling DOM events, understanding event propagation, using event delegation, and managing DOMContentLoaded events. Additionally, it includes guidance on working with forms and user inputs, providing a thorough understanding of dynamic web page manipulation.

7.1 Introduction to the DOM

The Document Object Model (DOM) is a crucial concept in web development, acting as the interface between JavaScript and the structure of web documents. The DOM represents an HTML or XML document as a tree-like structure, where each node is an object corresponding to a part of the document. Understanding this structure is essential for manipulating web pages dynamically.

At the core of the DOM is the `document` object, which serves as the entry point to the DOM tree. The `document` object allows JavaScript to interact with the browser's rendered HTML. By manipulating the elements via the `document` object, developers can create dynamic and interactive web pages.

```
const title = document.title;
console.log("Document title:", title);
```

The DOM defines several types of nodes, each serving a specific role:

- **Element Nodes**: Represent HTML tags.
- **Text Nodes**: Contain the text within an element.
- **Attribute Nodes**: Represent the attributes of an element.
- **Document Nodes**: Serve as the root of the entire document.

Each node type has properties and methods associated with it, allowing for sophisticated document manipulation. For example, Element nodes come with methods to access child nodes or to modify the element's attributes.

```
const heading = document.getElementById('main-heading');
heading.textContent = 'New Heading';
```

The example demonstrates accessing an element by its ID and modifying its text content, which showcases how developers can change the webpage dynamically.

The DOM tree's hierarchical structure mirrors the nested nature of HTML. Consider a simple HTML document:

```
<!DOCTYPE html>
<html>
<head>
    <title>Sample Page</title>
</head>
<body>
    <h1 id="main-heading">Welcome</h1>
    <p>This is a sample HTML document.</p>
</body>
</html>
```

This document will be represented in the DOM as follows:

```
Document
  html
      head
          title
      body
          h1
          p
```

Each tag, such as <html>, <head>, <body>, becomes an Element node within the DOM tree. Text contained within these tags, such as "Welcome" within the <h1> tag, becomes Text nodes.

A significant advantage of understanding the DOM is the ability to traverse and manipulate it. Traversal refers to navigating the DOM tree to access different nodes, which can be achieved using properties like `parentNode`, `childNodes`, `firstChild`, `lastChild`, `previousSibling`, and `nextSibling`. Here is an example to traverse the DOM tree to find an element's parent and its children:

```
const paragraph = document.querySelector('p');
const parent = paragraph.parentNode;
const children = parent.childNodes;
console.log('Parent:', parent);
console.log('Children:', children);
```

The manipulation aspect involves modifying specific nodes or attributes within the DOM. For example, using the `appendChild`, `removeChild`, `replaceChild`, and `insertBefore` methods allows adding, removing, replacing, and inserting elements respectively:

```
const newParagraph = document.createElement('p');
newParagraph.textContent = 'This is a new paragraph.';
document.body.appendChild(newParagraph);
```

In this example, a new paragraph element is created and appended to the body of the document, showcasing how seamlessly new content can be integrated into the existing structure.

Understanding the DOM forms the foundation for any web development practices. It equips developers with the knowledge required to create interactive and responsive web applications by dynamically manipulating the rendered HTML structure through JavaScript.

7.2 The DOM Tree and Nodes

The Document Object Model (DOM) is a programming interface for web documents. It represents the structure of a document as a tree of objects, making it easy for developers to manipulate web pages dynamically. Understanding the DOM tree and nodes within it is fundamental to harnessing its full potential in web development.

At the very top level of the DOM tree, we have the `document` object. This `document` object serves as the entry point to access and manipulate the nodes. These nodes are the primary elements in the DOM. Each node in the DOM represents a part of the document, such as elements, attributes, or text content.

Nodes are divided into several types, each serving different functions:

- **Element Nodes:** These represent HTML elements. For instance, an `<h1>` tag would be an element node.
- **Attribute Nodes:** These represent the attributes of HTML elements. For example, the `class` attribute in an `<h1 class="title">` would be an attribute node.
- **Text Nodes:** These represent the text content inside HTML elements.
- **Comment Nodes:** These represent comments in the HTML code.

Element nodes are perhaps the most crucial, as they can themselves contain other types of nodes, forming a nested structure. This hierarchical structure forms the "tree" of the Document Object Model.

In terms of hierarchy, consider the following example HTML:

```
<!DOCTYPE html>
<html>
  <head>
    <title>Document Title</title>
  </head>
  <body>
    <h1 id="main-heading">Main Heading</h1>
    <p class="intro">This is a paragraph of text.</p>
    <!-- This is a comment -->
    <div class="container">
      <p>Another paragraph within a div.</p>
    </div>
  </body>
</html>
```

When the browser parses this HTML, it creates a corresponding DOM tree:

```
Document
 |- html
     |- head
     |   |- title
     |- body
         |- h1 (id="main-heading")
         |- p (class="intro")
         |- #comment
         |- div (class="container")
             |- p
```

In the above tree structure:

- The `Document` node is the root node, as it represents the entire page. - The `html`, `head`, and `body` nodes are element nodes nested within the `Document` node. - The `title`, `h1`, `p`, and `div` nodes are also element nodes. - The text within the `h1` and `p` tags are represented by text nodes. - The comment within the `body` is represented by a comment node.

To programmatically interact with these nodes, JavaScript provides several essential properties and methods. For example, consider the following script:

```
let heading = document.getElementById("main-heading");
// Accessing the text content of the h1 element
console.log(heading.textContent);
```

Here, the `document.getElementById("main-heading")` method selects the `<h1>` element with the ID of `main-heading`. The `textContent` property retrieves the text within that element.

Traversal between nodes is facilitated by various properties:

- `parentNode`: Refers to the parent node of the current node.
- `childNodes`: A NodeList of all child nodes of the current node.
- `firstChild`, `lastChild`: Refer to the first and last child nodes of the current node, respectively.
- `previousSibling`, `nextSibling`: Refer to the previous and next sibling nodes of the current node, respectively.

Consider the following script to traverse the DOM tree created from the previous HTML:

```
let containerDiv = document.querySelector('.container');
console.log(containerDiv.parentNode); // Logs the body element
console.log(containerDiv.childNodes); // Logs the NodeList of child
    elements
console.log(containerDiv.firstChild); // Logs the first child (text node
    or element)
console.log(containerDiv.lastChild); // Logs the last child (text node
    or element)
```

Using the above traversal properties, we can navigate around the DOM tree with ease, accessing and manipulating nodes as required.

Understanding nodes' properties and behaviors is critical when building interactive web applications. Each node type interacts differently with DOM methods and properties, giving the developer fine-grained control over document structure and content. This foundational knowledge sets the stage for more advanced DOM manipulation techniques discussed in subsequent sections.

7.3 Selecting DOM Elements: getElementById, getElementsByClassName, getElementsByTagName

Selecting elements within the DOM is foundational to effectively manipulating and interacting with web pages. JavaScript provides several methods to accomplish this, focusing on specific and efficient selection strategies. This section provides a detailed examination of three primary DOM selection methods: `getElementById`, `getElementsByClassName`, and `getElementsByTagName`.

Individuals working with the DOM must develop a robust understanding of these selection methods to ensure precision in manipulating web page elements.

The `getElementById` method retrieves a single element that matches a given id attribute. It is one of the most straightforward methods, offering a unique identifier for elements which ensures a single, precise selection.

```
let element = document.getElementById('header');
```

In the above code snippet, the element with the `id` attribute of `header` is selected and assigned to the variable `element`. Given that `ids` should be unique within an HTML document, this method guarantees a one-to-one selection, simplifying subsequent manipulations of the element.

The `getElementsByClassName` method selects all elements that match a specified class name, returning a live HTMLCollection. This method is critical for scenarios requiring the manipulation of multiple elements sharing a common class.

```
let elements = document.getElementsByClassName('menu-item');
```

In this instance, all elements with the class `menu-item` are selected and stored in the `elements` variable. As an HTMLCollection, `elements` can be traversed using indexing or iteration methodologies, allowing for bulk operations on group member elements.

```
for (let i = 0; i < elements.length; i++) {
    elements[i].style.color = 'blue';
}
```

This loop iterates over each element in the `elements` collection, changing the text color to blue. The live nature of HTMLCollection means it automatically updates to reflect changes in the DOM structure, providing an up-to-date collection of elements matching the specified class name.

The `getElementsByTagName` method acquires all elements with a given tag name, also returned as a live HTMLCollection. This method is beneficial for broad, tag-based selections.

```
let paragraphs = document.getElementsByTagName('p');
```

With this command, every <p> (paragraph) element within the document is selected and stored in the `paragraphs` variable. As with class name selections, it is possible to iterate over these elements and apply collective transformations.

```
for (let i = 0; i < paragraphs.length; i++) {
    paragraphs[i].textContent = 'Updated text';
}
```

This code updates the text content in all paragraph elements to `'Updated text'`. Such manipulation underlines the utility of tag-based selection in uniformly updating content across multiple elements.

Adhering to these selection techniques, developers gain granular control over document elements. By utilizing `id`, `class`, or `tag name`, efficient element targeting can be performed, streamlining DOM manipulations and promoting modular, readable JavaScript code. Leading to sophisticated and dynamic web interactions, precise element selection is vital in contemporary web development practices.

7.4 Selecting DOM Elements: querySelector and querySelectorAll

The `querySelector` and `querySelectorAll` methods provide powerful and flexible means for selecting DOM elements using CSS selectors. Unlike more specialized methods such as `getElementById` or `getEle-`

`mentsByClassName`, these methods can employ complex selectors to retrieve elements that cannot be easily accessed otherwise. Understanding how to utilize these methods effectively can greatly enhance the capability to manipulate and traverse the DOM.

`querySelector` accepts a single argument, which is a CSS selector string. It returns the first element within the document (or a specific subtree) that matches the specified selector. If no matches are found, it returns `null`. This behavior makes `querySelector` especially useful when targeting specific elements that exist uniquely within a document.

```
const firstParagraph = document.querySelector('p');
console.log(firstParagraph); // Outputs the first <p> element in the
    document
```

In the example above, `querySelector` is used to select and log the first <p> element it encounters in the document. This method supports any valid CSS selector, making it extremely versatile. For instance, selecting elements by ID or class is straightforward:

```
const header = document.querySelector('#main-header');
const activeItems = document.querySelector('.active');
```

Here, `querySelector` selects an element with the ID `main-header` and the first element with the class `active`. Both ID and class selectors follow standard CSS syntax. Additionally, `querySelector` can combine selectors to target elements more precisely:

```
const mainSectionParagraph = document.querySelector('section#main p.
    intro');
```

In this example, `querySelector` finds the first <p> element with the class `intro` that is a descendant of the <`section`> element with the ID `main`. Compound selectors allow for hierarchical and attribute-based selection, greatly enhancing specificity.

On the other hand, `querySelectorAll` is used when targeting multiple elements matching a given selector. It returns a static `NodeList` representing a collection of elements from within the document that match the specified group of selectors. Despite its name, the `NodeList` returned is not live, meaning it does not automatically update if the document's structure changes.

```
const allParagraphs = document.querySelectorAll('p');
console.log(allParagraphs); // Outputs a NodeList of all <p> elements in
    the document
```

Unlike `getElementsByTagName`, which returns a live HTMLCollection, the `NodeList` from `querySelectorAll` is an array-like structure that can be iterated over, but it does not dynamically reflect changes in the DOM. Iteration over the `NodeList` can be achieved using standard loop constructs or higher-order functions provided by JavaScript.

```
const items = document.querySelectorAll('.item');
items.forEach((item) => {
   console.log(item);
});
```

The `forEach` method utilized above highlights the `NodeListś` compatibility with more modern JavaScript syntactic features and methods. This can make handling collections of elements more intuitive and concise.

Advanced usage of `querySelectorAll` includes leveraging complex CSS selectors to target elements based on a variety of conditions:

```
const evenItems = document.querySelectorAll('.item:nth-child(even)');
const visibleLinks = document.querySelectorAll('a[href\^="http"]:not([
    hidden])');
```

In this snippet, the first query selects all even children with the class `item`, while the second selects all <a> elements whose `href` attribute starts with `http` and that do not have the `hidden` attribute. These selectors take advantage of pseudo-classes and attribute selectors to create precise and powerful queries.

Both `querySelector` and `querySelectorAll` are essential tools in modern web development, enabling developers to write clear, expressive, and maintainable code when interacting with the DOM.

7.5 Traversing the DOM

To efficiently manipulate the structure and content of a webpage, a thorough understanding of DOM traversal is imperative. Traversal involves navigating through the elements of the DOM tree, which mirrors the hierarchical XML structure of the HTML document. Mastery of DOM traversal enables developers to seamlessly access and manipulate any node within the tree without relying on specific identifiers or classes.

In DOM traversal, we use various properties and methods provided by the DOM API to move through nodes in different directions. These directions include moving to parent, child, sibling, and ancestor nodes. Here are the essential properties and methods used for traversing the DOM:

Node Properties:

- `parentNode` - This property returns the parent node of the specified node, or null if the node has no parent. Knowing a node's parent is crucial for tasks that involve moving up the hierarchy or removing nodes.

```
let parent = document.getElementById('childElement').parentNode;
```

- `childNodes` - This property returns a live NodeList of all child nodes of the specified node, including text nodes. This property is useful for accessing a list of all children.

```
let children = document.getElementById('parentElement').childNodes;
```

- `firstChild` and `lastChild` - These properties return the first and last child nodes of the specified node, respectively. These are particularly useful for accessing boundary elements within a parent node.

```
let first = document.getElementById('parentElement').firstChild;
let last = document.getElementById('parentElement').lastChild;
```

- `nextSibling` and `previousSibling` - These properties return the next and previous sibling nodes of the specified node, respectively. They are used to navigate through nodes that share the same parent.

```
let next = document.getElementById('currentElement').nextSibling;
let prev = document.getElementById('currentElement').previousSibling;
```

- `children` - This property returns a live HTMLCollection containing all child elements of the specified node, excluding text nodes. This property provides a more concise view compared to `childNodes`.

```
let children = document.getElementById('parentElement').children;
```

Node Methods:

- `getElementsByTagName(tagName)` - This method returns a live

HTMLCollection of elements with the given tag name. It allows traversal by selecting nodes of a specific type within a subtree.

```
let paragraphs = document.getElementById('content').getElementsByTagName(
    'p');
```

- `getElementsByClassName(className)` - This method returns a live HTMLCollection of all child elements with the specified class name(s). It restricts the traversal to elements with a specific class.

```
let items = document.getElementById('list').getElementsByClassName('item'
    );
```

- `querySelector(selectors)` - This method returns the first element that matches a specified CSS selector(s) within the document or a subtree. It provides a powerful and flexible way to select nodes.

```
let mainTitle = document.getElementById('content').querySelector('h1.main
    -title');
```

- `querySelectorAll(selectors)` - This method returns a NodeList of all elements that match the specified CSS selector(s). It is useful for accessing multiple nodes simultaneously.

```
let allTitles = document.getElementById('content').querySelectorAll('h2.
    section-title');
```

Example of Traversing the DOM:

```
let section = document.querySelector('section');
while (section) {
    console.log(section.nodeName); // Outputs the tag name of each section element
    section = section.nextSibling; // Moves to the next sibling node
}
```

```
SECTION
#text
SECTION
#text
...
```

Understanding these traversal properties and methods allows developers to effectively manipulate the DOM structure. This skill is essential for dynamic content generation, responsive user interfaces, and complex web interactions. By harnessing DOM traversal, developers can create more interactive and user-friendly web applications.

7.6 Manipulating DOM Elements: InnerHTML, TextContent, and InnerText

Manipulating the content of DOM elements is a fundamental aspect of dynamic web development. Within the DOM API, three essential properties—`innerHTML`, `textContent`, and `innerText`—enable developers to manipulate HTML and text within elements effectively. Understanding the differences between these properties is crucial for making informed decisions while manipulating content programmatically.

`innerHTML` is a property of an element that allows you to get or set the HTML content inside the element. It parses any strings assigned to it as HTML, which can lead to significant performance overhead if used for large or complex markup.

```
let divElement = document.getElementById('exampleDiv');

// Setting HTML content
divElement.innerHTML = '<p>This is a <strong>paragraph</strong> with
    HTML content.</p>';

// Getting HTML content
console.log(divElement.innerHTML);
```

Listing 7.1: Using innerHTML to manipulate element content

The output of the above code will be:

```
<p>This is a <strong>paragraph</strong> with HTML content.</p>
```

While `innerHTML` is powerful, it should be used cautiously due to security concerns such as Cross-Site Scripting (XSS) attacks. Always sanitize user inputs before assigning them to `innerHTML` to prevent security vulnerabilities.

`textContent`, in contrast, represents the text content of an element and its descendants. It does not parse HTML and treats any provided content as plain text, preventing the execution of HTML tags or scripts.

```
let divElement = document.getElementById('exampleDiv');

// Setting text content
divElement.textContent = 'This is a paragraph with plain text content.';

// Getting text content
console.log(divElement.textContent);
```

Listing 7.2: Using textContent to manipulate element content

The output of the above code will be:

```
This is a paragraph with plain text content.
```

Using `textContent` ensures that any HTML tags will be displayed as text rather than rendered as HTML. This makes `textContent` a secure alternative to `innerHTML` when HTML parsing is unnecessary.

The `innerText` property is similar to `textContent` but has some notable differences. `innerText` takes into account CSS styles, including `display: none` and visibility of elements. Thus, it reflects the "rendered" text content of an element, considering the CSS properties applied.

```
let divElement = document.getElementById('exampleDiv');

// Setting inner text
divElement.innerText = 'This text is affected by CSS properties.';

// Getting inner text
console.log(divElement.innerText);
```

Listing 7.3: Using innerText to manipulate element content

The output of the above code will be:

```
This text is affected by CSS properties.
```

`innerText` also triggers reflow, meaning the browser will re-calculate the positions and geometries of elements in the DOM tree, which can affect performance on complex pages.

In practice, choosing between `innerHTML`, `textContent`, and `innerText` depends on the specific use case:

- Use `innerHTML` when you need to insert or manipulate HTML markup.
- Use `textContent` to insert or retrieve plain text, ensuring that HTML is treated as text.
- Use `innerText` when you need to consider CSS properties affecting visibility and layout of the text.

By mastering these properties, developers can manipulate DOM elements more effectively and make their web pages dynamic and responsive, while ensuring security and performance standards are met.

7.7 Creating and Appending Elements

Creating and appending elements to the DOM is a fundamental aspect of dynamic web development, enabling developers to alter the structure and content of web pages programmatically. This section provides an in-depth exploration of methods to create new elements and append them to the DOM using vanilla JavaScript.

To create a new element, we use the `document.createElement()` method. This function generates an element specified by its tag name. For instance, to create a new `<div>` element, the syntax is as follows:

```
let newDiv = document.createElement('div');
```

The element is created but not yet part of the DOM tree. To make it visible on the web page, it must be appended to an existing DOM node. The `appendChild()` method is commonly used to accomplish this task. Suppose we want to add the newly created `<div>` as a child to an existing element, say a `<body>` tag:

```
document.body.appendChild(newDiv);
```

The `appendChild()` method adds the new element as the last child of the specified parent element. If needed, we can also add multiple elements in sequence. Here is an example demonstrating this concept by appending several new `<li>` elements to an existing `<ul>` element:

```
let ulElement = document.querySelector('ul');
for (let i = 1; i <= 5; i++) {
    let liElement = document.createElement('li');
    liElement.textContent = 'Item ' + i;
    ulElement.appendChild(liElement);
}
```

In certain situations, appending an element at a specific position is necessary. The `insertBefore()` method inserts a node before a reference node as a child of a specified parent node. For instance:

```
let newItem = document.createElement('li');
newItem.textContent = 'New Item';
let ulElement = document.querySelector('ul');
let referenceNode = ulElement.children[2]; // third child
ulElement.insertBefore(newItem, referenceNode);
```

This example inserts `newItem` before the third child of the `<ul>` element.

It is also possible to create text nodes using the `docu-`

ment.createTextNode() method. Text nodes represent the text content of elements. For instance:

```
let textNode = document.createTextNode('Hello, World!');
let paragraph = document.createElement('p');
paragraph.appendChild(textNode);
document.body.appendChild(paragraph);
```

Here, a text node containing "Hello, World!" is created and appended to a <p> element, which is then appended to the body of the document.

Another important method is append(), which can add multiple nodes and strings:

```
let div = document.createElement('div');
div.append('Text part ', document.createElement('span'));
document.body.appendChild(div);
```

This method appends "Text part" and a new <span> element to the <div>.

Using the template element allows for creating HTML fragments that are not rendered until explicitly appended to the DOM. This can be particularly useful for creating complex structures before adding them to the document:

```
let template = document.createElement('template');
template.innerHTML = '<div>Template Content</div>';
let content = document.importNode(template.content, true);
document.body.appendChild(content);
```

The template element holds the HTML structure, and document.importNode() clones it for subsequent DOM insertion.

Understanding these methods empowers developers to create rich, interactive web applications by dynamically manipulating the DOM structure.

7.8 Removing and Replacing Elements

An essential aspect of dynamic web development is the ability to remove and replace elements within the Document Object Model (DOM). JavaScript provides several methods and properties to facilitate these tasks effectively. Understanding and accurately implementing these operations is crucial for maintaining responsive and interactive web applications.

To remove an element from the DOM, the `removeChild()` method is commonly utilized. This method is invoked on a parent node and requires the child node to be removed as its argument. Conversely, the entire element can be removed directly from its parent using the `remove()` method. This method does not require knowledge of the parent node.

Consider the following example where we remove a specific element from the DOM:

```
<!DOCTYPE html>
<html>
<head>
    <title>Remove Element Example</title>
    <script>
        function removeElement(){
            // Get the parent node
            var container = document.getElementById('container');

            // Get the child element to be removed
            var elementToRemove = document.getElementById('item');

            // Remove the child element
            container.removeChild(elementToRemove);
        }

        function removeElementDirectly(){
            var elementToRemove = document.getElementById('item');

            // Remove the element directly
            elementToRemove.remove();
        }
    </script>
</head>
<body>
    <div id="container">
        <p id="item">This is a removable paragraph.</p>
    </div>
    <button onclick="removeElement()">Remove with parent</button>
    <button onclick="removeElementDirectly()">Remove directly</button>
</body>
</html>
```

In this example, we have two buttons, each triggering a different method to remove the same element. The first button calls the `removeElement()` function, employing the `removeChild()` method on the parent node `container`. The second button calls the `removeElementDirectly()` function, which utilizes the `remove()` method on the element itself.

The `replaceChild()` method replaces an existing child node with a new node. This method requires two arguments: the new node and the node to be replaced. The following example illustrates the use of `replaceChild()` to substitute an existing paragraph with a new one:

```
<!DOCTYPE html>
<html>
<head>
    <title>Replace Element Example</title>
    <script>
        function replaceElement(){
            // Get the parent node
            var container = document.getElementById('container');

            // Create a new element
            var newParagraph = document.createElement('p');
            newParagraph.textContent = 'This paragraph is newly added.';

            // Get the existing element to be replaced
            var oldParagraph = document.getElementById('item');

            // Replace the old element with the new element
            container.replaceChild(newParagraph, oldParagraph);
        }
    </script>
</head>
<body>
    <div id="container">
        <p id="item">This paragraph will be replaced.</p>
    </div>
    <button onclick="replaceElement()">Replace Element</button>
</body>
</html>
```

Here, a new paragraph is created using the `createElement()` method and replaced with an existing paragraph within the same container by clicking the button.

JavaScript also allows replacing elements using modern approaches like the `replaceWith()` method. This method offers a straightforward way to replace an element directly without targeting the parent node. Here is an example:

```
<!DOCTYPE html>
<html>
<head>
    <title>Replace Element Directly Example</title>
    <script>
        function replaceElementDirectly(){
            var oldParagraph = document.getElementById('item');
            var newParagraph = document.createElement('p');
```

```
            newParagraph.textContent = 'This paragraph has replaced the
                old one directly.';

            // Replace the old element with the new element directly
            oldParagraph.replaceWith(newParagraph);
        }
    </script>
</head>
<body>
    <p id="item">This paragraph will be replaced directly.</p>
    <button onclick="replaceElementDirectly()">Replace Element Directly</
        button>
</body>
</html>
```

In this example, the `replaceWith()` method is applied to the old paragraph, seamlessly substituting it with a newly created paragraph without explicitly referencing the parent node.

Understanding these methods and effectively utilizing them ensures a smoother user experience and efficient DOM manipulation in modern web development practices. By leveraging `removeChild()`, `remove()`, `replaceChild()`, and `replaceWith()`, developers can dynamically manage the structure and content of a webpage, making it interactive and responsive to user actions.

7.9 Modifying Element Attributes

Understanding and manipulating DOM elements' attributes is a fundamental aspect of dynamic web development. Attributes in HTML elements provide additional information about elements; they are set within the start tag, and each attribute is composed of a name and a value pair. Various methods exist in JavaScript to interact with these attributes, enabling developers to modify the properties of HTML elements dynamically.

To manipulate attributes in the DOM, we primarily use methods from the `Element` interface such as `getAttribute()`, `setAttribute()`, `removeAttribute()`, in addition to properties directly reflecting HTML attributes, like setting `id`, `class`, `src`, etc.

```
// Selecting an element
var element = document.getElementById("myElement");

// Getting the value of an attribute
var attributeValue = element.getAttribute("data-custom");
```

```
console.log(attributeValue); // outputs the attribute value

// Setting a new attribute or modifying an existing one
element.setAttribute("data-custom", "newValue");

// Removing an attribute
element.removeAttribute("data-custom");
```

Listing 7.4: Modifying Element Attributes using JavaScript

1. **getAttribute**(attributeName): This method returns the value of the specified attribute on the element. If the attribute does not exist, it returns `null`.

```
var imgElement = document.querySelector("img");
var srcValue = imgElement.getAttribute("src");
console.log(srcValue); // Logs the src attribute of the image element
```

Listing 7.5: Using getAttribute() Method

2. **setAttribute**(attributeName, value): This method adds a new attribute or changes the value of an existing attribute on the specified element.

```
var linkElement = document.querySelector("a");
linkElement.setAttribute("href", "https://www.example.com");
```

Listing 7.6: Using setAttribute() Method

3. **removeAttribute**(attributeName): This method removes an attribute from the specified element if it exists.

```
var buttonElement = document.querySelector("button");
buttonElement.removeAttribute("disabled");
```

Listing 7.7: Using removeAttribute() Method

Moreover, for a faster and potentially more readable manipulation, direct properties corresponding to many attributes can be used:

```
// Direct property manipulation
var inputElement = document.querySelector("input");

// Setting the 'type' attribute via property
inputElement.type = "password";

// Getting the 'type' attribute via property
console.log(inputElement.type); // Outputs 'password'
```

Listing 7.8: Modifying Attributes via Direct Property Manipulation

Differences between Attributes and Properties

While HTML attributes initialize DOM properties and are generally in sync, they are not the same. Properties are a reflection of the current state of the DOM element whereas attributes are defined by the HTML and usually remain static unless explicitly altered.

```
var checkbox = document.querySelector("input[type='checkbox']");

// Set the 'checked' attribute
checkbox.setAttribute("checked", false);
console.log(checkbox.checked); // true - reflects the checked state of
    the checkbox

// Remove the 'checked' attribute
checkbox.removeAttribute("checked");
console.log(checkbox.checked); // false - reflects that the checkbox is
    not checked
```

Listing 7.9: Attributes vs Properties

Working with Data Attributes

Custom data attributes (prefixed with `data-`) are used to store extra information on standard, semantic HTML elements that cannot be handled by the other attributes. They are intended to store custom data private to the page or application.

```
var divElement = document.querySelector("div");

// Setting the data attribute
divElement.setAttribute("data-author", "Jane Doe");

// Accessing the data attribute
console.log(divElement.getAttribute("data-author")); // Jane Doe

// Using dataset property
divElement.dataset.book = "JavaScript Deep Dive";
console.log(divElement.dataset.book); // JavaScript Deep Dive
```

Listing 7.10: Working with Data Attributes

The `dataset` property provides convenient access to all the element's data attributes without needing to use `getAttribute` and `setAttribute` for each.

Understanding these methods and properties enables intricate control over the attributes of DOM elements. Detailed knowledge of these can significantly improve handling various dynamic behaviors required in modern web applications.

7.10 Working with CSS Classes and Styles

In JavaScript, manipulating CSS classes and styles is an essential aspect of dynamic web development. The ability to programmatically alter the presentation of HTML elements provides a powerful mechanism for enhancing user interaction and visual appeal. This section will delve into various methods offered by the Document Object Model (DOM) to work with CSS classes and inline styles.

The `classList` Property: One of the most efficient ways to manipulate CSS classes of an element is through the `classList` property. The `classList` property returns a live `DOMTokenList` collection of the class attributes for the element. This collection allows developers to add, remove, toggle, or check for the existence of a class without directly manipulating the `className` property.

```
const element = document.getElementById('myElement');

// Add a class
element.classList.add('newClass');

// Remove a class
element.classList.remove('oldClass');

// Toggle a class
element.classList.toggle('anotherClass');

// Check if an element has a class
if (element.classList.contains('newClass')) {
  console.log('Element has the class newClass');
}
```

Listing 7.11: Using classList to manipulate CSS classes

`element.className` Property: For situations where you need to manipulate the entire list of classes, the `element.className` property can be utilized. By setting the `className` property, you can assign a string value that contains a space-separated list of classes. However, this direct manipulation can overwrite existing classes, so it should be used with caution.

```
const element = document.getElementById('myElement');
```

```
// Set the complete class list
element.className = 'class1 class2 class3';

// Get the current class list
console.log(element.className);
```

Listing 7.12: Using className to manipulate classes

Inline Styles: Apart from CSS classes, JavaScript provides methods to manipulate an element's inline styles using the `style` property. The `style` property returns a `CSSStyleDeclaration` object that represents the element's inline styles.

```
const element = document.getElementById('myElement');

// Set a single inline style property
element.style.color = 'red';

// Set multiple inline style properties
element.style.cssText = 'background-color: yellow; width: 150px;';

// Remove an inline style property
element.style.removeProperty('color');

// Accessing computed styles
const computedStyles = getComputedStyle(element);
console.log(computedStyles.color);
```

Listing 7.13: Manipulating inline styles

`element.style.cssText`: The `cssText` property allows assigning or retrieving the entire inline style declaration for an element. This can be particularly useful for setting multiple inline styles at once.

```
const element = document.getElementById('myElement');

// Setting multiple styles simultaneously
element.style.cssText = 'color: blue; background: white; border: 1px
    solid black;';

// Reading the entire inline style declaration
console.log(element.style.cssText);
```

Listing 7.14: Using cssText to manipulate inline styles

Working with Vendor Prefixes: In certain cases, you might need to set styles with vendor-specific prefixes. JavaScript allows this by directly setting the style properties using camelCase.

```
const element = document.getElementById('myElement');
```

```
// Set a vendor-prefixed style property
element.style.webkitTransform = 'rotate(20deg)';
element.style.msTransform = 'rotate(20deg)';
element.style.transform = 'rotate(20deg)';
```

Listing 7.15: Setting vendor-prefixed styles

`getComputedStyle()`: The `getComputedStyle()` method helps retrieve the computed styles of an element, which include all CSS properties, whether they are set inline, embedded, or from external stylesheets.

```
const element = document.getElementById('myElement');

// Retrieve the computed styles for an element
const computedStyles = window.getComputedStyle(element);

// Access individual computed style properties
console.log(computedStyles.marginTop);
console.log(computedStyles['margin-top']); // Alternative syntax
```

Listing 7.16: Using getComputedStyle to read computed styles

By mastering these techniques, developers can exert a high degree of control over the presentation and responsiveness of web pages, ensuring a deeper and finer level of interaction with the DOM.

7.11 Handling DOM Events

Event handling forms a significant aspect of web development, enabling interactive and dynamic user experiences. In the context of the Document Object Model (DOM), events are actions or occurrences that happen in the system you are programming, which the system tells you about so your code can respond. Users interact with web pages by clicking, typing, scrolling, and more. Each of these interactions triggers specific events that can be handled using JavaScript.

To handle events in the DOM, there are several fundamental steps and techniques that are employed:

- Selecting the element where the event listener will be attached.
- Defining the event type to listen for.
- Writing the function to be executed when the event occurs.

- Attaching the event listener to the element.

The following provides a detailed, example-driven exploration of each aspect.

```
document.getElementById('myButton').addEventListener('click', function()
    {
   alert('Button was clicked!');
});
```

Listing 7.17: Adding an Event Listener

In the example above, the `getElementById` method selects an element with the ID `` `myButton' ``. The `addEventListener` method is then used to attach a click event to this element. When the button is clicked, the anonymous function provided to `addEventListener` executes and shows an alert.

Different event types include, but are not limited to:

- `click`
- `mouseover`
- `mouseout`
- `keydown`
- `keyup`
- `scroll`
- `submit`

Removing Event Listeners

There are scenarios where removing an event listener is necessary, for instance, to prevent memory leaks or when the element is no longer needed. For this purpose, the `removeEventListener` method is used, which requires the same function reference that was initially attached with `addEventListener`:

```
function showAlert() {
   alert('Event Triggered');
}
document.getElementById('myButton').addEventListener('click', showAlert);
```

```
document.getElementById('myButton').removeEventListener('click',
    showAlert);
```

Listing 7.18: Removing an Event Listener

Event Objects

Event objects provide extra information about the event. When an event occurs, the event object is automatically passed to the event handler, allowing us to access details like the element that triggered the event, mouse positions, key states, etc.

```
document.getElementById('myButton').addEventListener('click', function(
    event) {
   console.log('Event Type: ' + event.type);
   console.log('Element ID: ' + event.target.id);
});
```

Listing 7.19: Using Event Objects

In the above code, `event.type` provides the event type (`click`), and `event.target.id` gives the id of the element that triggered the event.

Event Propagation

Event propagation is a mechanism that defines how events travel through the DOM tree. Event propagation can occur in two main phases:

- **Capturing Phase**: The event travels from the root to the target element.
- **Bubbling Phase**: The event travels from the target element back up to the root.

By default, events are handled during the bubbling phase. The third parameter of the `addEventListener` can be set to `true` to handle the event during the capturing phase instead.

```
document.getElementById('parent').addEventListener('click', function() {
   console.log('Parent clicked');
}, true); // true indicates capturing phase

document.getElementById('child').addEventListener('click', function() {
```

```
    console.log('Child clicked');
});
```

Listing 7.20: Event Propagation Phases

Here, clicking on the child element will trigger the parent's event before the child's event, due to the capturing phase listener on the parent.

Preventing Default Behavior

Certain elements have default behaviors attached to events. For instance, a form submission or following a link. Using the `preventDefault` method on the event object, these can be stopped.

```
document.getElementById('myForm').addEventListener('submit', function(
    event) {
  event.preventDefault();
  console.log('Form submission canceled');
});
```

Listing 7.21: Preventing Default Behavior

Event Delegation

Event delegation takes advantage of event propagation to handle events at a higher level in the DOM rather than adding event listeners to individual elements. This is particularly useful in scenarios involving dynamically generated content.

```
document.getElementById('parentList').addEventListener('click', function
    (event) {
  if (event.target && event.target.nodeName == "LI") {
    console.log('List item clicked: ' + event.target.textContent);
  }
});
```

Listing 7.22: Event Delegation

In the code above, clicking on any `li` elements within the `parentList` will trigger the event handler, demonstrating efficient use of event delegation.

This section detailed the essential concepts and patterns for handling DOM events. With these techniques, developers can build interactive and efficient web applications.

7.12 Understanding Event Propagation: Capturing and Bubbling

Event propagation is a fundamental concept within the realm of web development, particularly when dealing with the DOM. It describes the process by which events traverse the DOM tree from the originating element to its intended target listeners. This traversal can occur in two distinct phases: capturing (also known as trickling) and bubbling.

The capturing phase begins at the root of the DOM tree and progresses downward towards the target element, whereas the bubbling phase starts from the target element and propagates upwards to the root. Understanding these phases is crucial for effective event handling.

```
document.body.addEventListener('click', function(event) {
  console.log('Body');
});

document.getElementById('parent').addEventListener('click', function(
    event) {
  console.log('Parent');
});

document.getElementById('child').addEventListener('click', function(
    event) {
  console.log('Child');
});
```

Listing 7.23: Event propagation phases example

In the example above, clicking on the 'child' element will generate the following output:

```
Child
Parent
Body
```

This output exemplifies the default bubbling behavior in which the event propagates from the innermost target ('child') outward to the ancestors ('parent' and 'body').

To capture events during the capturing phase, an additional parameter must be passed to the 'addEventListener' method. This parameter should be set to 'true' to denote that the event listener should be invoked during the capturing phase.

```
document.body.addEventListener('click', function(event) {
  console.log('Body');
}, true);
```

```
document.getElementById('parent').addEventListener('click', function(
    event) {
   console.log('Parent');
}, true);

document.getElementById('child').addEventListener('click', function(
    event) {
   console.log('Child');
}, true);
```

Listing 7.24: Catching events in the capturing phase

Now, clicking on the 'child' element yields:

```
Body
Parent
Child
```

This illustrates the capturing phase where the event is first intercepted by the outer elements ('body') before reaching the target ('child').

Event.stopPropagation() and Event.stopImmediatePropagation():

When handling events, it might be necessary to prevent them from continuing to propagate through the DOM. This can be accomplished using the 'stopPropagation' and 'stopImmediatePropagation' methods of the 'Event' interface.

```
document.body.addEventListener('click', function(event) {
   console.log('Body');
});

document.getElementById('parent').addEventListener('click', function(
    event) {
   event.stopPropagation();
   console.log('Parent');
});

document.getElementById('child').addEventListener('click', function(
    event) {
   console.log('Child');
});
```

Listing 7.25: Using stopPropagation to halt event propagation

Clicking on the 'child' element now results in:

```
Child
Parent
```

Here, the event propagation stops at the 'parent' element, and the event listener on 'body' is not executed. The 'stopImmediatePropagation' method differs in that it prevents other listeners of the same event from being called.

```
document.getElementById('parent').addEventListener('click', function(
     event) {
    event.stopImmediatePropagation();
    console.log('Parent - Listener 1');
});

document.getElementById('parent').addEventListener('click', function(
     event) {
    console.log('Parent - Listener 2');
});
```

Listing 7.26: Using stopImmediatePropagation to prevent other listeners

Upon clicking the 'parent' element, the result will be:

```
Parent - Listener 1
```

This example shows that only the first listener is triggered due to 'stopImmediatePropagation'.

A thorough grasp of capturing and bubbling in event propagation allows you to strategically place event listeners, optimize event handling, and create more efficient interactions within web applications.

7.13 Using Event Delegation

Event delegation is a technique in which a single event listener is added to a parent element in order to manage events for multiple child elements. This approach can optimize performance and simplify the management of dynamic content. Instead of attaching individual listeners to each child element, you attach one listener to their common ancestor and leverage event propagation to handle events efficiently.

To understand event delegation, it is crucial to first revisit the concept of event propagation. Event propagation in the DOM occurs in two main phases: the capture phase and the bubble phase. During the capture phase, the event travels from the window down through the parent elements to the target element. During the bubble phase, the event travels back up from the target element to the window. By adding an event listener to an ancestor element, you can catch events as they propagate up from the target element (bubbling phase).

Below is an example illustrating event delegation with a simple HTML structure:

```
<!DOCTYPE html>
<html lang="en">
<head>
    <title>Event Delegation Example</title>
</head>
<body>
    <ul id="parent-list">
        <li class="list-item">Item 1</li>
        <li class="list-item">Item 2</li>
        <li class="list-item">Item 3</li>
    </ul>
    <script src="script.js"></script>
</body>
</html}
```

In this example, instead of attaching an event listener to each `<li>` element, a single event listener is attached to the `<ul>` (the parent) element. The script (`script.js`) handles the click events for any `<li>` element inside the `<ul>` due to event delegation.

Here is the JavaScript code to utilize event delegation:

```
document.getElementById('parent-list').addEventListener('click',
    function(event) {
    if (event.target && event.target.matches('li.list-item')) {
        console.log('List item clicked: ', event.target.textContent);
    }
});
```

In the code above, we add an event listener to the `<ul>` element with the id `parent-list`. Inside the event handler function, we use the `event.target` property to determine which child element triggered the event. The `matches` method is used to check if the target element matches the specified CSS selector (`'li.list-item'` in this case).

This approach provides several benefits:

- **Improved Performance:** By reducing the number of event listeners, you can lower the amount of memory used and enhance performance, particularly when dealing with a large number of elements.
- **Simplified Management:** Event delegation simplifies the code structure, as all event handling logic is centralized in a single listener. This centralization is especially useful for managing dynamic content that may be added or removed from the DOM at runtime.
- **Dynamic Element Handling:** Since the event handler is set on

the parent element, it automatically applies to newly created child elements, making it unnecessary to add new listeners when the DOM is modified.

Consider an example where elements are dynamically added to the list:

```
// Function to add new list items
function addNewItem(text) {
    const newItem = document.createElement('li');
    newItem.className = 'list-item';
    newItem.textContent = text;
    document.getElementById('parent-list').appendChild(newItem);
}

// Adding new items
addNewItem('Item 4');
addNewItem('Item 5');
```

In this scenario, the newly added list items automatically benefit from the event delegation, as the click event listener on the parent `<ul>` element applies to them as well. There is no need to explicitly attach event listeners to the new list items.

Another commonly used pattern with event delegation is to employ it in combination with event propagation phases. While the previous examples handle events during the bubbling phase, it is also possible to handle events during the capture phase by setting the `useCapture` parameter to `true` in the `addEventListener` method:

```
document.getElementById('parent-list').addEventListener('click',
     function(event) {
    if (event.target && event.target.matches('li.list-item')) {
        console.log('List item clicked: ', event.target.textContent);
    }
}, true); // `true` enables capturing phase
```

This approach can be beneficial in certain scenarios where capturing the event during the capture phase is more appropriate. However, for most use cases in event delegation, handling events during the bubbling phase is the preferred method.

Understanding and implementing event delegation effectively can greatly enhance the efficiency and maintainability of your web applications, particularly when handling dynamic content or large numbers of similar elements within the DOM. This technique leverages the inherent properties of event propagation, streamlining event management by centralizing event handling logic.

7.14 The DOMContentLoaded Event

The `DOMContentLoaded` event is pivotal for ensuring that your JavaScript code executes effectively and efficiently after the initial HTML document has been fully loaded and parsed, without waiting for stylesheets, images, and subframes to finish loading. This makes `DOMContentLoaded` superior to other events like `window.onload` for scenarios where manipulating the DOM is required immediately after the basic structure of the document is accessible.

`DOMContentLoaded` fires when the HTML has been completely loaded and parsed, irrespective of stylesheets, images, and subframes, equipping developers with the flexibility to manipulate and interact with the DOM at an earlier stage of the page load process.

```
document.addEventListener("DOMContentLoaded", function(event) {
   console.log("DOM fully loaded and parsed");
   // Your DOM manipulation code goes here
});
```

Listing 7.27: Adding an event listener for DOMContentLoaded

In the example above, a `DOMContentLoaded` event listener is registered with the `document`. The callback function is executed as soon as the document is fully parsed, enabling immediate access and manipulation of the DOM elements. The output shown in the console demonstrates confirmation of the event:

```
DOM fully loaded and parsed
```

The `DOMContentLoaded` event contrasts with the `load` event, which waits until the entire page, including stylesheets, images, etc., has been fully loaded. This distinction is crucial when performance and timing for script execution are considered.

```
window.addEventListener("load", function(event) {
   console.log("Page fully loaded");
   // Additional operations on the fully loaded page
});
```

Listing 7.28: Adding an event listener for load event

Here's how the output comparison looks:

```
Page fully loaded
```

Employing `DOMContentLoaded` is optimal in single-page applications where dynamic content needs to be populated swiftly, enhancing the user experience by reducing the time before interactions can occur. Another scenario where `DOMContentLoaded` is valuable is when scripts are placed at the head of the document; without this event, premature script execution may lead to errors since the required DOM elements may not be available yet.

```
document.addEventListener("DOMContentLoaded", function(event) {
    let newElement = document.createElement("div");
    newElement.textContent = "New content here";
    document.body.appendChild(newElement);
});
```

Listing 7.29: Appending a new element during DOMContentLoaded

The above code demonstrates creating and appending a new `div` element to the body. This action occurs immediately after the document has been completely parsed.

It is also worth considering browser behavior. Older browsers like Internet Explorer 9 and earlier versions do not support the `DOMContentLoaded` event. For compatibility, fallback mechanisms with `document.readyState` can be utilized:

```
function onReady(callback) {
    if (document.readyState === "complete" || document.readyState === "
        interactive") {
        callback();
    } else {
        document.addEventListener("DOMContentLoaded", callback);
    }
}

onReady(function() {
    console.log("DOM is ready");
    // Your DOM manipulation code goes here
});
```

Listing 7.30: Cross-browser DOMContentLoaded event handling

This function ensures that the callback is executed once the DOM is ready to be manipulated, even if the document has already been loaded and parsed before the script was executed.

To appreciate the significance of `DOMContentLoaded`, understanding event timing is crucial. Here's an example to visually interpret timing differences:

```
document.addEventListener("DOMContentLoaded", function(event) {
    console.log("DOMContentLoaded:", event.timeStamp);
});
```

```
window.addEventListener("load", function(event) {
    console.log("Load:", event.timeStamp);
});
```

Listing 7.31: Logging event timings

Typical output would look like this:

```
DOMContentLoaded: 123.456
Load: 456.789
```

This clearly shows that `DOMContentLoaded` fires significantly earlier than the `load` event, offering a tangible benefit for performance-critical web applications.

The effective use of `DOMContentLoaded` can therefore serve as a robust tool for optimizing the initial load experience, allowing scripts to execute at an appropriate time to ensure smoother and more performant applications.

7.15 Working with Forms and Input

Working with forms and input elements in the DOM is essential for creating interactive web applications. Forms enable users to submit data that can be processed by web applications, and input elements provide various ways for users to enter data. This section covers the methods and properties for accessing and manipulating form and input elements, validating user input, and handling form submissions.

To start, consider the basic structure of an HTML form:

```
<form id="userForm">
    <label for="username">Username:</label>
    <input type="text" id="username" name="username">

    <label for="email">Email:</label>
    <input type="email" id="email" name="email">

    <button type="submit">Submit</button>
</form>
```

Accessing Form Elements: Forms and their input elements can be accessed using standard DOM selection methods covered previously. The `document.forms` collection provides a way to access all forms in a document. Additionally, form elements can be accessed by their `id`, `name`, or using `querySelector` and other DOM methods. Example:

```
var form = document.forms['userForm'];
```

```
var usernameInput = document.getElementById('username');
```

Alternatively, you can also use:

```
var form = document.querySelector('#userForm');
var emailInput = form.elements['email'];
```

Form Properties and Methods: Forms have an assortment of properties and methods that can be utilized to handle form data and submission. Some notable properties and methods include:

- `form.elements`: Returns a live HTMLCollection of all the elements contained in the form.
- `form.submit()`: Submits the form programmatically.
- `form.reset()`: Resets all elements in the form to their default values.
- `form.action`: Specifies where to send the form data.
- `form.method`: Specifies the HTTP method (GET or POST) to be used when submitting the form.

```
form.action = 'submitForm.php';
form.method = 'post';
```

Accessing Input Values: The values from input elements can be accessed and manipulated via their `value` property. For example:

```
var username = usernameInput.value;
var email = emailInput.value;
```

Setting a new value is straightforward:

```
usernameInput.value = 'newUsername';
```

Validating Input: HTML5 provides several built-in validation attributes such as `required`, `pattern`, `min`, `max`, `type`, etc. JavaScript can be utilized to manually validate inputs if more complex validation logic is needed.

```
if (usernameInput.value === '') {
    alert('Username is required.');
    return false;
}
if (!emailInput.value.includes('@')) {
    alert('Please enter a valid email.');
    return false;
}
```

Alternatively, constraint validation API methods like `checkValidity()` and properties like `validity` and `validationMessage` can be employed:

```
if (!form.checkValidity()) {
    var invalidFields = form.querySelectorAll(':invalid');
    invalidFields.forEach(function(field) {
        console.log(field.validationMessage);
    });
    return false;
}
```

Handling Form Submission: Handling form submission involves attaching an event listener to the form's `submit` event. This allows for processing or validating data before the form is submitted:

```
form.addEventListener('submit', function(event) {
    event.preventDefault(); // Prevents the default form submission
    var username = usernameInput.value;
    var email = emailInput.value;

    if (form.checkValidity()) {
        // Process the form data
        console.log('Username:', username);
        console.log('Email:', email);
    } else {
        console.log('Form is invalid.');
    }
});
```

`event.preventDefault()` is crucial in preventing the default form submission action, allowing JavaScript to handle the submission process. This is particularly useful in Single Page Applications (SPAs) where form data may be processed with AJAX requests rather than a full page reload.

Form Data Serialization: When dealing with form data, serialization into key-value pairs for submission is often necessary. The `FormData` object can be used:

```
var formData = new FormData(form);
formData.append('additionalField', 'extraValue');

// Logging all form data
for (var [key, value] of formData.entries()) {
    console.log(key, ':', value);
}
```

The `FormData` object is particularly useful when submitting forms using `XMLHttpRequest` or the Fetch API:

```
fetch('submitForm.php', {
    method: 'POST',
    body: formData
}).then(response => {
    return response.text();
```

```
}).then(data => {
    console.log(data);
});
```

Understanding and effectively managing forms and inputs in the DOM is fundamental for creating user-interactive applications, ensuring data integrity, and providing a seamless user experience.

Chapter 8

Event Handling

This chapter covers the essentials of event handling in JavaScript, emphasizing its role in creating interactive web applications. It explains how to add and remove event listeners, and provides an overview of different event types such as mouse, keyboard, and form events. The chapter delves into event objects and properties, event propagation (bubbling and capturing), and techniques for preventing default behavior and propagation. It also discusses custom events, debouncing, throttling, and handling touch events for mobile devices, ensuring comprehensive coverage of best practices for effective event management.

8.1 Introduction to Event Handling

Event handling is a cornerstone concept in JavaScript, essential for developing interactive web applications. Its primary role is to facilitate the communication between the user's actions and the browser. When a user interacts with a web page—be it through clicking a button, typing in a form, or scrolling down the page—events are generated. JavaScript provides mechanisms to detect these events and define responses to create dynamic behavior.

At the heart of event handling lies the concept of the *event*. An event in JavaScript represents the occurrence of some action or change in the web application's state. This could be a user action, such as a mouse click or a key press, or system-generated actions like page load or a timeout. The event handling mechanism allows developers to attach specific functions, called *event listeners*, to these events, thereby enabling the web page to respond in predefined ways.

To grasp the fundamentals of event handling, it is crucial to comprehend the primary components involved:

- **Events**: These are specific interactions or occurrences that can be detected by JavaScript.
- **Event Listeners**: Functions that are attached to an event and executed in response to the event's occurrence.
- **Event Objects**: Objects that provide contextual information about the event, such as the type of event, the target element, and other relevant properties.

Consider the following example to understand the basic structure of event handling:

```
// Selecting an element
let button = document.querySelector('#myButton');

// Defining an event listener function
function handleClick(event) {
   console.log('Button clicked');
}

// Attaching the event listener to the button
button.addEventListener('click', handleClick);
```

In this example, the desired element (a button with the ID `myButton`) is selected using the `document.querySelector` method. An event listener function `handleClick` is defined to log a message to the console when triggered. The `addEventListener` method is then used to associate the `handleClick` function with the `click` event on the selected button. When the button is clicked, the `handleClick` function is executed, demonstrating a basic event handling flow.

Event handling in JavaScript supports a wide variety of events, ranging from mouse and keyboard interactions to complex form events and custom-defined occurrences. The `addEventListener` method, as introduced in the example above, is the primary interface for registering event listeners. It allows binding one or more functions to specific events on DOM (Document Object Model) elements.

Events propagate through the DOM in a hierarchical manner, meaning that the same event may trigger multiple event listeners during its traversal. This propagation occurs in two phases:

- **Capturing Phase**: The event travels down from the document root to the target element.
- **Bubbling Phase**: The event bubbles back up from the target element to the document root.

By default, event listeners are triggered during the bubbling phase. However, developers can specify that an event listener should be activated during the capturing phase by passing a `true` value as the third argument to the `addEventListener` method, as shown below:

```
button.addEventListener('click', handleClick, true);
```

The `event` object, automatically passed as an argument to the event listener function, contains valuable information about the event. Essential properties and methods of the event object include:

- **type**: The type of event that was triggered (e.g., `'click'`, `'keypress'`).
- **target**: The element that triggered the event.
- **currentTarget**: The element to which the event listener is attached.
- **stopPropagation()**: A method to stop the propagation of the event in the bubbling or capturing phases.
- **preventDefault()**: A method to prevent the default action associated with the event.

Using the `event` object, developers can implement more sophisticated event handling logic tailored to the specific needs of their applications.

Moreover, advanced event handling techniques such as debouncing and throttling play a significant role in optimizing performance by controlling the frequency of event listener executions. These techniques ensure that costly operations are not performed excessively, improving the overall responsiveness of web applications.

Touch events enable handling user interactions on mobile devices, which often involve gestures rather than traditional mouse and keyboard input. JavaScript provides a set of touch events, including `touchstart`, `touchmove`, `touchend`, and `touchcancel`, to cater to these needs.

Best practices for event handling focus on aspects such as efficient memory usage, avoiding memory leaks, and ensuring that event listeners do not degrade the performance of the application. Properly managing the addition and removal of event listeners, handling asynchronous operations correctly, and leveraging event delegation are critical components in achieving effective event management.

8.2 Understanding Events and Event Handling

In JavaScript, events are actions or occurrences that happen in the system being programmed. These events are usually user-generated such as a mouse click, key press, or a form submission, but can also be generated by the system or by APIs. Event handling is the mechanism that captures these events and allows the developer to define the behavior when an event is detected.

To better understand events and event handling, it is crucial to note that events follow a well-defined lifecycle, which begins with the initiation of an event. The JavaScript runtime environment detects this event and subsequently triggers any associated event listeners. This section elucidates the fundamental principles of events, detailing the process of how these events are captured and handled using JavaScript.

JavaScript provides a comprehensive event handling model through the integration of event listeners and event handlers. The core method for attaching event listeners in JavaScript is `addEventListener`, which will be elaborated in subsequent sections.

```
document.addEventListener('click', function(event) {
    console.log('Document clicked');
});
```

Listing 8.1: Attaching an Event Listener

In the above example, an event listener is attached to the `document` object, responding to any 'click' events. Upon detecting a click event, the listener invokes the specified function, logging 'Document clicked' to the console.

Events are categorized into various types, each pertinent to a different user interaction or system-wide action:

- **UI Events:** These include general interactions with the user interface, such as loading a document (`load`) or resizing a window (`resize`).

- **Mouse Events:** These pertain to actions involving the mouse, such as `click`, `dblclick`, `mouseenter`, `mouseleave`.
- **Keyboard Events:** Key-related interactions such as `keydown`, `keyup`, and `keypress`.
- **Form Events:** Events that are triggered as a result of user interactions with form elements, like `submit`, `change`, `input`.
- **Touch Events:** Specific to touch screen devices, including `touchstart`, `touchmove`, and `touchend`.

When an event is triggered, an event object is created. This event object contains critical information about the event, such as the type of event, the element that triggered the event, and properties specific to the event type (like mouse coordinates for mouse events).

```
document.addEventListener('click', function(event) {
    console.log('Event Type: ' + event.type);
    console.log('Event Target: ' + event.target);
});
```

Listing 8.2: Event Object Properties

In the above snippet, the `event` object is passed to the event handler function, from which the event type and event target are extracted and logged.

Event propagation is integral to understanding event handling, involving two primary phases: event capturing and event bubbling. When an event is initiated, it first traverses down from the document root to the target element (*capturing phase*). Following this, it bubbles back up to the root (*bubbling phase*). During these phases, any event handlers attached to the traversed elements are invoked. This propagation mechanism allows for more versatile event handling strategies.

```
document.getElementById('parent').addEventListener('click', function(
     event) {
    console.log('Parent clicked');
}, true); // Capturing phase

document.getElementById('child').addEventListener('click', function(
     event) {
    console.log('Child clicked');
}); // Bubbling phase
```

Listing 8.3: Capturing and Bubbling

In this example, the event listener on the `parent` element is set to trigger during the capturing phase by passing `true` as the third argument to `addEventListener`. Conversely, the listener on the `child` element responds during the bubbling phase by default.

To manage events more effectively, JavaScript provides mechanisms to prevent default behaviors and stop propagation. The `event.preventDefault()` method can inhibit the default action associated with the event, such as preventing a form submission. The `event.stopPropagation()` method halts the event from propagating further, either up or down the DOM tree.

```
document.getElementById('link').addEventListener('click', function(event)
    {
  event.preventDefault(); // Prevents the default link action
  event.stopPropagation(); // Stops the event from bubbling
  console.log('Link clicked, default action prevented and propagation
      stopped');
});
```

Listing 8.4: Preventing Default Behavior and Stopping Propagation

The preceding code demonstrates preventing the default behavior of a hyperlink and stopping the event from propagating through the document.

Understanding these principles of events and event handling forms the foundation for creating interactive and responsive web applications.

8.3 Adding Event Listeners: addEventListener

The `addEventListener` method is fundamental in the context of JavaScript event handling. It allows the registration of event listeners on DOM elements, enabling the execution of specified functions in response to various events. The syntax for `addEventListener` is straightforward yet flexible:

```
element.addEventListener(event, function, useCapture);
```

Parameters:

- `event`: A string representing the type of event to listen for (e.g., 'click', 'mouseover', 'keydown').
- `function`: The function to be executed when the specified event is triggered. This is also known as the event handler.
- `useCapture` (optional): A boolean value indicating whether the event should be captured during the capturing phase (i.e., `true`) or the bubbling phase (i.e., `false`). The default value is `false`.

Example Usage

Consider a simple example where an event listener is added to a button element to handle its `click` event:

```
document.getElementById('myButton').addEventListener('click', function()
    {
    alert('Button was clicked!');
});
```

In this snippet, an alert will appear with the message 'Button was clicked!' whenever the button with the ID `myButton` is clicked.

Handling Events with External Functions

Instead of defining the event handler function inline, it is often beneficial to define the function separately. This approach supports code readability and reusability:

```
function handleClick() {
    alert('Button was clicked!');
}

document.getElementById('myButton').addEventListener('click',
    handleClick);
```

This code achieves the same effect as the previous example but uses an external function named `handleClick` to handle the `click` event.

Event Object in Event Handlers

When an event handler is invoked, it automatically receives an event object as its first argument. This object contains useful information about the event, such as the target element, event type, and various other properties:

```
document.getElementById('myButton').addEventListener('click', function(
    event) {
   console.log('Event Type:', event.type); // Output: Event Type: click
   console.log('Event Target:', event.target); // Output: Event Target:
       [object HTMLButtonElement]
});
```

Here, the event object is logged to the console, showing details about the event type and target element.

Use of `useCapture`

The optional `useCapture` parameter determines whether the event listener should capture the event during the capturing phase. Understanding event propagation phases—capturing and bubbling—is essential for effective event management. The following example illustrates the use of the `useCapture` parameter:

```
document.getElementById('outerDiv').addEventListener('click', function()
    {
   console.log('Outer DIV clicked during bubbling phase.');
}, false);

document.getElementById('outerDiv').addEventListener('click', function()
    {
   console.log('Outer DIV clicked during capturing phase.');
}, true);
```

In this case, two event listeners are added to the same element, `outerDiv`. The first listener logs a message during the bubbling phase, while the second listener does so during the capturing phase. If the `outerDiv` element is clicked, the captured output will be:

```
Outer DIV clicked during capturing phase.
Outer DIV clicked during bubbling phase.
```

The order of these messages demonstrates the capturing phase occurring before the bubbling phase.

Multiple Event Listeners for the Same Event

It is permissible to register multiple event listeners for the same event on a single element. These listeners will be invoked sequentially in the order in which they were added:

```
document.getElementById('myButton').addEventListener('click', function()
    {
  console.log('First listener.');
});

document.getElementById('myButton').addEventListener('click', function()
    {
  console.log('Second listener.');
});
```

Upon clicking the button, the console output will be:

```
First listener.
Second listener.
```

The first and second listeners are invoked in the order of their registration.

Passive Event Listeners

To improve performance, especially for touch and wheel events, flagging an event listener as passive is recommended. This informs the browser that the event listener will not invoke `preventDefault()`, potentially optimizing scrolling performance:

```
document.getElementById('myDiv').addEventListener('scroll', function(
    event) {
  // Handler code
}, { passive: true });
```

By marking the listener as passive, the browser can optimize the event handling process, as it no longer needs to check whether `preventDefault()` is called.

The `addEventListener` method provides a robust mechanism for event management in JavaScript, accommodating different phases of event propagation, passive listeners for performance improvements, and the capability of attaching multiple listeners to a single event. Effective utilization of this method is crucial for developing interactive and responsive web applications.

8.4 Removing Event Listeners: removeEventListener

Removing event listeners in JavaScript is crucial for optimizing application performance and avoiding potential memory leaks. It ensures that event handlers no longer respond to events after they are no longer needed, conserving system resources. The `removeEventListener` method is designed for this purpose.

The `removeEventListener` method takes the following parameters:

- **type:** The event type to stop listening for, such as `"click"`, `"keydown"`, etc.
- **listener:** The function that was initially passed to `addEventListener` when the event listener was added.
- **options:** (Optional) An options object or a boolean indicating whether the event listener was added with a capturing phase. It must match the options passed to `addEventListener`.

For a demonstration, consider an example where an event listener is attached to a button to log a message to the console when clicked:

```
document.getElementById('myButton').addEventListener('click', myFunction);

function myFunction() {
    console.log('Button was clicked!');
}
```

To remove this event listener, invoke `removeEventListener` with the same parameters used in `addEventListener`:

```
document.getElementById('myButton').removeEventListener('click', myFunction);
```

It is critical to ensure that the listener function reference is identical to the one used when adding the event listener. Using an anonymous function or recreating the function in-place will prevent the removal:

```
document.getElementById('myButton').removeEventListener('click', function() {
    console.log('Button was clicked!');
}); // This will not work
```

Moreover, if additional options were used when adding the event listener, the same options must be provided during removal. Consider an event listener added with the `capture` flag:

```
document.getElementById('myButton').addEventListener('click', myFunction, { capture
    : true });
```

The corresponding removal call must include the `capture` flag to be successful:

```
document.getElementById('myButton').removeEventListener('click', myFunction, {
    capture: true });
```

Illustrating with another scenario, we can utilize event listeners with options for passive or once attributes:

```
document.getElementById('myButton').addEventListener('click', myFunction, { passive
    : true });

document.getElementById('myButton').removeEventListener('click', myFunction, {
    passive: true });
```

The listener must be defined in the same manner when it needs to be manipulated or deactivated. Misalignment in the event listener definition, such as changes in options or listener function prototypes, causes failure in removal.

For example, storing and later referencing a bound function for removal might involve complexities. The function's original binding context must be maintained:

```
document.getElementById('myButton').addEventListener('click', myFunction.bind(this)
    );

// Attempt to remove the event listener (This will not work as expected)
document.getElementById('myButton').removeEventListener('click', myFunction.bind(
    this));
```

In the case above, using `bind` creates a new function reference, making the original listener function irretrievable for removal. Instead, one must maintain a reference to the bound function:

```
var boundFunction = myFunction.bind(this);
document.getElementById('myButton').addEventListener('click', boundFunction);

// To remove the event listener accurately
document.getElementById('myButton').removeEventListener('click', boundFunction);
```

Effective management and removal of event listeners, particularly in complex web applications, involve meticulous understanding and tracking of listener and option references. This ensures timely cleanup and optimal application performance.

8.5 Event Objects and Event Properties

In JavaScript event handling, an *event object* provides detailed information about an event that has occurred. Understanding the structure and properties of event objects is crucial for managing events effectively. When an event is triggered, the browser creates an event object, which is then passed to the event handler. This section explores the composition of event objects and highlights key properties, using both conceptual explanations and illustrative code examples.

When an event listener is registered for an event using `addEventListener`, the event handler function can have access to the event object by specifying a parameter. Consider the following code snippet:

```
// Adding an event listener with an event object
document.getElementById('myButton').addEventListener('click', function(
    event) {
   console.log(event);
});
```

In this example, the `event` parameter represents the event object associated with the click event on the element with the ID `myButton`. The properties of the event object contain valuable information about the event.

Common Properties of Event Objects The event object contains numerous properties. Some of the most commonly used properties are:

- **type**: A string specifying the event type, such as `click`, `keydown`, or `submit`.
- **target**: A reference to the element that triggered the event. This property is particularly useful for event delegation, where a single event listener handles events for multiple child elements.
- **currentTarget**: A reference to the element to which the event handler is attached. This is especially useful within the context of event delegation, helping to distinguish between the origin of the event and the element actually listening for the event.
- **timeStamp**: A long integer representing the time at which the event occurred. This can be useful for calculating the duration between events.
- **preventDefault()**, **stopPropagation()**: Methods used to control

event behavior, in terms of both default actions and event propagation, respectively.

Below is an example demonstrating the use of these event object properties:

```
// Example demonstrating common event object properties
document.getElementById('myButton').addEventListener('click', function(
    event) {
   console.log('Event Type:', event.type); // Output: "click"
   console.log('Target Element:', event.target); // Output: <button id="
       myButton">...</button>
   console.log('Handler Element:', event.currentTarget); // Output: <
       button id="myButton">...</button>
   console.log('Time Stamp:', event.timeStamp); // Output: [Time in
       milliseconds]

   event.preventDefault(); // Prevents default action
   event.stopPropagation(); // Stops event bubbling or capturing
});
```

MouseEvent and KeyboardEvent Properties In addition to the properties available on the generic event object, mouse and keyboard events expose additional properties relevant to their specific contexts.

For `MouseEvent` objects, properties include:

- **clientX, clientY**: Coordinates of the mouse pointer relative to the viewport.
- **pageX, pageY**: Coordinates of the mouse pointer relative to the entire document.
- **button**: Indicates which mouse button was pressed (0 for left button, 1 for middle button, 2 for right button).
- **altKey, ctrlKey, shiftKey, metaKey**: Boolean values indicating whether the Alt, Ctrl, Shift, or Meta keys were pressed during the mouse event.

The code example below illustrates the use of `MouseEvent` properties:

```
// Example demonstrating MouseEvent properties
document.addEventListener('click', function(event) {
   console.log('Mouse Coordinates (Viewport):', event.clientX, event.
       clientY);
   console.log('Mouse Coordinates (Document):', event.pageX, event.pageY
       );
```

```
    console.log('Mouse Button:', event.button);
    console.log('Alt key pressed:', event.altKey);
});
```

For `KeyboardEvent` objects, properties include:

- **key**: A string representing the key that was pressed, e.g., 'a', 'Enter'.
- **code**: A string representing the code of the physical key on the keyboard.
- **keyCode**: A numerical value representing the key code (deprecated, use `key` instead).
- **altKey, ctrlKey, shiftKey, metaKey**: Boolean values indicating whether the Alt, Ctrl, Shift, or Meta keys were pressed during the keyboard event.

The following example highlights the usage of `KeyboardEvent` properties:

```
// Example demonstrating KeyboardEvent properties
document.addEventListener('keydown', function(event) {
    console.log('Key Pressed:', event.key);
    console.log('Key Code:', event.code);
    console.log('Ctrl key pressed:', event.ctrlKey);
});
```

These examples highlight the utility of event object properties, facilitating robust and flexible event handling mechanisms. Users can leverage these detailed properties to implement precise, context-aware event responses, enhancing the interactivity and responsiveness of web applications.

8.6 Mouse Events: click, dblclick, mouseenter, mouseleave

Mouse events are integral to making web applications interactive and user-friendly. The most commonly used mouse events include `click`, `dblclick`, `mouseenter`, and `mouseleave`. Each of these events serves distinct purposes and understanding their behaviors is crucial for effective event handling.

The `click` event is triggered when an element is pressed and released by the mouse. It is important to remember that the `click` event only occurs after both the `mousedown` and `mouseup` events. Consider the following example where we attach a `click` event listener to a button:

```
document.getElementById('myButton').addEventListener('click', function() {
    alert('Button Clicked!');
});
```

In this example, whenever the button with the ID `myButton` is clicked, an alert box with the message "Button Clicked!" will appear.

The `dblclick` event is similar to the `click` event, but it is triggered when an element is double-clicked. Double-clicking involves clicking an element twice in quick succession. This can be useful for actions such as editing text or zooming into a section. For instance:

```
document.getElementById('myImage').addEventListener('dblclick', function() {
    this.style.width = '200%';
});
```

In this script, when the image with the ID `myImage` is double-clicked, its width will be doubled.

The `mouseenter` event occurs when the mouse pointer enters the boundary of an element. This event does not bubble, meaning it does not propagate up the document tree. This makes it distinct from the `mouseover` event, which does bubble. An illustration of using the `mouseenter` event is shown below:

```
document.getElementById('myDiv').addEventListener('mouseenter', function() {
    this.style.backgroundColor = 'lightblue';
});
```

Here, when the mouse pointer enters the area of the `div` element with the ID `myDiv`, its background color changes to light blue.

Conversely, the `mouseleave` event is fired when the mouse pointer exits the boundary of an element. Similar to `mouseenter`, it does not bubble. An application of the `mouseleave` event is demonstrated below:

```
document.getElementById('myDiv').addEventListener('mouseleave', function() {
    this.style.backgroundColor = 'white';
});
```

In this code, when the mouse pointer leaves the area of the `div` with the ID `myDiv`, its background color changes back to white.

Mouse event handlers can access the event object, which provides useful information about the event. For example, details such as the position of the mouse pointer when an event occurs can be extracted from the event object. Consider the following modification of the `click` event handler:

```
document.getElementById('myButton').addEventListener('click', function(event) {
   console.log('Mouse X: ' + event.clientX + ', Mouse Y: ' + event.clientY);
});
```

This handler logs the X and Y coordinates of the mouse pointer relative to the viewport when the button is clicked.

Handling mouse events efficiently can enhance user experience. It's often useful to distinguish between simple `click` events and double-click events, as well as to provide visual feedback for mouse interactions like `mouseenter` and `mouseleave` to improve interactivity and user engagement. It is also essential to manage performance, especially in applications where mouse events trigger intensive operations.

Effective mouse event handling forms an integral part of responsive web design, ensuring applications behave intuitively and meet user expectations. Properly implemented mouse event listeners can significantly contribute to the usability and interactivity of web applications.

8.7 Keyboard Events: keydown, keyup, keypress

Keyboard events in JavaScript facilitate the interaction between the user and the application by detecting and responding to the user's keystrokes. Among the various keyboard events, the primary ones include `keydown`, `keyup`, and `keypress`. Each of these events serves specific purposes and understanding their differences is crucial for implementing robust and efficient key event handling.

The `keydown` event is fired when a key is pressed down. This event continues to trigger as long as the key is being held down, making it particularly useful for tasks that require continuous user action, such as navigating a game character.

```
// Example of a keydown event listener
int main() {
   cout << 'Hello World!';
   return 0;
}
```

In the provided example, every time a key is pressed down, a message indicating the key pressed is logged to the console. The `event` object passed to the function contains the property `key`, which indicates the key pressed by the user.

The `keyup` event is triggered when a key is released. It is useful for detecting the end of a key action or performing actions that should only occur once a key press is completed.

```
// Example of a keyup event listener
document.addEventListener('keyup', function(event) {
    console.log('Keyup event fired: ' + event.key);
});
```

Here, the event handler logs a message to the console each time the user releases a key. Similar to the `keydown` event, the `keyup` event handler utilizes the `event` object to determine the key that was released.

The `keypress` event is slightly different and is fired only for character keys, making it irrelevant for non-character keys such as the `Ctrl`, `Shift`, or `Alt` keys. This event captures the character produced by the key press, respecting the current keyboard layout and the state of any modifier keys (e.g., `Shift`, `Caps Lock`).

```
// Example of a keypress event listener
document.addEventListener('keypress', function(event) {
    console.log('Keypress event fired: ' + event.key);
});
```

The event handler in this example logs the character that is produced by the key press. It is important to note that the `keypress` event is deprecated and is not recommended for new projects. Instead, using `keydown` and `keyup`, in combination with checking for specific character properties, is the modern approach.

For instance, implementing a form validation feature that requires users to input only numeric values can be achieved using the `keydown` event:

```
// Example of validating numeric input
document.getElementById('numericInput').addEventListener('keydown', function(event)
      {
    if (!/[0-9]/.test(event.key)) {
        event.preventDefault();
    }
});
```

In this scenario, an `input` field with the ID `numericInput` listens for the `keydown` event. The regular expression `/[0-9]/` checks whether the key pressed is a numeric character. If it is not, the `event.preventDefault()` method is called to prevent the keystroke from being registered.

Handling common combinations of keys, such as `Ctrl+C` for copying, can be performed by examining the `event` object's properties:

```
// Example of handling Ctrl+C key combination
document.addEventListener('keydown', function(event) {
    if (event.ctrlKey && event.key === 'c') {
        console.log('Ctrl+C pressed');
    }
});
```

This snippet demonstrates listening for the `Ctrl+C` key combination. The `event.ctrlKey` property indicates whether the `Ctrl` key is pressed, and the `event.key` property specifies the character 'c'. By combining these checks, one can determine if the specific key combination is activated.

To distinguish among different key events, especially for non-character keys or handling combinations, the `key` and `code` properties provide additional specificity:

- `event.key`: Returns the value of the key pressed (e.g., 'a', 'Enter', 'Shift').
- `event.code`: Returns the physical key on the keyboard pressed (e.g., 'KeyA', 'Enter', 'ShiftLeft').

Using `event.code` is advantageous in distinguishing between keys that produce the same `event.key` value but are located at different physical positions.

Consider a scenario where distinguishing between the left and right `Shift` keys is necessary:

```
// Example of distinguishing between left and right Shift keys
document.addEventListener('keydown', function(event) {
    if (event.code === 'ShiftLeft') {
        console.log('Left Shift key pressed');
    } else if (event.code === 'ShiftRight') {
        console.log('Right Shift key pressed');
    }
});
```

This example illustrates using the `event.code` property to differentiate between the left and right `Shift` keys. Such distinctions can be critical in applications requiring unique handling for specific keys or combinations.

Overall, understanding and properly utilizing `keydown`, `keyup`, and `keypress` events, alongside modern best practices, is essential for effective keyboard event handling in JavaScript applications, enabling richer and more intuitive user interactions.

8.8 Form Events: submit, change, input

Form events play a crucial role in handling user interactions with web forms. In JavaScript, the most common form events are `submit`, `change`, and `input`. Each of these events is associated with different user actions and requires distinct handling techniques. Understanding how to manage these events effectively is essential for creating dynamic and responsive web applications.

`submit`: The `submit` event is triggered when a form is submitted. This event is particularly useful for validating form data before it is sent to the server.

```
document.querySelector('form').addEventListener('submit', function(event)
    {
   event.preventDefault(); // Prevents the default form submission
   // Code to handle form submission, such as validation
   console.log('Form submitted!');
});
```

In the code above, the `event.preventDefault()` method is used to prevent the form from submitting in the traditional manner, allowing the custom form handling code to execute.

`change`: The `change` event is fired when the value of an input element changes and the element loses focus. This event is suitable for handling scenarios where the user's input needs to be processed when they finish editing a form field and move on to another one.

```
document.querySelector('input[type="text"]').addEventListener('change',
    function(event) {
   // Code to handle the change in the input value
   console.log('Input value changed to:', event.target.value);
});
```

The event handler retrieves the updated value from the `event.target.value` property and processes it accordingly.

`input`: The `input` event is triggered whenever the value of an input, textarea, or select element is changed. This event is fired immediately as the user interacts with the field, providing real-time feedback and updates which are useful for features like live validation or instant search.

```
document.querySelector('input[type="text"]').addEventListener('input',
    function(event) {
   // Code to handle real-time updates
   console.log('Current input value:', event.target.value);
});
```

This event handler also uses the `event.target.value` property to retrieve and process the current value of the input element.

When handling form events, it is crucial to ensure compatibility across different browsers and form elements. For instance, certain form elements such as checkboxes and radio buttons may exhibit slightly different behaviors depending on the event being used. Testing form interactions across various scenarios ensures consistent user experiences.

Additionally, ensuring accessibility by binding event handlers to appropriate form elements can significantly improve usability for users relying on assistive technologies. For example, labeling form fields appropriately and providing meaningful feedback upon user interactions maintains accessibility standards.

Managing form events efficiently often involves combining multiple event listeners and utilizing the Document Object Model (DOM) to access and manipulate form elements dynamically. Considering performance implications, particularly when handling a large number of form elements or complex validation logic, enhances the overall efficiency and responsiveness of web applications.

Careful orchestration of form events like `submit`, `change`, and `input` enables developers to craft refined and user-friendly interfaces, ensuring robust data collection and validation mechanisms within web forms.

Finally, integrating backend validation processes with frontend form handling provides a powerful combination that enhances both user experience and data integrity.

8.9 Focus and Blur Events

Focus and blur events play a crucial role in user interaction within web forms and other interactive elements. In JavaScript, the `focus` event is triggered when an element gains focus, typically via user interaction like clicking on an input field or tabbing to it. Conversely, the `blur` event is dispatched when an element loses focus.

The primary elements that harness `focus` and `blur` events include form inputs such as text fields, radio buttons, checkboxes, and select dropdowns. Understanding how to manage these events effectively is critical for tasks such as form validation, input field styling, and ensuring a seamless user experience.

To handle these events in JavaScript, one can employ the standard event listener methods such as `addEventListener`:

```
// Example: Adding focus and blur event listeners to an input element
const inputElement = document.querySelector('input');

inputElement.addEventListener('focus', (event) => {
  console.log('Input field has gained focus.');
});

inputElement.addEventListener('blur', (event) => {
  console.log('Input field has lost focus.');
});
```

It is essential to understand that `focus` and `blur` events do not bubble up the DOM hierarchy. This characteristic makes it necessary to attach these events directly to the elements of interest rather than leveraging event delegation. If event delegation is required, one might opt for `focusin` and `focusout` events, which do bubble.

```
// Example: Using focusin and focusout events for delegation
document.addEventListener('focusin', (event) => {
  console.log('Element gained focus:', event.target);
});

document.addEventListener('focusout', (event) => {
  console.log('Element lost focus:', event.target);
});
```

Managing Focus Programmatically

In addition to user-triggered focus events, JavaScript allows programmatically focusing and blurring elements using the `focus()` and `blur()` methods. These methods can be used to guide user behavior or prepare the interface for specific user input windows.

```
// Example: Programmatically focusing and blurring an element
const secondInputElement = document.querySelectorAll('input')[1];

// Focus the second input field
secondInputElement.focus();
```

```
// Blur the second input field
secondInputElement.blur();
```

Practical Applications

- Input Field Highlighting

  A common application of handling focus and blur events is input field highlighting to enhance visual feedback for users. When the input field gains focus, its border or background can be styled to indicate readiness for user input.

```
inputElement.addEventListener('focus', (event) => {
  event.target.style.backgroundColor = '#e0f7fa'; // Light blue
      background
});

inputElement.addEventListener('blur', (event) => {
  event.target.style.backgroundColor = ''; // Reset background
});
```

- Form Validation

  Focus and blur events are also integral to form validation techniques. Real-time validation can be achieved by providing immediate feedback upon input field blur, ensuring that users are informed of potential errors as they interact with the form.

```
function validateInput(event) {
  const inputField = event.target;
  if (inputField.value.trim() === '') {
    inputField.setCustomValidity('This field cannot be empty.');
  } else {
    inputField.setCustomValidity(''); // Clear any previous error
        message
  }
}

inputElement.addEventListener('blur', validateInput);
```

Event Properties

Both focus and blur events provide a standard set of event properties that can be utilized for further processing within the event handler functions. These properties include the event `target`, which represents the element that triggered the event. Understanding and using these properties can provide more control and context in event handling.

```
inputElement.addEventListener('focus', (event) => {
  console.log('Focus event on:', event.target);
});

inputElement.addEventListener('blur', (event) => {
  console.log('Blur event on:', event.target);
});
```

By harnessing the power of focus and blur events alongside other JavaScript capabilities, developers can ensure more interactive, accessible, and user-friendly web applications. Proper handling of these events fortifies form validation processes, augments user experience through real-time feedback, and maintains overall application robustness.

8.10 Custom Events and Event Emission

Custom events in JavaScript provide a mechanism for developers to define and dispatch their own events. This enhances the interactivity and modularity of web applications, permitting communication between different parts of the application that may be loosely connected. The `Event` constructor and the `dispatchEvent` method are fundamental to implementing custom events.

To create a custom event, the `Event` constructor is utilized. This constructor allows the specification of the event type and an object that can define additional properties such as `bubbles` and `cancelable`. These properties determine the event's behavior concerning propagation and default action prevention, respectively.

```
// Creating the custom event
const customEvent = new Event('myCustomEvent', {
  bubbles: true,
  cancelable: true
});
```

Once the custom event is created, it can be dispatched using the `dispatchEvent` method which is called on the target element that should dispatch the event. This method initiates the event propagation mechanism, including the capturing and bubbling phases based on the `bubbles` property defined in the event.

```
// Dispatching the custom event
```

```
document.dispatchEvent(customEvent);
```

Event listeners can be added to elements to listen for custom events in the same way they listen for built-in events. This involves using the `addEventListener` method specifying the custom event type as the first parameter.

```
// Adding an event listener for the custom event
document.addEventListener('myCustomEvent', function (e) {
  console.log('Custom event triggered.');
});
```

Custom events can convey additional data by using the `CustomEvent` constructor, which extends the `Event` constructor with the ability to pass additional information through the `detail` property.

```
// Creating a custom event with additional data
const customEventWithDetail = new CustomEvent('myCustomEventWithDetail', {
  detail: { message: 'Hello, world!' },
  bubbles: true,
  cancelable: true
});

// Dispatching the custom event with additional data
document.dispatchEvent(customEventWithDetail);

// Adding an event listener that utilizes the additional data
document.addEventListener('myCustomEventWithDetail', function (e) {
  console.log(e.detail.message);
});
```

The above approach can facilitate complex interactions within applications, enabling elements to communicate states or occurrences with detailed contextual information. Proper handling of custom events involves ensuring that the event type string and event listener functions are well-documented to maintain code clarity.

For finer control over event propagation and to cater to more complicated scenarios, the behavior of custom events during the capture, target, and bubble phases can be customized. This allows developers to create nuanced interactions within web applications. Consider the scenario where an event must trigger on multiple elements along the event propagation path:

```
// Adding event listeners on different levels of the DOM
document.body.addEventListener('myCustomEvent', function (e) {
  console.log('Body caught the event.');
});

document.getElementById('targetElement').addEventListener('myCustomEvent', function
    (e) {
  console.log('Target element got the event.');
});
```

```
// Dispatching the custom event from the target element
document.getElementById('targetElement').dispatchEvent(customEvent);
```

In the example, the event will propagate through the DOM, illustrating how the event flows from the dispatch point outward. The combination of `addEventListener`, `dispatchEvent`, and the `Event` or `CustomEvent` constructors empowers developers to build sophisticated event-driven applications while adhering to structured and scalable code practices.

8.11 Event Bubbling and Capturing

Event propagation in JavaScript can be understood through two distinct phases: **event capturing** and **event bubbling**. These phases define the path an event takes from the origin point (where the event occurs) through the DOM (Document Object Model) towards the root element, and possibly back again.

When an event is triggered, the browser first checks if there are any capturing event listeners. It then moves down the DOM tree to the target element, executing any capturing listeners it encounters. This phase is known as the **capture phase**.

After reaching the target element, the event then begins to ascend the DOM tree, executing any bubbling event listeners it encounters along the way. This phase is known as the **bubble phase**.

To set an event listener to execute during the capture phase, an additional argument needs to be passed to 'addEventListener'. This third argument is a boolean value that, when set to 'true', registers the event listener for the capture phase. By default, this value is 'false', making the event listener execute in the bubble phase.

The following example demonstrates the event capturing and bubbling phases:

```
<!DOCTYPE html>
<html>
<head>
<title>Event Bubbling and Capturing Example</title>
<script>
document.addEventListener('DOMContentLoaded', (event) => {
    document.getElementById('outer').addEventListener('click', () => {
        console.log('Outer Clicked - Capturing or Bubbling');
    }, false);
```

```
    document.getElementById('middle').addEventListener('click', () => {
        console.log('Middle Clicked - Capturing or Bubbling');
    }, false);

    document.getElementById('inner').addEventListener('click', () => {
        console.log('Inner Clicked - Capturing or Bubbling');
    }, false);

    document.getElementById('outer').addEventListener('click', () => {
        console.log('Outer Clicked - Capturing');
    }, true);

    document.getElementById('middle').addEventListener('click', () => {
        console.log('Middle Clicked - Capturing');
    }, true);

    document.getElementById('inner').addEventListener('click', () => {
        console.log('Inner Clicked - Capturing');
    }, true);
});
</script>
</head>
<body>
    <div id="outer" style="padding: 50px; border: 1px solid red;">
        Outer Div
        <div id="middle" style="padding: 50px; border: 1px solid green;">
            Middle Div
            <div id="inner" style="padding: 50px; border: 1px solid blue;"
                >
                Inner Div
            </div>
        </div>
    </div>
</body>
</html>
```

In this example, two sets of event listeners are added to the elements: one set for capturing and one set for bubbling. When you click on the "Inner Div," the following sequence of events occurs:

```
Inner Clicked - Capturing
Middle Clicked - Capturing
Outer Clicked - Capturing
Inner Clicked - Capturing or Bubbling
Middle Clicked - Capturing or Bubbling
Outer Clicked - Capturing or Bubbling
```

To elaborate further:

- **Capture Phase**: The event travels from the window down to the innermost element (`#inner`). Along this path, it invokes any capturing event listeners first.

- **Bubble Phase**: After executing all capture phase listeners and reaching the target element, the event starts bubbling. It then invokes all bubbling event listeners from the target (`#inner`) up to `document`.

This propagation model can be controlled to prevent certain events from reaching specific elements or to enhance event handling efficiency.

To stop the propagation of an event during its traversal through the DOM, either in the capturing or bubbling phase, you can call the `stopPropagation` method on the event object. For example:

```
document.getElementById("middle").addEventListener("click", (event) => {
    console.log("Middle Clicked - Bubbling");
    event.stopPropagation();
}, false);
```

This will prevent any listeners on ancestors from executing during the bubble phase after the `Middle Clicked - Bubbling` logs to the console when the middle div is clicked.

Understanding the behavior of event propagation is critical for designing sophisticated and responsive user interfaces. Properly managing event flow through capturing and bubbling ensures that listeners perform optimally, while avoiding unintended side effects from event propagation.

8.12 Preventing Default Behavior and Event Propagation

In JavaScript event handling, controlling an event's default behavior and propagation mechanism is crucial for creating sophisticated web applications. This section details the methodologies for preventing default behaviors and understanding the nuances of event propagation.

To prevent the default behaviour of an event, we use the `preventDefault()` method. This method ensures that the default action of the event does not occur. For instance, when a hyperlink is clicked, it typically directs the browser to another URL. Calling `preventDefault()` on the click event stops this redirection.

```
document.getElementById("myLink").addEventListener("click", function(
    event) {
  event.preventDefault();
```

```
  console.log("Default action prevented. No redirection.");
});
```

In this example, clicking on the element with the ID `myLink` logs a message to the console instead of redirection.

Event propagation comprises two phases: capturing and bubbling. Event capturing starts from the window object and proceeds down the DOM tree to the target element. Bubbling, on the other hand, proceeds in the opposite direction, moving from the target element up to the window object. By default, most events bubble.

The third optional parameter of `addEventListener()` can be set to `true` to register an event listener for the capturing phase.

```
document.getElementById("myButton").addEventListener("click", function(
    event) {
  console.log("Button clicked. Event bubbling.");
}, false);

document.getElementById("container").addEventListener("click", function(
    event) {
  console.log("Container clicked. Event bubbling.");
}, false);

document.getElementById("container").addEventListener("click", function(
    event) {
  console.log("Container clicked. Event capturing.");
}, true);
```

If the button with ID `myButton` is nested within an element with ID `container`, clicking the button results in the following console output:

```
Container clicked. Event capturing.
Button clicked. Event bubbling.
Container clicked. Event bubbling.
```

To stop the event from propagating either during the capturing or bubbling phase, we use the `stopPropagation()` method. This method ensures the event doesn't travel further up or down the DOM tree.

```
document.getElementById("myButton").addEventListener("click", function(
    event) {
  event.stopPropagation();
  console.log("Propagation stopped.");
}, false);

document.getElementById("container").addEventListener("click", function(
    event) {
  console.log("This will not be logged if myButton is clicked.");
}, false);
```

In the instance above, clicking on myButton logs "Propagation stopped." but prevents the container's click event from logging any messages, effectively isolating the button's event.

Combining preventDefault() and stopPropagation() within a single event listener is common, especially in complex applications requiring a high level of interaction control.

Furthermore, understanding the concept of stopImmediatePropagation() is important. This method halts the execution of remaining listeners on the current target after being called. Such precision is vital in specific scenarios where subsequent event listeners might otherwise interfere.

```
document.getElementById("myButton").addEventListener("click", function(
    event) {
  event.stopImmediatePropagation();
  console.log("Immediate propagation stopped.");
}, false);

document.getElementById("myButton").addEventListener("click", function(
    event) {
  console.log("This will not execute due to stopImmediatePropagation.");
}, false);
```

Here, clicking the button results in the following console output:

```
Immediate propagation stopped.
```

In this context, the second event listener on myButton does not execute due to stopImmediatePropagation() preventing any further event listeners from being triggered on the same element.

These methods (preventDefault(), stopPropagation(), and stopImmediatePropagation()) empower developers to fine-tune event management in web applications, ensuring efficient and precise event control across myriad interactive scenarios.

8.13 Debouncing and Throttling Events

In managing JavaScript events, especially those that can occur rapidly such as keystrokes or window resizing, it is crucial to optimize performance by controlling the execution rate of event handlers. Two essential techniques to achieve this are debouncing and throttling. Both serve to limit the frequency with which a function gets executed, yet they operate differently.

Debouncing delays the execution of a function until after a certain period of inactivity, resetting the timer each time the event is triggered during the wait period. This approach ensures that the function is called only once after the event flow has ceased.

Throttling, on the other hand, guarantees the function executes at regular intervals during the event stream, but no more frequently than the specified wait time. This can be immensely effective when continuous feedback is necessary, but overloading resources is a concern.

```
function debounce(func, wait) {
    let timeout;
    return function executedFunction(...args) {
        const later = () => {
            clearTimeout(timeout);
            func.apply(this, args);
        };
        clearTimeout(timeout);
        timeout = setTimeout(later, wait);
    };
};
```

Listing 8.5: Debouncing Function

The ‘debounce‘ function takes two parameters: ‘func‘, the function to be debounced, and ‘wait‘, the delay in milliseconds. Within ‘debounce‘, a variable ‘timeout‘ is maintained to keep track of the timer. The returned function, ‘executedFunction‘, uses spread syntax (‘...args‘) to capture arguments and the ‘later‘ function is defined to call ‘func‘ with the provided ‘args‘ using ‘apply‘ to preserve ‘this‘ context. By calling ‘clearTimeout(timeout)‘ first, it ensures that any previous timer is canceled before setting a new one.

```
Executed debounced function after the user has stopped typing for the specified wait time.
```

```
const inputField = document.getElementById('inputField');
inputField.addEventListener('input', debounce(function(event) {
    console.log('Debounced Input:', event.target.value);
}, 300));
```

Listing 8.6: Implementation of Debounce on Input Event

In this implementation, an input event listener is added to ‘inputField‘. The event handler is passed through the ‘debounce‘ function with a delay of 300 milliseconds. Consequently, the handler executes only after user input has stopped for 300 milliseconds, optimizing performance by reducing the number of function calls triggered by continuous user input.

```
function throttle(func, limit) {
    let lastFunc;
    let lastRan;
    return function() {
        const context = this;
        const args = arguments;
        if (!lastRan) {
            func.apply(context, args);
            lastRan = Date.now();
        } else {
            clearTimeout(lastFunc);
            lastFunc = setTimeout(function() {
                if ((Date.now() - lastRan) >= limit) {
                    func.apply(context, args);
                    lastRan = Date.now();
                }
            }, limit - (Date.now() - lastRan));
        }
    }
}
```

Listing 8.7: Throttling Function

The 'throttle' function similarly takes 'func' and 'limit' as parameters. It uses 'lastRan' to track the last time 'func' executed, ensuring the function runs initially and subsequently at fixed intervals determined by 'limit'. If the time since 'lastRan' is less than 'limit', it schedules the function to run using 'setTimeout'. This ensures the function executes at most once per specified 'limit' period.

The throttled function provides periodic updates within a defined time interval.

```
const handleScroll = () => {
    console.log('Scroll event at', new Date().toISOString());
};

window.addEventListener('scroll', throttle(handleScroll, 1000));
```

Listing 8.8: Implementation of Throttling on Scroll Event

In this example, the scroll event listener uses 'throttle' to invoke 'handleScroll' at maximum once per second (1000 milliseconds). This preventive measure ensures that performance is maintained even during rapid scroll events by limiting the volume of executed callbacks.

Both debouncing and throttling are pivotal in resource optimization and improving user experience. While debouncing is ideal for wait-until-stop scenarios such as validation or suggestions, throttling is suited for maintaining responsive applications by providing periodic updates without overwhelming system resources. Selecting the appropriate technique depends on the specific requirement of your event handling logic for efficient and performant web applications.

8.14 Touch Events for Mobile Devices

Touch events enable developers to create interactive and dynamic user experiences on mobile devices. Modern browsers and devices support a variety of touch events, which are crucial for implementing features such as swiping, pinching, and long pressing. Understanding and properly using touch events allows developers to create responsive, intuitive interfaces for touch-based devices.

JavaScript provides several touch event types, including `touchstart`, `touchmove`, `touchend`, and `touchcancel`. These events are akin to mouse events but are designed specifically for touch-enabled devices.

The `touchstart` event triggers when a finger touches the screen. The `touchmove` event fires whenever a finger moves on the touch surface. The `touchend` event occurs when a finger is lifted off the screen. Lastly, the `touchcancel` event fires when the system cancels the touch event, such as when a context menu appears or the device switches applications.

To handle these touch events, the `addEventListener` method is used in a similar manner to mouse and keyboard events. Below is an example of how to set up event listeners for basic touch events:

```
document.addEventListener('touchstart', handleTouchStart, false);
document.addEventListener('touchmove', handleTouchMove, false);
document.addEventListener('touchend', handleTouchEnd, false);
document.addEventListener('touchcancel', handleTouchCancel, false);

function handleTouchStart(event) {
    // Handle touch start event
}

function handleTouchMove(event) {
    // Handle touch move event
}

function handleTouchEnd(event) {
    // Handle touch end event
}

function handleTouchCancel(event) {
    // Handle touch cancel event
```

```
}
```

Touch Event Properties

Touch event objects contain valuable information regarding the touch interactions. These properties can be accessed to obtain details about the touch points:

- `touches`: A list of all touch points currently in contact with the surface. - `targetTouches`: A list of all touch points that are currently in contact with the surface and were started on the same target element. - `changedTouches`: A list of touch points that have changed since the last touch event.

Each entry in these lists is a `Touch` object which includes properties such as `identifier`, `target`, `clientX`, `clientY`, `screenX`, and `screenY`. Here's an example that uses these properties:

```
function handleTouchStart(event) {
    const touch = event.changedTouches[0];
    console.log('Touch started at:', touch.clientX, touch.clientY);
}

function handleTouchMove(event) {
    const touch = event.touches[0];
    console.log('Touch moved to:', touch.clientX, touch.clientY);
}

function handleTouchEnd(event) {
    const touch = event.changedTouches[0];
    console.log('Touch ended at:', touch.clientX, touch.clientY);
}
```

Handling Multi-touch

Detecting and managing multiple touch points is essential for implementing gestures such as pinch-to-zoom and rotate. The following example demonstrates how to distinguish between single-touch and multi-touch events:

```
function handleTouchStart(event) {
    if (event.touches.length === 1) {
        console.log('Single touch detected.');
    } else if (event.touches.length === 2) {
        console.log('Multi-touch detected.');
```

```
    }
}
```

Preventing Default Behavior and Optimizing Performance

Just as with mouse events, preventing the default behavior of touch events can be necessary to ensure smooth and expected user interactions. This is particularly important when implementing custom touch gestures. The event method `preventDefault` can be used to stop the default behaviors that browsers may apply to touch events, such as scrolling or zooming:

```
function handleTouchMove(event) {
    event.preventDefault(); // Prevent scrolling
    const touch = event.touches[0];
    console.log('Custom handling for touch move at:', touch.clientX,
         touch.clientY);
}
```

Additionally, touch events can generate a high frequency of callbacks, which may degrade performance. Techniques like debouncing and throttling are effective ways to limit the invocation rate of touch event handlers, ensuring the application remains responsive:

```
let lastTouchMove = 0;

function handleTouchMove(event) {
    event.preventDefault();

    const now = Date.now();
    if (now - lastTouchMove > 16) { // Throttle to ~60fps
        lastTouchMove = now;
        const touch = event.touches[0];
        console.log('Throttled touch move at:', touch.clientX, touch.
             clientY);
    }
}
```

By properly handling touch events and optimizing performance, developers can create fluid and natural-feeling interactions on mobile devices.

8.15 Best Practices for Event Handling

When crafting interactive web applications, adhering to best practices in event handling is essential for performance efficiency and code maintainability. Below, we will discuss several important strategies to optimize event handling in JavaScript.

- **Minimize the Number of Event Handlers**

  Adding too many event handlers can significantly impact performance, especially in applications that require responsiveness. Instead of attaching an event handler to every element, consider event delegation. Event delegation leverages the concept of event bubbling by adding a single event listener to a parent element to manage events for all its children.

```
document.querySelector('#parent').addEventListener('click', function(event)
    {
    if (event.target.matches('.child-element')) {
        console.log('Child element clicked!');
    }
});
```

- **Throttling and Debouncing**

  To avoid excessive event firing, particularly with high-frequency events like 'resize' or 'scroll', use throttling or debouncing. Throttling enforces a maximum number of times that a function can be called over time, while debouncing ensures that the function is called only once after a specified delay.

  A simple throttling function:

```
function throttle(func, limit) {
    let lastFunc;
    let lastRan;
    return function() {
        const context = this;
        const args = arguments;
        if (!lastRan) {
            func.apply(context, args);
            lastRan = Date.now();
        } else {
            clearTimeout(lastFunc);
            lastFunc = setTimeout(function() {
                if ((Date.now() - lastRan) >= limit) {
                    func.apply(context, args);
                    lastRan = Date.now();
                }
            }, limit - (Date.now() - lastRan));
        }
    }
}
```

An example of using debounce function:

```
function debounce(func, delay) {
    let debounceTimer;
    return function() {
        const context = this;
        const args = arguments;
        clearTimeout(debounceTimer);
        debounceTimer = setTimeout(() => func.apply(context, args), delay);
    };
}
```

- **Event Listener Removal**

  Always remove event listeners when they are no longer needed. This reduces memory leaks and improves performance. Use the 'removeEventListener' method, ensuring that the function reference matches the one used in 'addEventListener'.

```
function handleClick(event) {
   console.log('Element clicked');
}

const element = document.querySelector('.clickable');
element.addEventListener('click', handleClick);

// Later, remove the event listener
element.removeEventListener('click', handleClick);
```

- **Avoid Anonymous Functions**

  Using named functions instead of anonymous ones with 'addEventListener' provides multiple benefits, including the ease of removing event listeners and improved stack traces for debugging.

```
// Preferred way with named function
function handleClick(event) {
   console.log('Element clicked');
}
element.addEventListener('click', handleClick);
element.removeEventListener('click', handleClick);

// Less preferred with anonymous function
element.addEventListener('click', function(event) {
   console.log('Element clicked');
});
```

- **Use Passive Event Listeners**

  For events like 'touchstart' and 'touchmove' on mobile devices, where preventing default behavior is unnecessary, using passive event listeners can improve scrolling performance.

```
document.addEventListener('touchstart', function(event) {
   console.log('Touch started');
}, { passive: true });
```

- **Event Normalization**

  Browser inconsistencies can result in varied behavior across different browsers. Consider using libraries like 'jQuery' or implementing polyfills to normalize events, ensuring consistent functionality.

```
// Example with jQuery for event normalization
$(document).on('click', '.element', function(event) {
    console.log('Element clicked, normalized event');
});
```

- **Prevent Overlapping Handlers**

  Ensure that adding multiple event listeners on the same event does not result in overlapping functionality. Design the event handlers to be modular and single-responsibility, reducing potential conflicts.

- **Monitoring and Logging**

  Implement logging within event handlers for debugging and monitoring purposes. Tracking the event flow and handler execution can identify issues related to performance or logic errors.

```
function logEvent(event) {
    console.log(`Event ${event.type} fired on ${event.target}`);
}
element.addEventListener('click', logEvent);
```

Adhering to these best practices will significantly enhance the performance, maintainability, and reliability of your event handling in modern JavaScript applications.

Chapter 9

Asynchronous JavaScript: Callbacks, Promises, and Async/Await

This chapter examines asynchronous JavaScript, focusing on the mechanisms that enable non-blocking operations. It begins with an overview of synchronous and asynchronous execution, followed by detailed discussions on callbacks, including error handling and the pyramid of doom. The chapter then introduces promises, explaining their creation, usage, chaining, and error handling, along with methods like Promise.all and Promise.race. Finally, it covers the async/await syntax, providing examples of async functions and error management. By comparing callbacks, promises, and async/await, the chapter highlights best practices for writing efficient and readable asynchronous code.

9.1 Introduction to Asynchronous JavaScript

Asynchronous programming is a key feature that enables JavaScript to handle tasks without blocking the execution of other operations. This capability allows JavaScript to manage multiple operations concurrently, which is crucial for responsive web applications. In this section, we delve into the fundamental concepts that distinguish asynchronous JavaScript from synchronous execution, setting the stage for a comprehensive understanding of more advanced topics like callbacks, promises, and the async/await syntax.

Synchronous execution processes tasks one at a time in the sequence they are encountered. When a function is called, it must complete before the next function can begin. This straightforward approach, while simple to understand, can lead to performance bottlenecks. For example, if a synchronous JavaScript function makes a network request, it will block the entire execution thread until a response is received, rendering the web application unresponsive during that period.

Consider the following JavaScript code snippet demonstrating synchronous execution:

```
console.log('Start');
function synchronousNetworkCall() {
    const response = synchronousHttpRequest('https://example.com/data');
    console.log(response);
}
synchronousNetworkCall();
console.log('End');
```

The output, which happens sequentially, will showcase how the 'synchronousNetworkCall' blocks the further execution until it completes:

```
Start
<Data returned from network>
End
```

In asynchronous execution, tasks can be initiated and then continue to run concurrently with other operations. This non-blocking behavior allows JavaScript to perform other tasks while waiting for the completion of time-consuming operations like network requests, file reading, and other I/O tasks.

To accomplish asynchronous execution, JavaScript employs several mechanisms, the most fundamental of which are callbacks, promises, and async/await. These tools provide different levels of abstraction and control over asynchronous operations.

- **Callbacks:** Callbacks are functions passed as arguments to other functions, which are then invoked once a specific task is completed. This method enables the continuation of code execution without waiting for non-blocking operations to finish. The following code illustrates the use of callbacks for asynchronous programming:

```
console.log('Start');
function asynchronousNetworkCall(callback) {
    setTimeout(() => {
        const response = 'Data returned from network';
        callback(response);
    }, 2000);
}
asynchronousNetworkCall((response) => {
    console.log(response);
});
console.log('End');
```

  In this example, the 'setTimeout' function simulates an asynchronous network call. The function takes a callback, which is invoked once the simulated delay (representing network latency) is complete. The output, in this case, will be:

```
Start
End
Data returned from network
```

  The code demonstrates how JavaScript can continue execution (logging 'End') while waiting for the asynchronous operation to complete ('Data returned from network').

- **Promises:** Promises provide a cleaner, more manageable way to handle asynchronous operations. They represent a value that may be available now, or in the future, or never. A promise can be in one of three states: pending, fulfilled, or rejected. This allows structured handling of asynchronous code, paving the way for chaining operations and handling errors more gracefully. An example of a promise-based approach is:

```
console.log('Start');
function asyncNetworkCall() {
    return new Promise((resolve, reject) => {
        setTimeout(() => {
            const response = 'Data returned from network';
            resolve(response);
        }, 2000);
    });
}
```

```
asyncNetworkCall().then((response) => {
    console.log(response);
}).catch((error) => {
    console.error(error);
});
console.log('End');
```

In this code, the ‘asyncNetworkCall‘ function returns a promise that resolves with a simulated network response. The ‘then‘ method is used to handle the successful resolution of the promise, allowing us to process the response without nesting callbacks. The output remains:

```
Start
End
Data returned from network
```

- **Async/await:** Async/await syntax, introduced in ECMAScript 2017 (ES8), provides a more synchronous feel to asynchronous code. It is built on top of promises, allowing asynchronous code to be written in a cleaner and more readable manner. By employing ‘async‘ functions and the ‘await‘ keyword, developers can write asynchronous operations as though they were synchronous. The example below demonstrates this approach:

```
console.log('Start');
async function asyncFunction() {
    try {
        const response = await asyncNetworkCall();
        console.log(response);
    } catch (error) {
        console.error(error);
    }
}
asyncFunction();
console.log('End');
```

Here, ‘asyncFunction‘ is an ‘async‘ function, and ‘await‘ pauses its execution until the promise returned by ‘asyncNetworkCall‘ is resolved or rejected. This paradigm significantly simplifies error handling and improves code readability. The output, showing the order of operations, will be:

```
Start
End
Data returned from network
```

In summary, asynchronous JavaScript effectively manages tasks without blocking the main execution thread, using mechanisms like callbacks, promises, and async/await to handle non-blocking operations efficiently. Understanding these concepts provides the foundation for writing more responsive and performant web applications.

9.2 Understanding Synchronous vs. Asynchronous

To understand the intricacies of asynchronous JavaScript, it is essential first to delineate the concepts of synchronous and asynchronous execution. These paradigms define how tasks are performed and managed in JavaScript, impacting the performance and responsiveness of applications significantly.

Synchronous code is executed in a sequential manner, where each line of code runs one after another. This means that a task cannot proceed until the preceding task has completed. Consider the following synchronous JavaScript code:

```
// Synchronous code example
console.log('Task 1');
console.log('Task 2');
console.log('Task 3');
```

The above code will produce the following output:

```
Task 1
Task 2
Task 3
```

Each `console.log` statement waits for the previous one to complete before executing. This process ensures a predictable, linear execution flow but can lead to inefficient resource usage when longer operations (such as network requests or file I/O) are required, as the application will be unresponsive during these operations.

In contrast, asynchronous code allows other tasks to run while waiting for the completion of time-consuming operations. This non-blocking behavior is essential for maintaining a responsive user interface and enhancing performance. JavaScript achieves asynchronous execution mainly through callbacks, promises, and the async/await syntax.

Consider the following example of asynchronous execution using a callback function:

```
// Asynchronous code example with a callback
function fetchData(callback) {
    setTimeout(() => {
```

```
        callback('Data received');
    }, 1000);
}

console.log('Start fetching data');
fetchData((message) => {
    console.log(message);
});
console.log('Other operations');
```

The above code will produce the following output:

```
Start fetching data
Other operations
Data received
```

Here, the `setTimeout` function simulates an asynchronous operation, which delays the execution of the provided callback by 1000 milliseconds (1 second). The message `Data received` is logged after the delay, while other operations can continue running in the meantime.

To understand the underlying mechanics, let's delve into the event loop. The JavaScript runtime environment includes a call stack, an event queue, and a message loop.

1. **Call Stack**: This stack structure manages the execution context, handling function invocations and returns. When a function is called, it is pushed onto the stack, and when it returns, it is popped off. 2. **Event Queue**: This queue collects asynchronous operations' callbacks (such as I/O operations, timers, and event listeners) until the call stack is empty and ready to process them. 3. **Message Loop (Event Loop)**: This loop continuously checks the call stack and the event queue. If the call stack is empty, it moves the first callback from the event queue to the call stack for execution.

Here's a more detailed look at asynchronous operations involving the event loop:

```
// Event Loop demonstration
console.log('Start');

setTimeout(() => {
    console.log('Timeout callback');
}, 0);

console.log('End');
```

Despite the timeout being set to 0 milliseconds, the output will be:

```
Start
End
Timeout callback
```

The timeout callback is not executed immediately, even with a zero delay, because it is placed in the event queue and will only be executed once the call stack is clear.

Asynchronous behavior can significantly enhance performance and user experience. However, it also introduces complexity, such as managing state across asynchronous operations and handling errors effectively. Understanding the distinction between these paradigms and the role of the event loop is crucial for writing efficient and maintainable JavaScript.

This understanding paves the way for the upcoming discussions on callbacks, promises, and the async/await syntax, each providing different mechanisms and abstractions for managing asynchronous code. Mastering these concepts will allow you to handle asynchronous operations proficiently in modern JavaScript applications.

9.3 Callbacks: Definition and Usage

One of the fundamental mechanisms to achieve asynchronous execution in JavaScript is through callbacks. A callback is a function that is passed as an argument to another function, to be executed once an event or action has completed. This approach allows for the main flow of a program to continue while waiting for potentially time-consuming tasks to complete, thus enabling non-blocking operations.

Definition of a Callback Function

In JavaScript, a callback function can be defined as any function that is passed as an argument to another function and is then invoked within that outer function to complete some kind of routine or action. Consider the following simple example:

```
function fetchData(callback) {
    // Simulate a delay
    setTimeout(() => {
        const data = 'Data fetched from server';
        callback(data);
    }, 1000);
}

function displayData(data) {
    console.log(data);
```

```
}

fetchData(displayData);
```

In this example, ‘fetchData‘ is a function that takes a callback function as an argument. It simulates fetching data with a delay using ‘setTimeout‘. Once the data is "fetched" (after 1 second), the callback function is invoked with the fetched data. Here, ‘displayData‘ is passed as the callback function and is responsible for logging the data to the console.

Usage of Callbacks

Callbacks are widely used in various scenarios including event handling, server requests, and reading files. The following sections provide detailed explanations and examples of these uses.

Event Handling

One of the most common uses of callbacks is in event handling. In a web application, events such as user interactions (clicks, mouse movements, key presses) are handled using callbacks. For instance:

```
document.getElementById('myButton').addEventListener('click', function()
     {
   alert('Button clicked!');
});
```

Here, the ‘addEventListener‘ function is used to attach an event listener to an HTML element with the ID ‘myButton‘. The function passed to ‘addEventListener‘ is the callback that executes when the 'click' event occurs, in this case, it simply shows an alert box.

Server Requests

Callbacks are crucial in handling server requests, for instance, using the ‘XMLHttpRequest‘ object or ‘fetch‘ API. Here is an example using ‘XMLHttpRequest‘:

```
function makeRequest(url, callback) {
    const xhr = new XMLHttpRequest();
    xhr.open('GET', url);
    xhr.onload = function() {
        if (xhr.status === 200) {
            callback(null, xhr.responseText);
        } else {
            callback(xhr.status, null);
        }
    };
    xhr.send();
}
```

```
makeRequest('https://api.example.com/data', function(error, data) {
    if (error) {
        console.error('Request failed with status', error);
    } else {
        console.log('Data received:', data);
    }
});
```

This example illustrates a simple 'makeRequest' function that makes an HTTP GET request to a specified URL. It takes a URL and a callback function as arguments. The 'onload' event handler of 'XMLHttpRequest' is a callback that gets called when the request completes. Depending on the status of the request, the callback function passed to 'makeRequest' processes the response or logs an error.

Reading Files

Callbacks are also often used when reading files in Node.js. For example, using the 'fs' module to read a file:

```
const fs = require('fs');

fs.readFile('example.txt', 'utf8', function(err, data) {
    if (err) {
        return console.log(err);
    }
    console.log(data);
});
```

The 'fs.readFile' function reads the contents of a file asynchronously. It accepts the path to the file, the character encoding, and a callback function. The callback is invoked with an error object (if an error occurred) and the file data. This allows the rest of the program to continue executing while the file is being read.

Error-First Callbacks

A common pattern in Node.js and other JavaScript environments is the error-first callback. This pattern ensures that the first parameter of the callback is an error object (or null if no error occurred), and the subsequent parameters contain the results of the operation. This pattern allows for a consistent way of handling errors and results in asynchronous functions. Consider the following example:

```
function performOperation(callback) {
    // Simulate an operation
    setTimeout(() => {
        const success = Math.random() > 0.5;
```

```
        if (success) {
            callback(null, 'Operation successful');
        } else {
            callback('Operation failed');
        }
    }, 1000);
}

performOperation(function(error, result) {
    if (error) {
        return console.log('Error:', error);
    }
    console.log('Result:', result);
});
```

In this example, 'performOperation' simulates an asynchronous operation. The callback function checks for errors first. If an error occurs, it logs the error message. Otherwise, it logs the result.

Using callbacks for asynchronous tasks allows JavaScript developers to write non-blocking code that efficiently handles time-consuming operations such as file I/O, network requests, and user interactions. Although callbacks are powerful, they come with their own set of challenges, particularly in terms of readability and maintainability when dealing with complex asynchronous workflows. This leads to phenomena such as the "Pyramid of Doom," which will be discussed in the following sections.

9.4 Handling Errors with Callbacks

In the context of asynchronous JavaScript, handling errors effectively within callback functions is crucial to maintaining robust, maintainable code. Callbacks, by their nature, can introduce complexities in error management that require careful consideration. This section will delve into the methodologies and best practices for managing errors in callback-based asynchronous operations.

When working with callbacks, it is a common pattern to pass an error object as the first argument to the callback function. This convention, known as the "Node.js callback pattern" or "error-first callback pattern," allows the callback to distinguish between successful and erroneous outcomes of the asynchronous operation.

Consider the following example of an asynchronous file read operation using Node.js:

```
const fs = require('fs');

fs.readFile('example.txt', 'utf8', function(err, data) {
    if (err) {
        console.error('Error reading file:', err);
        return;
    }
    console.log('File content:', data);
});
```

In this example, the `fs.readFile` function initiates an asynchronous file read. The callback function passed to `fs.readFile` takes two parameters: `err` and `data`. If an error occurs during the file read operation, the `err` parameter will contain an error object, and the `data` parameter will be `undefined`. The callback checks for the presence of `err` and handles it accordingly by logging the error message and terminating further execution within the callback using `return;`.

Failing to handle errors appropriately can result in unhandled exceptions, which can be particularly problematic in asynchronous code, as the stack trace may not provide sufficient context to diagnose the issue. Therefore, every asynchronous callback should explicitly account for potential errors.

Another aspect to consider is the propagation of errors in callbacks. In some cases, an error encountered in one asynchronous operation must be propagated to a broader context to be handled effectively. This can be implemented by nesting callbacks and passing error objects up the callback chain.

Consider the following nested callback example:

```
function asyncOperation(callback) {
    setTimeout(function() {
        const error = new Error('An error occurred');
        callback(error, null);
    }, 1000);
}

function anotherAsyncOperation(data, callback) {
    setTimeout(function() {
        if (!data) {
            const error = new Error('No data provided');
            callback(error, null);
            return;
        }
        callback(null, 'Processed: ' + data);
    }, 1000);
}
```

```
asyncOperation(function(err, result) {
    if (err) {
        console.error('Error in asyncOperation:', err);
        return;
    }
    anotherAsyncOperation(result, function(err, finalResult) {
        if (err) {
            console.error('Error in anotherAsyncOperation:', err);
            return;
        }
        console.log('Final result:', finalResult);
    });
});
```

In this example, `asyncOperation` and `anotherAsyncOperation` are two functions that perform asynchronous tasks. Both functions follow the error-first callback pattern. The callback provided to `asyncOperation` handles its errors and, upon success, initiates `anotherAsyncOperation`. Each callback explicitly checks for errors and handles them before proceeding to the next step. This example illustrates the necessity of considering error propagation at each level of nested callbacks.

To manage complex scenarios involving multiple asynchronous operations, libraries such as `async` provide utility functions for handling errors more elegantly. For example, the `async.series` method can be used to perform a series of asynchronous functions in succession, with error handling centralized in a final callback:

```
const async = require('async');

async.series([
    function(callback) {
        asyncOperation(callback);
    },
    function(callback) {
        anotherAsyncOperation('Some data', callback);
    }
], function(err, results) {
    if (err) {
        console.error('Error in async series:', err);
        return;
    }
    console.log('Results:', results);
});
```

In this snippet, the `async.series` method accepts an array of functions to execute in series. Each function takes a single `callback` parameter, following the error-first pattern. The final callback is called after all the functions have executed, or immediately if an error occurs in any function. This structure separates the logic of error handling from the individual operations, simplifying the management of complex asynchronous workflows.

Understanding and implementing proper error handling in callback functions is essential for building resilient JavaScript applications. By adhering to the error-first callback convention, carefully propagating errors, and leveraging utility libraries, developers can effectively manage asynchronous errors and improve code maintainability.

9.5 The Pyramid of Doom

The "Pyramid of Doom" refers to the increasingly nested structure of callback functions, which can make asynchronous code difficult to read and maintain. This typically occurs when performing a series of asynchronous operations that depend on each other. The term derives from the way the code visually resembles a pyramid or triangle due to successive levels of indentation.

Consider a scenario where we need to perform three asynchronous operations in sequence: fetching data from an API, processing the fetched data, and then saving the processed data to a database. Using callback-based asynchronous programming, the structure might look something like this:

```
fetchDataFromAPI(function(err, data) {
    if (err) {
        console.error('Error fetching data:', err);
    } else {
        processData(data, function(err, processedData) {
            if (err) {
                console.error('Error processing data:', err);
            } else {
                saveToDatabase(processedData, function(err) {
                    if (err) {
                        console.error('Error saving data:', err);
                    } else {
                        console.log('Data successfully saved.');
                    }
                });
            }
        });
    }
});
```

Listing 9.1: Example of Pyramid of Doom

In this example, each callback function is nested inside the previous one. This nesting occurs because each subsequent asynchronous operation depends on the completion of the preceding one.

Such deeply nested structures can lead to several problems. First, the code becomes difficult to read and comprehend. When developers need to understand how the operations flow from one to another, they must trace through multiple levels of indentation. Additionally, this structure complicates debugging, as errors may need to be propagated through multiple nested levels. It becomes challenging to manage error handling, leading to potentially unhandled exceptions.

The Pyramid of Doom can be mitigated using several techniques, the most notable of which are Promises and the asyncawait syntax. Promises provide a means to write asynchronous code without deeply nested callbacks. Instead of passing a callback function, the asynchronous function returns a Promise object. This object represents an eventual completion (or failure) of the asynchronous operation and allows chaining of subsequent operations.

Here's how the same example can be reorganized using promises to avoid the Pyramid of Doom:

```
fetchDataFromAPI()
    .then(data => processData(data))
    .then(processedData => saveToDatabase(processedData))
    .then(() => console.log('Data successfully saved.'))
    .catch(err => console.error('Error:', err));
```

Listing 9.2: Avoiding Pyramid of Doom with Promises

In this version, each asynchronous function returns a promise, and subsequent operations are chained using the `.then()` method. If any error occurs during any of the asynchronous operations, it will be caught by the `.catch()` method at the end of the chain. This approach significantly improves readability by flattening the callback structure.

Furthermore, the introduction of asyncawait syntax in ES2017 offers an even more straightforward and readable way to write asynchronous code. It allows you to write asynchronous code that looks synchronous, which further eliminates the Pyramid of Doom.

Here is the same example using asyncawait:

```
async function performOperations() {
    try {
        const data = await fetchDataFromAPI();
        const processedData = await processData(data);
        await saveToDatabase(processedData);
        console.log('Data successfully saved.');
    } catch (err) {
        console.error('Error:', err);
    }
}
performOperations();
```

Listing 9.3: Avoiding Pyramid of Doom with AsyncAwait

Using asyncawait, the function `performOperations()` handles the sequence of asynchronous operations without nested callbacks. The `await` keyword suspends the execution of the `performOperations()` function until the Promise is resolved, thus making the asynchronous code look synchronous. This approach also makes error handling more straightforward, as we can use trycatch blocks to catch any thrown exceptions.

In essence, while the Pyramid of Doom poses significant challenges in callback-based asynchronous programming, modern JavaScript features such as Promises and asyncawait provide effective mechanisms to write more maintainable and readable asynchronous code.

9.6 Introduction to Promises

JavaScript promises provide a robust and elegant approach to handling asynchronous operations by avoiding some common pitfalls associated with callbacks, such as the "pyramid of doom" or callback hell. Promises represent a value which may be available now, or in the future, or never. They streamline the process of executing, handling, and chaining asynchronous calls, making the code more manageable and readable.

A promise is an object that represents the eventual completion (or failure) of an asynchronous operation and its resulting value. This abstraction allows developers to attach callbacks to handle the asynchronous completion or failure rather than pass callbacks directly into a function.

```
let myPromise = new Promise((resolve, reject) => {
    let isSuccessful = true; // This simulates an asynchronous operation'
        s outcome
```

```
    if (isSuccessful) {
        resolve('Operation Successful!');
    } else {
        reject('Operation Failed.');
    }
});
```

Listing 9.4: Creating a Simple Promise

In the above snippet, a new promise object `myPromise` is created. The `Promise` constructor takes a single argument, which is a function called the executor. This executor function has two arguments: `resolve` and `reject`. These are callbacks provided by the JavaScript engine. The `resolve` callback is used if the asynchronous operation is successful, whereas `reject` is used if it fails.

States of a Promise

A promise can be in one of three states:

- **Pending**: The initial state. The promise is neither fulfilled nor rejected.
- **Fulfilled**: The operation completed successfully, and the `resolve` was called.
- **Rejected**: The operation failed, and the `reject` was called.

```
let promise = new Promise((resolve, reject) => {
    const success = true;
    if (success) resolve("Success!");
    else reject("Failure!");
});

console.log(promise); // Promise {<fulfilled>: 'Success!'}
```

Listing 9.5: Promise States

Handling Promise Results

To handle the outcome of a promise, two principal methods are provided: `.then()` and `.catch()`. The `.then()` method registers callbacks to handle the fulfillment case, while `.catch()` handles the rejection case.

```
myPromise.then((message) => {
    console.log(message); // Output: 'Operation Successful!'
}).catch((error) => {
    console.error(error); // Handles rejected case
```

```
});
```

Listing 9.6: Handling Promise Resolution

Promise Chaining

Promises allow chaining by returning another promise from within the `.then()` method. This enables the handling of sequences of asynchronous operations in a more readable manner.

```
let firstPromise = new Promise((resolve, reject) => {
    resolve('First success');
});

firstPromise.then((message) => {
    console.log(message); // Output: 'First success'
    return 'Second success';
}).then((secondMessage) => {
    console.log(secondMessage); // Output: 'Second success'
});
```

Listing 9.7: Chaining Promises

In the example, the first promise resolves, and its success message is logged. The `.then()` method also returns another string which is subsequently handled by another `.then()` call, forming a chain of promises.

Catching Errors

Error handling in promises chains is streamlined through the `.catch()` method. If any promise in the chain is rejected, control is passed to the nearest `.catch()` method.

```
let failingPromise = new Promise((resolve, reject) => {
    reject('An error occurred');
});

failingPromise.then((message) => {
    console.log(message);
}).catch((error) => {
    console.error(error); // Output: 'An error occurred'
});
```

Listing 9.8: Catching Errors in Promises

In this section, we establish the foundation of JavaScript promises, covering their creation, states, handling results, chaining, and error management. Promises pave the way for handling asynchronous operations in a more structured and readable manner, setting the stage for further understanding their advanced usage and integration with modern JavaScript practices.

9.7 Creating and Using Promises

Promises in JavaScript represent a value that may be available now, in the future, or never. They provide a way to handle asynchronous operations in a more manageable fashion compared to callbacks. A promise can be in one of three states: pending, fulfilled, or rejected.

To create a new promise, use the `Promise` constructor with a function as its argument. This function is called the executor function, and it takes two parameters: `resolve` and `reject`. The `resolve` function is called when the promise is fulfilled (success), and the `reject` function is called when the promise is rejected (failure).

```
let promise = new Promise(function(resolve, reject) {
    // executor function
});
```

Inside the executor function, you write the asynchronous code. For example, let's create a promise that resolves after 2 seconds:

```
let promise = new Promise(function(resolve, reject) {
    setTimeout(function() {
        resolve('Promise fulfilled!');
    }, 2000);
});
```

In this example, the promise will transition to the fulfilled state after 2 seconds, passing the message 'Promise fulfilled!' to the `resolve` function.

To consume a promise, use the `then` method. The `then` method takes up to two arguments: the first is a callback function for when the promise is fulfilled, and the second is a callback function for when the promise is rejected. Here is how you use the promise created above:

```
promise.then(function(value) {
    console.log(value);
});
```

The above code outputs the following after 2 seconds:

```
Promise fulfilled!
```

If the promise gets rejected, you can handle the error with the second argument of `then` or by chaining a `catch` method.

```
let promise = new Promise(function(resolve, reject) {
    setTimeout(function() {
        reject('Promise rejected!');
    }, 2000);
});

promise.then(
    function(value) { console.log(value); },
    function(error) { console.log(error); }
);
```

Or equivalently, using `catch`:

```
promise.catch(function(error) {
    console.log(error);
});
```

The output after 2 seconds will be:

```
Promise rejected!
```

You can chain multiple promises together by returning a promise from the `then` method:

```
let promise = new Promise(function(resolve, reject) {
    setTimeout(function() {
        resolve(1);
    }, 1000);
});

promise
    .then(function(value) {
        console.log(value); // 1
        return value * 2;
    })
    .then(function(value) {
        console.log(value); // 2
        return value * 2;
    })
    .then(function(value) {
        console.log(value); // 4
    });
```

In this chain, each `then` method creates a new promise resolved with the value returned by the callback. This feature allows for sequential asynchronous operations, making the code more readable and easier to maintain.

To handle errors in a promise chain, use the `catch` method at the end:

```
let promise = new Promise(function(resolve, reject) {
    setTimeout(function() {
        reject(new Error('Something went wrong!'));
    }, 1000);
});

promise
    .then(function(value) {
        console.log(value);
    })
    .catch(function(error) {
        console.error(error.message);
    });
```

The `catch` method catches errors in the entire chain, allowing you to handle all errors in one place, thereby simplifying error management in complex asynchronous code sequences.

Promises simplify asynchronous programming by avoiding the pitfalls of callbacks and providing a more structured way to handle asynchronous operations, chaining, and error management.

9.8 Chaining Promises

Promises provide a powerful way to handle asynchronous operations in JavaScript. One of their most significant strengths is the ability to chain multiple operations together, allowing for sequential execution of asynchronous tasks. Chaining promises simplifies complex operations and makes code more readable and maintainable.

When a promise is resolved, it can return another promise, facilitating the chaining mechanism. This strategy enables sequential execution where each operation starts only after the preceding one completes. To understand how chaining works, consider the following example where we fetch user data and then their corresponding posts:

```
// Simulating API requests with promises
function getUser(id) {
    return new Promise((resolve) => {
        setTimeout(() => {
            resolve({ id: id, name: 'John Doe' });
        }, 1000);
    });
}
```

```
function getPosts(userId) {
    return new Promise((resolve) => {
        setTimeout(() => {
            resolve([{ id: 1, content: 'Post 1'}, {id: 2, content: 'Post 2
                '}]);
        }, 1000);
    });
}

// Chaining Promises
getUser(1)
    .then(user => {
        console.log('User:', user);
        return getPosts(user.id);
    })
    .then(posts => {
        console.log('Posts:', posts);
    })
    .catch(error => {
        console.error('Error:', error);
    });
```

In this example, the `getUser` function simulates fetching user data and returns a promise that resolves after one second. The `getPosts` function simulates fetching posts for a user and also returns a promise that resolves after one second. Notice how the `getPosts` function is called within the `then` block of the `getUser` function. This ensures `getPosts` executes only after `getUser` has resolved.

The key aspects of promise chaining involve handling intermediate results and any potential errors along the chain. Each `then` block processes the resolved value and can return either a value or another promise.

Returning Plain Values

If a `then` block returns a plain value (not a promise), the next `then` block receives this value and continues execution. Consider the following example:

```
getUser(2)
    .then(user => {
        console.log('User:', user);
        return user.name;
    })
    .then(userName => {
        console.log('User Name:', userName);
    })
```

```
    .catch(error => {
        console.error('Error:', error);
    });
```

In this case, the first `then` block returns a plain string, `user.name`. This value is passed to the next `then` block, demonstrating that returned plain values are directly used in subsequent promise chains.

Returning Promises

Often, returning promises in a chain is necessary when performing asynchronous operations sequentially. For example:

```
getUser(3)
    .then(user => {
        console.log('User:', user);
        return getPosts(user.id);
    })
    .then(posts => {
        console.log('Posts:', posts);
        return getPostComments(posts[0].id);
    })
    .then(comments => {
        console.log('Comments on first post:', comments);
    })
    .catch(error => {
        console.error('Error:', error);
    });
```

Here, the promise returned by `getPosts` will resolve and pass its result (the posts) to the subsequent `then` block. If another asynchronous operation is needed, like fetching comments for the first post, it can be chained by returning another promise (`getPostComments` in this case).

Error Handling in Chained Promises

Properly handling errors is crucial when chaining promises, as an error in any part of the chain can propagate downwards. The `catch` method can be used to handle errors. If an error occurs, it bypasses all subsequent `then` blocks until a `catch` block is encountered. For example:

```
getUser(4)
    .then(user => {
        console.log('User:', user);
        return getPosts(user.id);
    })
```

```
    .then(posts => {
        throw new Error('Fetching comments failed');
        return getPostComments(posts[0].id);
    })
    .then(comments => {
        console.log('Comments on first post:', comments);
    })
    .catch(error => {
        console.error('Caught an error:', error.message);
    });
```

If any `then` block throws an error or a promise within the chain is rejected, the `catch` block captures it. It is good practice to place a `catch` block at the end of a promise chain to handle any errors that might occur.

The `finally` Method

Introduced in ECMAScript 2018, the `finally` method provides a way to execute code regardless of the promise's fate (whether it was resolved or rejected). It's particularly useful for cleanup operations like closing files or stopping loaders. For instance:

```
getUser(5)
    .then(user => {
        console.log('User:', user);
        return getPosts(user.id);
    })
    .then(posts => {
        console.log('Posts:', posts);
    })
    .catch(error => {
        console.error('Error:', error);
    })
    .finally(() => {
        console.log('Operation complete.');
    });
```

In this example, the `finally` block will execute after all the `then` and `catch` blocks, regardless of whether the operations succeeded or failed.

9.9 Handling Errors in Promises

Error handling in promises is vital for building robust and reliable asynchronous applications. When working with promises, there are multiple ways to handle errors to ensure that the application can gracefully manage unexpected situations and debug effectively.

A promise represents a value that may be available now, in the future, or never. This value can either be resolved successfully or rejected with an error. Handling rejections properly is crucial to maintaining the integrity of the application. This section will examine the mechanisms for dealing with errors in promises, detailing various methods to capture, handle, and propagate errors effectively.

Catching Errors with `.catch()`:

The `.catch()` method is used to handle any errors in a promise chain. It can be appended to the end of a promise chain and will catch any rejection that occurs, either from the initial promise or any subsequent `.then()` operations. Below is an example illustrating the use of `.catch()`:

```
let promise = new Promise((resolve, reject) => {
    // Simulate an asynchronous operation
    setTimeout(() => {
        let success = false;
        if (success) {
            resolve('Operation succeeded');
        } else {
            reject(new Error('Operation failed'));
        }
    }, 1000);
});

promise
    .then(result => {
        console.log(result);
    })
    .catch(error => {
        console.error('Caught in .catch:', error.message);
    });
```

In this example, if the asynchronous operation fails, the promise is rejected with an error. The `.catch()` method captures the error and logs it to the console.

Error Propagation in Promise Chains:

Errors can propagate through promise chains if they are not handled immediately. This allows for centralized error handling at the end of a promise chain. Here is an illustration:

```
let promise = new Promise((resolve, reject) => {
    reject(new Error('Initial failure'));
});

promise
    .then(result => {
        console.log(result);
        return 'Step 1';
    })
    .then(result => {
        console.log(result);
        return 'Step 2';
    })
    .catch(error => {
        console.error('Error propagated to the end:', error.message);
    });
```

In this code, the initial promise is rejected. Since this rejection is not handled immediately, it propagates through the subsequent `.then()` calls and is finally caught by the `.catch()` at the end.

Catching Errors in Specific Steps:

It is possible to handle errors at specific steps within a promise chain, allowing different steps to have their own error handling logic:

```
let promise = new Promise((resolve, reject) => {
    resolve('Initial success');
});

promise
    .then(result => {
        console.log(result);
        throw new Error('Error in Step 1');
    })
    .catch(error => {
        console.error('Caught error in Step 1:', error.message);
        return 'Recovered from Step 1';
    })
    .then(result => {
        console.log(result);
        return 'Step 2';
    })
    .catch(error => {
        console.error('Error in Step 2:', error.message);
    });
```

In this snippet, an error is thrown intentionally in the first `.then()` method. The subsequent `.catch()` handles this specific error and returns a recovery value. This allows the promise chain to continue its normal execution.

Using `Promise.reject()`:

The `Promise.reject()` method returns a promise that is rejected with a given reason. This is useful for testing error handling mechanisms or initializing a promise chain with a rejection:

```
let rejectedPromise = Promise.reject(new Error('Explicit rejection'));

rejectedPromise
    .catch(error => {
        console.error('Handled explicit rejection:', error.message);
    });
```

This example shows a promise that is explicitly rejected using `Promise.reject()`. The rejection is then handled by the `.catch()` method.

Error Handling in `Promise.all()`:

The `Promise.all()` method returns a single promise that resolves when all of the promises in the iterable have resolved or when the iterable contains no promises. If any promise is rejected, the returned promise is immediately rejected with that reason:

```
let promise1 = Promise.resolve('First');
let promise2 = Promise.reject(new Error('Failure in second promise'));
let promise3 = Promise.resolve('Third');

Promise.all([promise1, promise2, promise3])
    .then(results => {
        console.log(results);
    })
    .catch(error => {
        console.error('Caught error in Promise.all:', error.message);
    });
```

In this example, `promise2` is rejected, causing the promise returned by `Promise.all()` to be rejected immediately. The `.catch()` method captures the rejection and logs the error message.

Chaining `Promise.all()`:

When working with multiple asynchronous operations, it is often necessary to handle errors collectively or individually. Combining `Promise.all()` with chained `.catch()` methods allows for sophisticated error handling strategies:

```
let promise1 = Promise.resolve('First');
let promise2 = new Promise((resolve, reject) =>
    setTimeout(() => reject(new Error('Async failure')), 1000));
let promise3 = Promise.resolve('Third');

Promise.all([
    promise1.catch(error => ({ status: 'rejected', reason: error })),
    promise2.catch(error => ({ status: 'rejected', reason: error })),
    promise3.catch(error => ({ status: 'rejected', reason: error }))
])
.then(results => {
    results.forEach(result => {
        if (result.status === 'rejected') {
            console.error('Handled error:', result.reason.message);
        } else {
            console.log('Success:', result);
        }
    });
});
```

Here, each promise in `Promise.all()` individually handles its own rejection and transforms the error into a more manageable format. The final `.then()` processes the results, differentiating between successful and rejected promises.

These techniques and examples illustrate the fundamental practices of handling errors in promises effectively. By understanding and implementing these methods, developers can write asynchronous JavaScript code that is both resilient and maintainable.

9.10 The Promise.all and Promise.race Methods

In the domain of asynchronous programming, handling multiple asynchronous operations concurrently is a frequent requirement. JavaScript's Promises API offers two powerful methods, `Promise.all` and `Promise.race`, to manage such scenarios efficiently. These methods are essential for orchestrating multiple promises and provide control over their resolution behavior.

`Promise.all` is pivotal when the completion of all asynchronous tasks is indispensable before proceeding. This method takes an iterable of promises and returns a single promise that resolves when all the included promises have resolved. The resultant promise resolves with an array of the fulfilled values. Conversely, if any promise in the iterable rejects, `Promise.all` immediately rejects with the reason of the first promise that rejects.

Here is a detailed example illustrating `Promise.all`:

```
const promise1 = Promise.resolve(3);
const promise2 = 42;
const promise3 = new Promise((resolve, reject) => {
  setTimeout(resolve, 100, 'foo');
});

Promise.all([promise1, promise2, promise3]).then((values) => {
  console.log(values);
});
// expected output: Array [3, 42, "foo"]
```

Listing 9.9: Using Promise.all

In this scenario, three promises are combined: `promise1` which resolves instantly, `promise2` which is simply a value (which will be implicitly converted into a resolved promise), and `promise3` which resolves after 100 milliseconds. `Promise.all` returns a promise that resolves once all three promises have resolved, producing the array `[3, 42, "foo"]`.

The significance of error handling in `Promise.all` cannot be understated. If any promise rejects, the resultant promise from `Promise.all` will reject immediately with the rejection reason, and subsequent fulfillment values are disregarded.

```
const promise1 = Promise.resolve(3);
const promise2 = new Promise((resolve, reject) => {
  setTimeout(reject, 100, 'error occurred');
});
const promise3 = new Promise((resolve) => {
  setTimeout(resolve, 200, 'foo');
});

Promise.all([promise1, promise2, promise3])
  .then((values) => {
    console.log(values);
  })
  .catch((error) => {
    console.error(error);
  });
// expected output: "error occurred"
```

Listing 9.10: Error Handling in Promise.all

In this example, although `promise1` resolves and `promise3` would eventually resolve, the rejection of `promise2` after 100 milliseconds causes the entire `Promise.all` to reject with the error `"error occurred"`.

In contrast, `Promise.race` is designed for scenarios where the quickest response is essential. It takes an iterable of promises and returns a promise that resolves or rejects as soon as one of the promises in the iterable settles (i.e., resolves or rejects). This provides flexibility when the task's timing is critical.

Here is a detailed example of `Promise.race`:

```
const promise1 = new Promise((resolve) => {
  setTimeout(resolve, 500, 'one');
});

const promise2 = new Promise((resolve) => {
  setTimeout(resolve, 100, 'two');
});

Promise.race([promise1, promise2]).then((value) => {
  console.log(value);
});
// expected output: "two"
```

Listing 9.11: Using Promise.race

In this case, `promise2` resolves before `promise1`, leading `Promise.race` to resolve to `"two"` when `promise2` fulfills after 100 milliseconds.

The behavior when promises in the iterable settle in different ways within `Promise.race` must be keenly understood. The method's resultant promise will adopt the state of the first settled promise, be it resolved or rejected.

```
const promise1 = new Promise((resolve, reject) => {
  setTimeout(reject, 100, 'failed');
});

const promise2 = new Promise((resolve) => {
  setTimeout(resolve, 500, 'successful');
});

Promise.race([promise1, promise2])
  .then((value) => {
    console.log(value);
  })
  .catch((error) => {
    console.error(error);
  });
```

```
// expected output: "failed"
```

Listing 9.12: Promise.race with rejection

Here, `promise1` rejects first, causing `Promise.race` to reject with the error `"failed"`, despite `promise2` ultimately resolving successfully after 500 milliseconds.

Interleaving `Promise.all` and `Promise.race` within complex asynchronous workflows allows for sophisticated control over concurrent operation handling. Mastery of these methods is essential for building robust, performant, and efficient asynchronous applications in JavaScript.

9.11 Async/Await: Introduction and Basics

Async/await, introduced in ECMAScript 2017 (ES8), provides a new way to handle asynchronous operations in JavaScript, aiming to simplify the process and make asynchronous code look more like synchronous code. This syntactic sugar around Promises allows for more readable and maintainable code, offering a linear flow of asynchronous actions, which significantly improves the clarity of error handling and logical sequences.

The 'async' keyword is used to declare an asynchronous function, which returns an 'AsyncFunction' object. The 'await' keyword can only be used inside an 'async' function. When encountering an 'await' expression, the execution of the 'async' function pauses until the Promise is resolved (fulfilled or rejected). Afterward, it resumes with the resolved value. This mechanism ensures that asynchronous code execution can be written in a blocking style without actually blocking the main thread.

To declare an asynchronous function, you prepend the function declaration with the 'async' keyword:

```
async function fetchData() {
    // Implementation will go here
}
```

Alternatively, for function expressions and arrow functions, the syntax would be:

```
const fetchData = async () => {
    // Implementation will go here
};
```

The simplest use of the 'await' keyword is to wait for a Promise to resolve and return its result:

```
async function fetchData() {
    let response = await fetch('https://api.example.com/data');
    let data = await response.json();
    return data;
}
```

In this example, the 'fetch' function returns a Promise that resolves with a 'Response' object when the network request completes. By using 'await', the code execution pauses until the 'fetch' Promise resolves, then the 'response.json()' method is called, also returning a Promise, which is awaited again to obtain the final data.

The key advantage of async/await is its ability to handle errors in a more straightforward and synchronous-like manner using try/catch blocks. Consider the following code for error handling:

```
async function fetchData() {
    try {
        let response = await fetch('https://api.example.com/data');
        if (!response.ok) {
            throw new Error('Network response was not ok');
        }
        let data = await response.json();
        return data;
    } catch (error) {
        console.error('Fetch error: ', error);
    }
}
```

Here, a 'try' block contains the asynchronous code. If any part of the code throws an error (e.g., network issues or JSON parsing errors), the 'catch' block will handle it. This approach enhances readability and debuggability compared to traditional Promise-based error handling using '.catch()'.

When multiple asynchronous operations need to be performed sequentially, async/await makes the code concise and clear:

```
async function fetchAllData() {
    let data1 = await fetchData('https://api.example.com/data1');
    let data2 = await fetchData('https://api.example.com/data2');
    let data3 = await fetchData('https://api.example.com/data3');
    return [data1, data2, data3];
}
```

If these operations are independent and can be performed concurrently, 'Promise.all()' can be combined with async/await to further improve efficiency:

```
async function fetchAllData() {
```

```
    let [data1, data2, data3] = await Promise.all([
        fetchData('https://api.example.com/data1'),
        fetchData('https://api.example.com/data2'),
        fetchData('https://api.example.com/data3')
    ]);
    return [data1, data2, data3];
}
```

This pattern allows the program to wait for all promises to resolve before proceeding, reducing total wait time compared to sequentially awaiting each Promise.

Another important aspect is handling retry logic for operations that may fail intermittently. With async/await, retrying becomes less cumbersome:

```
async function fetchWithRetry(url, retries = 3) {
    for (let i = 0; i < retries; i++) {
        try {
            let response = await fetch(url);
            if (!response.ok) {
                throw new Error('Network response was not ok');
            }
            return await response.json();
        } catch (error) {
            if (i === retries - 1) {
                console.error('Fetch error: ', error);
                throw error;
            }
        }
    }
}
```

By enclosing the fetch call within a loop and utilizing 'try/catch' for each attempt, this function retries the operation the specified number of times before propagating the error.

In comparison to callbacks and Promises, async/await offers a more intuitive structure for handling asynchronous workflows. The reduction in boilerplate code and enhanced ability to handle errors synchronously provide a robust approach to managing asynchronous operations.

9.12 Using Async Functions

Async functions provide a more convenient and readable way to work with asynchronous code compared to traditional methods such as callbacks and promises. An async function is a function declared with the `async` keyword, enabling the use of `await` within the function body. The `await` keyword pauses the execution of the async function, yielding control back to the calling function until the awaited promise resolves or rejects.

To begin with, let's examine the syntax of declaring an async function:

```
async function fetchData() {
  const response = await fetch('https://api.example.com/data');
  const data = await response.json();
  return data;
}
```

In this example, the `fetchData` function is declared with the `async` keyword. Inside the function, the `await` keyword is used to pause the execution until the `fetch` promise is resolved. Once the response is received, it pauses again to convert the response to JSON format. Finally, it returns the data.

Notably, an async function always returns a promise. Thus, the call to `fetchData()` will return a promise that resolves with the data or rejects with an error. Here is how you might call `fetchData` and handle its result:

```
fetchData().then(data => {
  console.log(data);
}).catch(error => {
  console.error('Error fetching data:', error);
});
```

An async function can contain multiple `await` expressions. Each `await` pauses the function execution until the corresponding promise is settled:

```
async function sequentialSteps() {
  const step1 = await doStep1();
  console.log(step1);

  const step2 = await doStep2(step1);
  console.log(step2);

  const step3 = await doStep3(step2);
  console.log(step3);

  return step3;
}
```

In this example, the `sequentialSteps` function performs a series of asynchronous operations in sequence, waiting for each one to complete before proceeding to the next. This behavior simplifies the logic and increases the readability compared to promise chaining.

`await` can also be used with any promise, not just those returned by the fetch API. For instance, one might use it with custom promises:

```
function delay(ms) {
  return new Promise(resolve => setTimeout(resolve, ms));
}

async function delayedOperation() {
  console.log('Wait for 2 seconds...');
  await delay(2000);
  console.log('Done waiting!');
}
```

Here, the `delay` function returns a promise that resolves after a specified number of milliseconds. The `delayedOperation` function then uses `await delay(2000)` to pause for 2 seconds before logging "Done waiting!".

One critical point to consider when using async functions is error handling. If an awaited promise is rejected, the rejected value will be thrown as an exception. This allows for enhanced error handling using try-catch blocks within async functions:

```
async function fetchAndHandle() {
  try {
    const response = await fetch('https://api.example.com/data');
    if (!response.ok) {
      throw new Error(`HTTP error! status: ${response.status}`);
    }
    const data = await response.json();
    return data;
  } catch (error) {
    console.error('Failed to fetch data:', error);
    throw error; // Rethrow the error after logging it
  }
}
```

In the `fetchAndHandle` function, the try block encompasses the asynchronous operations. If an error occurs during fetching or processing the response, it is caught in the catch block where it is logged and then rethrown. This pattern ensures that errors are managed and propagated appropriately.

One common use case of async functions is handling multiple asynchronous operations concurrently. This can be achieved using `Promise.all` in conjunction with async functions:

```
async function fetchMultipleData() {
  const urls = [
```

```
    'https://api.example.com/data1',
    'https://api.example.com/data2',
    'https://api.example.com/data3'
  ];

  const promises = urls.map(url => fetch(url).then(response => response.
      json()));

  try {
    const results = await Promise.all(promises);
    console.log('All data fetched:', results);
    return results;
  } catch (error) {
    console.error('Error fetching one or more sources:', error);
  }
}
```

In this example, `fetchMultipleData` function fetches data from multiple URLs concurrently by mapping each URL to a promise. The `Promise.all` method waits for all promises to resolve or for any to reject, aggregating the results or catching any errors.

Proper use of async functions can greatly enhance code readability and maintainability in asynchronous JavaScript programming.

9.13 Error Handling with Async/Await

Handling errors in asynchronous code is crucial for developing robust and maintainable applications. The `async/await` syntax in JavaScript not only simplifies writing asynchronous code but also provides intuitive mechanisms for error handling.

Consider an asynchronous function decorated with the `async` keyword:

```
async function fetchData(url) {
    const response = await fetch(url);
    const data = await response.json();
    return data;
}
```

Error handling in this `async` function can be efficiently managed using `try-catch` blocks. The basic structure for catching exceptions thrown by `await` statements is as follows:

```
async function fetchData(url) {
    try {
        const response = await fetch(url);
        const data = await response.json();
        return data;
```

```
    } catch (error) {
        console.error('Error fetching data:', error);
        throw error; // Re-throwing the error after logging it
    }
}
```

In the example above, any error encountered either during the `fetch` operation or while parsing the JSON response will be caught by the `catch` block, which then logs the error and re-throws it.

This pattern allows for handling asynchronous errors similarly to synchronous code, improving readability. Additionally, the re-thrown error can be captured by calling functions, creating a propagation mechanism for error handling across different layers of the application.

The `try-catch` mechanism integrates well with other standard error-handling patterns. For instance, wrapping `async` function calls in a higher-level `try-catch` block ensures centralized error management:

```
async function main() {
    try {
        const data = await fetchData('https://example.com/api/data');
        console.log('Data received:', data);
    } catch (error) {
        console.error('Error in main function:', error);
    }
}

main();
```

In this scenario, any errors from `fetchData` propagate to the `main` function's `catch` block, which can further manage or log the error appropriately.

Temporary failure scenarios, such as transient network errors, often require retry mechanisms. The following example demonstrates a basic retry logic using `async/await`:

```
async function fetchDataWithRetry(url, retries = 3, delay = 1000) {
    for (let i = 0; i < retries; i++) {
        try {
            const response = await fetch(url);
            if (!response.ok) {
                throw new Error(`HTTP error! status: ${response.status}`);
            }
            const data = await response.json();
            return data;
        } catch (error) {
            if (i < retries - 1) {
                console.warn(`Retrying (${i + 1}/${retries})...`);
                await new Promise(res => setTimeout(res, delay)); // Pause before
                    retry
            } else {
                console.error('Exhausted all retries:', error);
                throw error;
```

```
            }
        }
    }
}
```

The function `fetchDataWithRetry` repeatedly attempts to fetch data according to the specified number of retries. In case of failure, it waits for a defined delay before retrying. Upon exhausting all retries, it logs the error and re-throws it.

When dealing with multiple asynchronous operations, grouping them using `Promise.all` while ensuring robust error handling becomes important. Here's an example integrating `async/await` with `Promise.all`:

```
async function fetchMultipleData(urls) {
    try {
        const fetchPromises = urls.map(url => fetchData(url));
        const results = await Promise.all(fetchPromises);
        return results;
    } catch (error) {
        console.error('Error fetching multiple data:', error);
        throw error;
    }
}

async function main() {
    const urls = ['https://example.com/api/data1', 'https://example.com/api/data2'];

    try {
        const data = await fetchMultipleData(urls);
        console.log('All data received:', data);
    } catch (error) {
        console.error('Error in main when fetching multiple data:', error);
    }
}

main();
```

In the `fetchMultipleData` function, `Promise.all` manages multiple fetch promises concurrently. If any of the fetch operations fail, the catch block captures and manages the error.

Finally, special cases such as cleanup operations can be handled using the `finally` block, which executes regardless of the `try` or `catch` outcome. Here is an example:

```
async function fetchData(url) {
    try {
        const response = await fetch(url);
        const data = await response.json();
        return data;
    } catch (error) {
        console.error('Error fetching data:', error);
        throw error;
    } finally {
        console.log('Fetch attempt completed');
```

```
    }
}
```

`finally` ensures critical steps, such as resource cleanup or UI state reset, are executed irrespective of success or failure. This pattern is essential for maintaining application stability and user experience consistency.

Understanding and implementing these error-handling patterns ensures that your asynchronous JavaScript code remains reliable, and maintains smooth and user-friendly operations under various circumstances.

9.14 Comparison of Callbacks, Promises, and Async/Await

When developing asynchronous JavaScript applications, the choice between callbacks, promises, and `async/await` can significantly impact code readability, maintainability, and error handling efficiency. Understanding these three techniques in-depth allows developers to leverage their respective strengths and mitigate their weaknesses. This section dives into a detailed comparison across various dimensions such as syntax complexity, error handling, and composability.

Syntax Complexity

Callbacks traditionally employ a nested function approach, which is straightforward for simple tasks but becomes challenging to manage as complexity grows. Consider a scenario where we need to perform three asynchronous tasks in sequence:

```
function task1(callback) {
    // ... perform task 1
    callback(null, result1);
}

function task2(result1, callback) {
    // ... perform task 2 using result1
    callback(null, result2);
}

function task3(result2, callback) {
    // ... perform task 3 using result2
```

```
    callback(null, result3);
}

task1((err1, result1) => {
    if (err1) {
        // handle error
    } else {
        task2(result1, (err2, result2) => {
            if (err2) {
                // handle error
            } else {
                task3(result2, (err3, result3) => {
                    if (err3) {
                        // handle error
                    } else {
                        console.log(result3);
                    }
                });
            }
        });
    }
});
```

As depicted, callbacks can quickly lead to deeply nested structures, often referred to as "callback hell" or the "pyramid of doom."

Promises offer a cleaner, more linear way of handling asynchronous operations by promoting method chaining:

```
const task1 = () => {
    return new Promise((resolve, reject) => {
        // ... perform task 1
        resolve(result1);
    });
};

const task2 = (result1) => {
    return new Promise((resolve, reject) => {
        // ... perform task 2 using result1
        resolve(result2);
    });
};

const task3 = (result2) => {
    return new Promise((resolve, reject) => {
        // ... perform task 3 using result2
        resolve(result3);
    });
};

task1()
    .then(result1 => task2(result1))
```

```
    .then(result2 => task3(result2))
    .then(result3 => console.log(result3))
    .catch(error => {
        // handle error
    });
```

The introduction of `async/await` elevates readability by allowing asynchronous code to appear synchronous.

```
async function executeTasks() {
    try {
        const result1 = await task1();
        const result2 = await task2(result1);
        const result3 = await task3(result2);
        console.log(result3);
    } catch (error) {
        // handle error
    }
}

executeTasks();
```

Here, asynchronous functions are defined using the `async` keyword, and `await` pauses the execution until the promise is resolved, resulting in code that is easier to read and maintain.

Error Handling

Error handling with callbacks often requires manual checks and nested conditions:

```
task1((err1, result1) => {
    if (err1) {
        console.error(err1);
    } else {
        task2(result1, (err2, result2) => {
            if (err2) {
                console.error(err2);
            } else {
                task3(result2, (err3, result3) => {
                    if (err3) {
                        console.error(err3);
                    } else {
                        console.log(result3);
                    }
                });
            }
        });
    }
```

```
});
```

Promises improve error handling by chaining `.catch()` methods, which can capture errors occurring at any point in the promise chain:

```
task1()
    .then(result1 => task2(result1))
    .then(result2 => task3(result2))
    .then(result3 => console.log(result3))
    .catch(error => {
        console.error(error);
    });
```

`async/await` leverages `try...catch` blocks, simplifying error handling across multiple asynchronous operations:

```
async function executeTasks() {
    try {
        const result1 = await task1();
        const result2 = await task2(result1);
        const result3 = await task3(result2);
        console.log(result3);
    } catch (error) {
        console.error(error);
    }
}

executeTasks();
```

Composability

Composability refers to the ability to combine multiple asynchronous operations in a flexible and maintainable way. Callbacks, due to their nested nature, provide less room for reusability and composability.

Promises inherently promote composability by allowing operations to be structured as a chain, enabling better modularity:

```
const task1 = () => { /* Task 1 implementation */ };
const task2 = (result1) => { /* Task 2 implementation */ };
const task3 = (result2) => { /* Task 3 implementation */ };
task1().then(task2).then(task3).then(console.log).catch(console.error);
```

With `async/await`, composability is further enhanced. Functions can be defined autonomously and composed more freely:

```
async function task1() { /* Task 1 implementation */ }
async function task2(result1) { /* Task 2 implementation */ }
```

```
async function task3(result2) { /* Task 3 implementation */ }

async function executeTasks() {
    try {
        const result1 = await task1();
        const result2 = await task2(result1);
        const result3 = await task3(result2);
        console.log(result3);
    } catch (error) {
        console.error(error);
    }
}

executeTasks();
```

In scenarios where multiple asynchronous operations need to be executed concurrently, promises provide methods like `Promise.all()` and `Promise.race()` for effective parallel processing:

```
Promise.all([task1(), task2(), task3()])
    .then(([result1, result2, result3]) => {
        console.log(result1, result2, result3);
    })
    .catch(error => {
        console.error(error);
    });
```

The `async/await` paradigm can achieve similar concurrency by combining `Promise.all()` with the `await` keyword:

```
async function executeConcurrentTasks() {
    try {
        const [result1, result2, result3] = await Promise.all([task1(),
              task2(), task3()]);
        console.log(result1, result2, result3);
    } catch (error) {
        console.error(error);
    }
}

executeConcurrentTasks();
```

Choosing between callbacks, promises, and `async/await` depends on the specific requirements and constraints of the project at hand. Each approach offers unique advantages, particularly in enhancing code readability, maintaining better error handling, and improving composability.

9.15 Best Practices for Asynchronous Programming

To ensure robust and maintainable asynchronous code in JavaScript, developers should adhere to a set of best practices. These guidelines help manage complexity and reduce potential pitfalls associated with asynchronous operations.

1. Prefer Promises and Async/Await Over Callbacks

Although callbacks are the foundation of asynchronous programming in JavaScript, their use can lead to complex and difficult-to-maintain code structures. Promises and `async/await` syntax offer cleaner, more readable alternatives. Promises flatten nested callback structures, and `async/await` further simplifies handling asynchronous code by making it look synchronous. Here's a comparison:

```
fs.readFile('file1.txt', (err, data1) => {
    if (err) {
        // Handle error
    } else {
        fs.readFile('file2.txt', (err, data2) => {
            if (err) {
                // Handle error
            } else {
                console.log(data1, data2);
            }
        });
    }
});
```

Listing 9.13: Callback Example

```
async function readFileContents() {
    try {
        const data1 = await fs.promises.readFile('file1.txt');
        const data2 = await fs.promises.readFile('file2.txt');
        console.log(data1, data2);
    } catch (err) {
        // Handle error
    }
}
```

Listing 9.14: Async/Await Example

2. Handle Errors Effectively

Error handling is crucial in asynchronous programming. When using callbacks, it's important to consistently check and handle errors.

Promises and `async/await` offer centralized error handling with `.catch()` and `try...catch`. This centralization makes the code more robust and easier to manage.

```
fetchData()
    .then(response => processData(response))
    .then(result => displayResult(result))
    .catch(error => {
        // Handle error across all steps
        console.error('Error:', error);
    });
```

Listing 9.15: Promise Error Handling

```
async function fetchDataAndProcess() {
    try {
        const response = await fetchData();
        const result = await processData(response);
        displayResult(result);
    } catch (error) {
        // Handle error in a single location
        console.error('Error:', error);
    }
}
```

Listing 9.16: Async/Await Error Handling

3. Use the Most Specific Scope Possible

Limiting the scope of asynchronous operations helps reduce unintended side effects. Define variables within the smallest scope where they are needed, and avoid using global variables. This is especially important in `async/await` functions where variables can easily leak into unintended scopes.

```
async function fetchDataAndProcess() {
    try {
        const response = await fetchData();
        if (response) {
            const data = await processData(response);
            displayResult(data);
        }
    } catch (error) {
        console.error('Error:', error);
    }
    // The variable 'data' is not accessible here, avoiding potential
        conflicts
}
```

Listing 9.17: Proper Use of Scope

4. Avoid Excessive Use of `Promise.all`

While `Promise.all` is beneficial for running multiple asynchronous operations concurrently, its misuse can lead to performance issues and hard-to-diagnose errors. Only use `Promise.all` when all promises are independent of each other and should be executed in parallel. Always handle rejections properly, as a single rejection can fail the entire operation.

```
async function loadData() {
    try {
        const [data1, data2] = await Promise.all([
            fetchData1(),
            fetchData2()
        ]);
        // Process data1 and data2
    } catch (error) {
        // Handle individual errors
        console.error('Loading data failed:', error);
    }
}
```

Listing 9.18: Using Promise.all Correctly

5. Be Cautious with Unhandled Rejections

Unhandled promise rejections can cause silent failures that are difficult to debug. It's essential to always attach `.catch()` handlers to promises or use `try...catch` with `async/await`. Modern JavaScript environments will warn about unhandled promise rejections, but explicit handling is a safer practice.

```
fetchData()
    .then(response => processData(response))
    .catch(error => {
        console.error('Error occurred while processing data:', error);
    });
```

Listing 9.19: Handled Promise Rejection

```
async function fetchDataAndProcess() {
    try {
        const response = await fetchData();
        const result = await processData(response);
        displayResult(result);
    } catch (error) {
        console.error('An error occurred:', error);
    }
}
```

Listing 9.20: Using try...catch with async/await

6. Leverage Asynchronous Iteration

For handling a series of asynchronous operations, consider using asynchronous iteration with `for await...of` loops. This pattern is particularly useful when dealing with streams of data or when the operations need to be performed sequentially but the source of data is asynchronous.

```
async function processStream(stream) {
    try {
        for await (const chunk of stream) {
            processChunk(chunk);
        }
    } catch (error) {
        console.error('Stream processing error:', error);
    }
}
```

Listing 9.21: Using for await...of

7. Modularize and Abstract Asynchronous Logic

Code readability and reusability are enhanced by modularizing asynchronous logic into functions or classes. Isolate different responsibilities and reuse common patterns to avoid redundancy.

```
async function fetchData(url) {
    const response = await fetch(url);
    if (!response.ok) {
        throw new Error('Network response was not ok');
    }
    const data = await response.json();
    return data;
}

async function processAllData(urls) {
    for (const url of urls) {
        try {
            const data = await fetchData(url);
            processData(data);
        } catch (error) {
            console.error('Failed to process data from', url, error);
        }
    }
}
```

Listing 9.22: Modularized Asynchronous Function

8. Debounce and Throttle Asynchronous Calls

To optimize performance and reduce unnecessary network requests, implement debouncing and throttling mechanisms. This is particularly important in event-driven applications such as those involving user input or scrolling.

```
function debounce(func, wait) {
    let timeout;
    return function(...args) {
        clearTimeout(timeout);
        timeout = setTimeout(() => func.apply(this, args), wait);
    };
}

// Usage example
const debouncedFetch = debounce(() => fetchData(), 300);
window.addEventListener('resize', debouncedFetch);
```

Listing 9.23: Debounce Function

```
function throttle(func, limit) {
    let lastFunc;
    let lastRan;
    return function(...args) {
        if (!lastRan) {
            func.apply(this, args);
            lastRan = Date.now();
        } else {
            clearTimeout(lastFunc);
            lastFunc = setTimeout(() => {
                if ((Date.now() - lastRan) >= limit) {
                    func.apply(this, args);
                    lastRan = Date.now();
                }
            }, limit - (Date.now() - lastRan));
        }
    };
}

// Usage example
const throttledScroll = throttle(() => fetchData(), 1000);
window.addEventListener('scroll', throttledScroll);
```

Listing 9.24: Throttle Function

Effective asynchronous programming requires balancing readability, performance, and error handling. Prioritizing promises and `async/await`, leveraging modern JavaScript features, and structuring code for maintainability are essential practices. By adhering to these standards, developers can create robust and scalable asynchronous applications.

Chapter 10

Modules and Modern JavaScript Features

This chapter explores the use of modules and modern JavaScript features that enhance code organization and functionality. It covers the ES6 module system, including exporting and importing modules, and the differences between named and default exports. Topics such as dynamic imports, CommonJS modules, and tools for transpiling and bundling are addressed. The chapter also introduces modern syntax features like let and const, destructuring assignments, template literals, spread and rest operators, and enhanced object literals. Additional discussions include ES6 class syntax, iterators, generators, the Fetch API, and new built-in methods, ensuring a thorough understanding of contemporary JavaScript practices.

10.1 Introduction to Modules

In JavaScript development, modularity plays a pivotal role in code organization and maintainability. A module is a self-contained piece of code that encapsulates related functionality, enabling developers to break down complex applications into manageable units. The concept of modularity is not novel; it has been employed in various programming languages to facilitate code reuse, testing, and separation of concerns. In JavaScript, modules allow developers to encapsulate code logic, export relevant components, and import them where needed, leading to cleaner and more modular codebases.

JavaScript modules are implemented differently depending on the context. The evolution from script-based inclusions to the standardized ES6 module system (ESM) represents a significant advancement in modern JavaScript practices. Understanding the various types of modules and their respective use cases is crucial for effective development in contemporary JavaScript environments.

Historical Context and Evolution

Historically, JavaScript did not have a native module system. Developers resorted to concatenating multiple script files using HTML `<script>` tags. This approach had several limitations, such as global scope pollution and dependency management issues. As projects grew, the need for a robust module system became evident, leading to the development of various solutions, such as CommonJS, AMD (Asynchronous Module Definition), and ultimately, ES6 modules.

CommonJS and AMD

CommonJS modules were primarily designed for server-side JavaScript using environments like Node.js. They use the `require()` function to import dependencies and `module.exports` to export modules. This synchronous approach worked well for server-side applications but was less suited for the asynchronous nature of web browsers.

```
// Example of CommonJS module export
const utilities = {
    add: (a, b) => a + b,
    multiply: (a, b) => a * b
};

module.exports = utilities;

// Example of CommonJS module import
const util = require('./utilities'); // Assumes utilities.js is the
    file name
console.log(util.add(2, 3)); // Outputs: 5
```

On the other hand, AMD was designed specifically for browser environments, emphasizing asynchronous loading of modules to improve performance and responsiveness. It achieved this using a `define()` function to define modules and their dependencies.

```
// Example of AMD module
```

```
define(['dependency1', 'dependency2'], function(dep1, dep2) {
    function add(a, b) {
        return a + b;
    }
    return {
        add: add
    };
});

// Example of loading an AMD module
require(['module'], function(module) {
    console.log(module.add(2, 3)); // Outputs: 5
});
```

The Standardization with ES6 Modules

With the advent of ES6, also known as ECMAScript 2015, a standardized module system was introduced. ES6 modules (ESM) brought a more declarative syntax and were designed to be statically analyzable, allowing for advanced build-time optimizations like tree-shaking. This standardization simplifies JavaScript development by providing a uniform approach for both client-side and server-side applications.

Modules in ES6 are defined in distinct files, with `export` statements used to expose functions, objects, or values from a module, and `import` statements used to access these exported entities in other modules.

```
// Example of ES6 module export (utilities.js)
export function add(a, b) {
    return a + b;
}

export function multiply(a, b) {
    return a * b;
}

// Example of ES6 module import (main.js)
import { add, multiply } from './utilities.js';

console.log(add(2, 3)); // Outputs: 5
console.log(multiply(2, 3)); // Outputs: 6
```

ES6 modules enforce strict mode automatically, providing a more secure and predictable coding environment. The explicit nature of imports and exports helps in identifying dependencies, facilitating easier module management and debugging.

Benefits of Using Modules

Modules offer numerous advantages, enhancing code quality and development workflows. These benefits include:

- **Encapsulation**: Modules enable developers to encapsulate functionality, isolating it from other parts of the application. This reduces the risk of naming collisions and unintended interactions.
- **Reusability**: Modules promote code reuse by allowing developers to define reusable components that can be imported and utilized across different parts of an application or even across different projects.
- **Maintainability**: Breaking down an application into smaller, self-contained modules makes it easier to manage, debug, and update. Changes in one module have minimal or no impact on others, reducing the risk of introducing bugs.
- **Dependency Management**: Modern module systems provide mechanisms for handling dependencies, ensuring that required modules are loaded in the correct order. This eliminates the manual management of script tags and interdependencies.
- **Improved Performance**: Particularly with ES6 modules, static analysis and advanced optimizations like tree-shaking (removing unused code from the final bundle) can be performed during the build process, leading to optimized and performant applications.

The shift from monolithic script files to a modular architecture represents a fundamental improvement in JavaScript development. By leveraging the power of modules, developers can build more robust, scalable, and maintainable applications, aligning with modern development best practices.

10.2 The ES6 Module System (ESM)

The ES6 module system, also known as ECMAScript modules (ESM), provides an organized approach for structure and maintainability in JavaScript projects. Modules allow developers to break down program components into smaller, reusable pieces of code. This modular approach enhances readability, testability, and manageability, especially in larger codebases.

Key Concepts and Syntax

In ESM, every file is encapsulated as a module. By default, variables, functions, objects, etc., are local to the module unless they are explicitly exported. Import statements are used to bring these exports into other modules.

```
// mathUtils.js - Module file

// Named export
export function add(a, b) {
    return a + b;
}

// Default export
const PI = 3.14159265359;
export default PI;
```

Listing 10.1: Basic Module Example

```
// app.js - Importing module

import PI, { add } from './mathUtils.js';

console.log(`Value of PI: ${PI}`);
console.log(`Addition: ${add(2, 3)}`);
```

Listing 10.2: Import Example

The `import` statement is used to bring functionalities into the current file from the specified module.

Exporting Modules

There are principally two types of exports in ESM: named exports and default exports.

1. `Named Exports`: These allow you to export multiple bindings (variables, functions, classes) from a module. Each export is referenced by its name and must be imported with the same identifier. 2. `Default Exports`: Each module can have one default export. This is beneficial when a module is exporting a singular primary value, like a function or class.

Examples:

```
// utils.js
export function multiply(a, b) {
    return a * b;
}

export function subtract(a, b) {
    return a - b;
```

```
}
```

Listing 10.3: Named Exports

```
// config.js
const config = { apiUrl: 'https://api.example.com', timeout: 5000 };

export default config;
```

Listing 10.4: Default Export

Importing Modules

`Named Exports` should be imported using curly braces:

```
import { multiply, subtract } from './utils.js';
```

`Default Exports` can be imported directly without braces:

```
import config from './config.js';
```

Renaming Imports and Exports

Both named and default imports/exports can be renamed for convenience or to avoid naming conflicts.

```
// renamable.js
function printMessage() {
   console.log("Hello World");
}

function fetchData() {
   // Fetching data logic
}

export { printMessage as showMsg, fetchData as getData };
```

Listing 10.5: Renaming at Export

```
// anotherFile.js
import { showMsg, getData } from './renamable.js';
```

Listing 10.6: Renaming at Import

Similarly, when importing the default export, it can be given any name, irrespective of the original module's default export name.

```
import conf from './config.js'; // 'conf' is now an alias for the
    default export
console.log(conf.apiUrl);
```

Importing All Exports

An asterisk (*) can be used to import all exports from a module as a namespace. This technique aliases all exported functions/variables under a single name.

```
// utilImport.js
import * as Utils from './utils.js';

console.log(Utils.multiply(2, 3));
console.log(Utils.subtract(5, 2));
```

Module Execution Order and Synchronization

When a module first imports another module, the imported module is executed only once. Subsequent imports retrieve the initialized module. The module dependency graph is traversed to ensure correct execution order. This guarantees synchronization and prevents file dependency conflicts.

Consider a scenario where `moduleA.js` depends on `moduleB.js`, and `moduleC.js` depends on both. The execution order will be determined by the import statements.

Notice the following:

```
// moduleA.js
console.log('Module A');
import './moduleB.js';

// moduleB.js
console.log('Module B');
import './moduleC.js';

// moduleC.js
console.log('Module C');
```

On execution, the output will be:

```
Module C
Module B
Module A
```

These concepts form the cornerstone of the ES6 module system, fostering maintainability and scalability in modern JavaScript applications. Proper understanding and usage of ESM enable developers to write cleaner, more modular code.

10.3 Exporting and Importing Modules

Modules in JavaScript allow for a more modular approach to code organization, enhancing maintainability and reusability. The ES6 module system introduced a standardized syntax for exporting and importing modules. This system helps developers isolate pieces of code into separate files which can be managed independently and integrated seamlessly.

Exporting Modules

To make code available from a module, it must be explicitly exported. JavaScript provides two primary ways to export bindings: named exports and default exports.

Named exports allow you to export multiple bindings (variables, functions, or classes) from a module. Each binding is exported by its name and can be imported using the same name.

```
// math.js
export const pi = 3.14159;
export function add(a, b) {
  return a + b;
}
```

Listing 10.7: {Example of Named Exports}

In this example, `pi` and `add` are named exports.

Default exports are used when a module exports a single binding, which is likely the primary functionality of that module. There can only be one default export per module.

```
// math.js
const pi = 3.14159;
export default function add(a, b) {
  return a + b;
}
```

Listing 10.8: {Example of Default Export}

In this example, the `add` function is the default export of the module.

Importing Modules

To use the exported functionality from a module, you import it into your script. Imports can be done using either their named or default syntax depending on how they were exported.

Named imports allow you to import specific bindings using the same names as the ones used in the export statement.

```
// app.js
import { pi, add } from './math.js';
console.log(pi); // 3.14159
console.log(add(2, 3)); // 5
```

Listing 10.9: {Example of Named Imports}

Default imports bring in the default export from a module. The name used to refer to the default import can be different from the name of the import in the module.

```
// app.js
import add from './math.js';
console.log(add(2, 3)); // 5
```

Listing 10.10: {Example of Default Import}

It is possible to combine both named and default imports in a single statement.

```
// mathExtra.js
export const pi = 3.14159;
export default function multiply(a, b) {
  return a * b;
}

// app.js
import multiply, { pi } from './mathExtra.js';
console.log(pi); // 3.14159
console.log(multiply(2, 3)); // 6
```

Listing 10.11: {Combining Named and Default Imports}

Modules can re-export bindings from other modules using the export statement.

```
// constants.js
export const pi = 3.14159;

// functions.js
export function add(a, b) {
  return a + b;
}
export function subtract(a, b) {
  return a - b;
}

// index.js
export { pi } from './constants.js';
```

```
export { add, subtract } from './functions.js';

// app.js
import { pi, add, subtract } from './index.js';
console.log(pi); // 3.14159
console.log(add(5, 2)); // 7
console.log(subtract(5, 2)); // 3
```

Listing 10.12: {Re-exporting Bindings}

This modular approach not only improves code organization but also enhances its maintainability. By keeping the code for different functionalities in separate modules, it is easier to update, debug, and collaborate. Users can selectively import only the parts of the modules they need, optimizing performance and reducing unnecessary code.

Dynamic imports allow for modules to be loaded asynchronously, which is useful for lazy loading parts of the application, thus improving performance.

```
// app.js
async function loadMathModule() {
  const math = await import('./math.js');
  console.log(math.add(2, 3)); // 5
}
loadMathModule();
```

Listing 10.13: {Dynamic Import Example}

Dynamic imports return a promise that resolves to the module object. This feature is particularly useful for on-demand loading of parts of the application, such as routes in a single-page application manifest.

The ES6 module system provides a robust and standard way to manage dependencies and modularize code, promoting cleaner and more maintainable codebases. Through named and default exports, developers have fine-grained control over what is exposed from their modules, and with the flexibility of dynamic imports, modern JavaScript applications can be optimized for performance by loading resources only as needed.

10.4 Named Exports vs Default Exports

In the ES6 module system, JavaScript modules can export functionalities such as variables, functions, and classes using two primary approaches: named exports and default exports. Understanding the distinction between these two forms is essential for effectively organizing and managing code in large-scale applications.

Named Exports:

Named exports allow the export of multiple variables, functions, or classes from a module. Each entity exported using named exports must be explicitly named, enabling other modules to import them selectively. A module can have any number of named exports. The syntax for named exports is straightforward, as demonstrated below:

```
// file: mathUtils.js
export const add = (a, b) => a + b;
export const subtract = (a, b) => a - b;
export const multiply = (a, b) => a * b;
export const divide = (a, b) => a / b;
```

In this example, the `mathUtils.js` module exports four named exports: `add`, `subtract`, `multiply`, and `divide`. Other modules can import these functions using the following syntax:

```
// file: app.js
import { add, multiply } from './mathUtils.js';

console.log(add(2, 3)); // Output: 5
console.log(multiply(4, 5)); // Output: 20
```

Here, only the `add` and `multiply` functions are imported from `mathUtils.js`. This customizability is one of the main advantages of named exports, allowing modules to import only the needed functionalities, potentially reducing the overall bundle size.

Default Exports:

In contrast, default exports facilitate the export of a single value or entity per module. The primary advantage of default exports is that they provide a default behavior or object from the module, which can ease the use-cases where a module's primary function is intended to be the main export.

The syntax for default exports is akin to named exports but without the explicit naming of the exported entity:

```
// file: calculator.js
const calculator = {
  add(a, b) { return a + b; },
  subtract(a, b) { return a - b; },
  multiply(a, b) { return a * b; },
  divide(a, b) { return a / b; }
};
```

```
export default calculator;
```

In this example, the `calculator` object is exported as the default export from the `calculator.js` module. Importing a default export is straightforward and does not necessitate curly braces:

```
// file: main.js
import calculator from './calculator.js';

console.log(calculator.add(2, 3)); // Output: 5
console.log(calculator.divide(10, 2)); // Output: 5
```

The `calculator` object is imported directly without using curly braces. This behavior is particularly useful when a module is designed to export a single main component or function, thereby simplifying the import process.

Mixing Named and Default Exports:

It is worth noting that a single module can include both named and default exports. This flexibility allows module authors to define a primary export alongside additional supporting exports.

```
// file: myModule.js
const mainExport = () => {
  console.log('This is the main export');
};

const auxiliaryFunction = () => {
  console.log('This is an auxiliary function');
};

export default mainExport;
export { auxiliaryFunction };
```

In this case, `myModule.js` has a default export `mainExport` and a named export `auxiliaryFunction`. Consumers of this module can choose to import whichever export is relevant:

```
// file: app2.js
import mainExport, { auxiliaryFunction } from './myModule.js';

mainExport(); // Output: This is the main export
auxiliaryFunction(); // Output: This is an auxiliary function
```

Import Aliasing:

When importing named exports, developers have the option to alias the imported entities, which can be useful to avoid naming conflicts or to clarify the purpose of the import in the consuming module:

```
// file: app3.js
import { add as sum, subtract as difference } from './mathUtils.js';

console.log(sum(10, 20)); // Output: 30
console.log(difference(10, 5)); // Output: 5
```

In this example, the `add` and `subtract` functions from `mathUtils.js` are imported with aliases `sum` and `difference`, respectively. This feature plays a significant role in enhancing code maintainability and readability, especially in large applications.

By judiciously using named and default exports, developers can significantly enhance the modularity and clarity of their JavaScript codebases. Effective use of these export types fosters better separation of concerns, code reuse, and collaboration among development teams.

10.5 Dynamic Imports and Lazy Loading

Dynamic imports and lazy loading serve as powerful tools for optimizing JavaScript applications, enabling the conditional loading of dependencies and improving page load performance. This section delves into the syntax and practical applications of dynamic imports, followed by their implementation in lazy loading.

Dynamic imports in JavaScript are employed using the 'import()' function, which returns a promise that resolves to the module. This feature allows developers to conditionally load modules at runtime based on various factors such as user interactions, application state, or environmental conditions. The primary advantage is a reduction in initial load time, deferring the loading of non-essential code until it is actually needed.

The syntax for a dynamic import is straightforward:

```
const modulePromise = import('./module.js');
modulePromise.then((module) => {
  // Use the module here
  module.defaultFunction();
}).catch((error) => {
  // Handle any errors that occurred during the import
  console.error('Error loading module:', error);
});
```

In this example, 'import('./module.js')' initiates the dynamic import of 'module.js'. The promise resolves to the module object, from which functions and variables can be accessed.

Dynamic imports can also be utilized in 'async' functions, providing a more concise and readable syntax:

```
async function loadModule() {
    try {
        const module = await import('./module.js');
        module.defaultFunction();
    } catch (error) {
        console.error('Error loading module:', error);
    }
}
loadModule();
```

This approach integrates seamlessly with modern asynchronous coding practices using 'async'/'await', improving code clarity and maintainability.

A practical application of dynamic imports is lazy loading, which involves loading parts of an application only when they are required. This is particularly beneficial for large applications where loading all code upfront would lead to slower performance and longer load times.

Consider an example of a single-page application (SPA) with multiple routes where each route corresponds to a different feature or module. Lazy loading can be applied to load the necessary modules only when the user navigates to the corresponding route. In a typical routing setup, this can be achieved as follows:

```
const routes = {
    home: './home.js',
    about: './about.js',
    contact: './contact.js'
};

async function loadRoute(route) {
    if (routes[route]) {
        try {
            const module = await import(routes[route]);
            module.initialize();
        } catch (error) {
            console.error('Error loading route module:', error);
        }
    } else {
        console.error('Route not found:', route);
    }
}
```

```
// Example usage
document.getElementById('homeLink').addEventListener('click', () =>
    loadRoute('home'));
document.getElementById('aboutLink').addEventListener('click', () =>
    loadRoute('about'));
document.getElementById('contactLink').addEventListener('click', () =>
    loadRoute('contact'));
```

In this scenario, the ‘loadRoute‘ function dynamically imports the module corresponding to the selected route and invokes its initialization function. This pattern ensures that only the code necessary for the active route is loaded, reducing the application’s initial load time and improving performance.

Lazy loading components in frameworks like React can also benefit from dynamic imports. The ‘React.lazy‘ function enables components to be loaded dynamically, combined with ‘Suspense‘ to handle loading states:

```
import React, { Suspense } from 'react';

const Home = React.lazy(() => import('./Home'));
const About = React.lazy(() => import('./About'));
const Contact = React.lazy(() => import('./Contact'));

function App() {
    return (
        <div>
            <Suspense fallback={<div>Loading...</div>}>
                <Route path="/home" component={Home} />
                <Route path="/about" component={About} />
                <Route path="/contact" component={Contact} />
            </Suspense>
        </div>
    );
}
export default App;
```

Here, the ‘React.lazy‘ function creates components that are loaded only when required, while the ‘Suspense‘ component manages the loading state, providing a fallback UI until the component is ready.

By leveraging dynamic imports and lazy loading, developers can enhance the performance and responsiveness of their applications. These techniques facilitate modularity and efficiency, ensuring that resources are loaded only as needed, aligning with modern web development best practices.

10.6 CommonJS Modules

The CommonJS module system provides a foundation for a modular structure in JavaScript, particularly for server-side applications. Unlike the ES6 module system, which is designed with native support in mind and can be used both in browsers and on servers, CommonJS is primarily used in Node.js environments. The design focuses on simplicity and synchronous loading, which suits server-side scripting where input/output operations often dominate.

CommonJS modules are encapsulated in files, each having its own scope. To export functionality from a module, the object `module.exports` is used. To import a module, the `require` function is employed. These mechanisms bring clarity and organization to the codebase, making dependencies and module interfaces explicit.

```
/* add.js - A module to perform addition. */
function add(a, b) {
   return a + b;
}
module.exports = add;

/* main.js - Importing and using the add module. */
const add = require('./add');
console.log(add(2, 3)); // Output: 5
```

Listing 10.14: A Basic Example of CommonJS Module Export and Import

The example demonstrates how `add.js` exports a single function, `add`, and `main.js` imports this function and utilizes it. This modular structure allows the `add` function to be easily tested, reused, and maintained independently.

In more complex modules, `module.exports` could be an object containing multiple properties or methods. This facilitates exporting multiple pieces of functionality from a single module.

```
/* math.js - A module with multiple mathematical operations. */
function add(a, b) {
   return a + b;
}

function multiply(a, b) {
   return a * b;
}

module.exports = {
```

```
    add: add,
    multiply: multiply
};

/* main.js - Importing and using the math module. */
const math = require('./math');
console.log(math.add(2, 3)); // Output: 5
console.log(math.multiply(2, 3)); // Output: 6
```

Listing 10.15: Exporting Multiple Functions in CommonJS

A further advantage of CommonJS is the ease of creating singleton objects. Modules are cached upon their first load; subsequent `require` calls return the cached instance, fostering a design where a module can maintain state across an application.

```
/* config.js - A configuration module. */
let configuration = null;

function getConfig() {
    if (!configuration) {
        configuration = initializeConfig();
    }
    return configuration;
}

function initializeConfig() {
    // Simulate loading configuration from a file or environment
    return { appName: 'DemoApp', version: '1.0' };
}

module.exports = { getConfig };

/* main.js - Using the configuration module as a singleton. */
const config1 = require('./config').getConfig();
const config2 = require('./config').getConfig();
console.log(config1 === config2); // Output: true
```

Listing 10.16: Singleton Pattern with CommonJS Modules

CommonJS supports circular dependencies where two or more modules depend on each other. While circular dependencies can complicate the code, they are sometimes necessary. CommonJS handles this by exposing partly initialized exports to the modules involved in the cycle.

```
/* moduleA.js */
const moduleB = require('./moduleB');
module.exports = {
    greet: function() {
        return 'Hello ' + moduleB.getName();
```

```
    }
};

/* moduleB.js */
const moduleA = require('./moduleA');
module.exports = {
    getName: function() {
        return 'CommonJS';
    },
    getGreeting: function() {
        return moduleA.greet();
    }
};

/* main.js */
const moduleB = require('./moduleB');
console.log(moduleB.getGreeting()); // Output: Hello CommonJS
```

Listing 10.17: Handling Circular Dependencies in CommonJS

Due to its synchronous nature, CommonJS is unsuitable for contexts where asynchronous module loading is necessary, such as modern web browsers. As a result, newer environments and tools are transitioning to the ES6 module system, which supports asynchronous loading patterns.

Despite that, legacy systems and many Node.js applications continue to rely on CommonJS, and understanding this module system remains crucial for maintaining and transitioning existing codebases. This knowledge also helps in comprehending the differences between CommonJS and ES6 modules, aiding in the selection of appropriate module systems for different application contexts.

10.7 Transpiling and Bundling Modules

Modern JavaScript applications often employ the use of modules and advanced language features that are not universally supported in all environments. Consequently, developers use tools such as transpilers and bundlers to ensure compatibility and optimize the deployment process. This section explores the significance of these tools and breaks down their functionalities and configurations.

Transpiling, short for source-to-source compiling, is the process of converting source code written in one programming language into another language of similar or lower abstraction level. In the context of

JavaScript development, transpiling typically refers to converting ECMAScript 6 (ES6) or later code into ECMAScript 5 (ES5) to ensure compatibility with older browsers and environments. Commonly used tools for this purpose include Babel and TypeScript.

Bundling involves combining multiple JavaScript files into a single file or a few files to reduce the number of HTTP requests made by a webpage. This process can also entail code minification and optimization, which enhances performance. Webpack and Rollup are among the most popular bundlers in the JavaScript ecosystem.

Babel is a widely-used JavaScript transpiler that supports the latest ECMAScript features. It translates modern JavaScript into a version compatible with older environments. A basic Babel configuration involves installing the necessary packages and setting up the `.babelrc` configuration file.

```
npm install --save-dev @babel/core @babel/cli @babel/preset-env
```

Listing 10.18: Install Babel CLI and Preset

The `.babelrc` file defines the presets and plugins Babel uses to transpile the code.

```
{
  "presets": ["@babel/preset-env"]
}
```

Listing 10.19: .babelrc Configuration

`@babel/preset-env` automatically determines the necessary transformations and polyfills based on the target environments specified in a project's `package.json` file.

```
{
  "browserslist": "> 0.25%, not dead"
}
```

Listing 10.20: package.json Browserslist Configuration

Once configured, Babel can be used to transpile JavaScript files. The following command transpiles all `.js` files in the `src` directory and outputs them to the `dist` directory.

Listing 10.21: Babel CLI Command

```
npx babel src --out-dir dist
```

Webpack is a powerful module bundler capable of managing complex dependency graphs efficiently. To illustrate its capabilities, we begin with the installation of Webpack and the Webpack CLI.

Listing 10.22: Install Webpack and Webpack CLI

```
npm install --save-dev webpack webpack-cli
```

A basic Webpack configuration is defined in a `webpack.config.js` file. This configuration specifies the entry point, output file, and various loaders and plugins.

```
const path = require('path');

module.exports = {
  entry: './src/index.js',
  output: {
    filename: 'bundle.js',
    path: path.resolve(__dirname, 'dist')
  },
  module: {
    rules: [
      {
        test: /\.js$/,
        exclude: /node_modules/,
        use: {
          loader: 'babel-loader'
        }
      }
    ]
  },
  mode: 'development'
};
```

Listing 10.23: Basic Webpack Configuration

In this configuration, Webpack starts from `src/index.js` as the entry point, processes it with `babel-loader` to transpile the ES6 code, and outputs the bundled file as `dist/bundle.js`.

Rollup is another popular JavaScript bundler, particularly favored for library development due to its tree-shaking capabilities, which eliminate dead code to optimize the final bundle size. To set up Rollup, the following installation command is used.

Listing 10.24: Install Rollup and Babel Plugin

```
npm install --save-dev rollup @rollup/plugin-babel @rollup/plugin-node-resolve
    @rollup/plugin-commonjs
```

The Rollup configuration is defined in a `rollup.config.js` file.

```
import babel from '@rollup/plugin-babel';
import resolve from '@rollup/plugin-node-resolve';
import commonjs from '@rollup/plugin-commonjs';

export default {
  input: 'src/index.js',
  output: {
    file: 'dist/bundle.js',
    format: 'cjs'
  },
  plugins: [
    resolve(),
    commonjs(),
    babel({ babelHelpers: 'bundled' })
  ]
};
```

Listing 10.25: Basic Rollup Configuration

This configuration specifies the input file, output format, and the plugins needed to resolve node modules, convert CommonJS modules, and transpile using Babel.

Both Webpack and Rollup offer various plugins and features to handle different types of files, optimize assets, and enhance development workflows. Transpiling and bundling are integral steps in modern JavaScript development, ensuring that the code is both forward-compatible and optimized for performance. Understanding and leveraging these tools is essential for efficient and maintainable codebases.

10.8 Modern JavaScript Syntax: let and const

The introduction of `let` and `const` in ES6 represents a significant improvement over the traditional variable declaration keyword, `var`. The use of `let` and `const` addresses several shortcomings of `var` and introduces block-scoping to JavaScript, enhancing code readability and maintainability.

The primary distinction between `let` and `const` is mutability. `let` allows for the re-assignment of variables, whereas `const` ensures that a variable is immutable once it has been assigned a value.

Block Scope and `let`

A critical feature of `let` is block scope. Unlike `var`, which is function-scoped, `let` is confined to the block in which it is defined. This confines the variable's visibility to the block, reducing the likelihood of namespace collisions and unintended reference issues.

Consider the following example to illustrate block-scoping with `let`:

```
{
    let x = 10;
    console.log(x); // Outputs: 10
}
console.log(x); // ReferenceError: x is not defined
```

The variable `x` is only accessible within the block where it is defined. Attempting to access `x` outside the block results in a `ReferenceError`.

Temporal Dead Zone

Another aspect of `let` is the Temporal Dead Zone (TDZ). The TDZ refers to the time between entering the scope in which the variable is bound and its actual declaration and initialization. Accessing the variable in this zone results in a `ReferenceError`.

```
console.log(a); // ReferenceError: a is not defined
let a = 5;
```

Despite being declared with `let`, attempting to access `a` before its declaration and initialization throws a `ReferenceError` due to the TDZ.

Immutability with `const`

The keyword `const` provides a mechanism to declare constants, ensuring the variable's value cannot be re-assigned. However, it is crucial to understand that `const` enforces immutability on the variable binding, not on the data itself. This means that while a `const` variable cannot be re-assigned, the contents of the object or array it references can still be modified.

Let us consider an example demonstrating `const`:

```
const PI = 3.14159;
console.log(PI); // Outputs: 3.14159

// Attempting to re-assign a const variable results in an error
PI = 3.14; // TypeError: Assignment to constant variable.
```

In this example, reassigning `PI` results in a `TypeError`. However, if `PI` were an object, its properties could still be modified:

```
const config = {
    host: 'localhost',
    port: 8080
};
config.port = 3000; // This is allowed
```

```
console.log(config.port); // Outputs: 3000
```

Here, the `port` property of the `config` object is successfully modified, even though `config` is a constant.

Block Scope with `const`

Similar to `let`, `const` is also block-scoped:

```
{
    const y = 30;
    console.log(y); // Outputs: 30
}
console.log(y); // ReferenceError: y is not defined
```

Attempting to access `y` outside its block results in a `ReferenceError`.

Best Practices

To leverage the full benefits of `let` and `const`, some best practices should be adhered to:

- **Prefer `const` over `let`**: Use `const` by default and only use `let` if re-assignment of the variable is required.
- **Avoid `var`**: The use of `var` should be avoided due to its function-scoping behavior, potential for hoisting-related bugs, and loss of the benefits provided by block-scoping.
- **Use meaningful names**: Whether using `let` or `const`, variable names should be descriptive and meaningful in the context of their use.

The advent of `let` and `const` in ES6 has significantly streamlined variable declaration in JavaScript. By facilitating block-level scoping and allowing developers to clearly express their intentions regarding variable immutability, these keywords have contributed to more robust, maintainable codebases in modern JavaScript development.

10.9 Destructuring Assignment

Destructuring assignment is a syntactic feature introduced in ES6 that allows the unpacking of values from arrays or properties from objects into distinct variables. This feature provides a concise way to extract values and is particularly useful for handling complex data structures with minimal code.

Array Destructuring

Using destructuring assignment with arrays allows us to assign values to variables directly from the array. The syntax involves placing a comma-separated list of variable names within square brackets on the left-hand side of the assignment.

```
const numbers = [1, 2, 3];
const [a, b, c] = numbers;

console.log(a); // 1
console.log(b); // 2
console.log(c); // 3
```

Unpacking a subset of the array can be done by using commas to skip items:

```
const numbers = [1, 2, 3, 4];
const [first, , third] = numbers;

console.log(first); // 1
console.log(third); // 3
```

Array destructuring can also handle rest elements using the rest parameter syntax, which stores all remaining items into a new array:

```
const numbers = [1, 2, 3, 4, 5];
const [first, second, ...rest] = numbers;

console.log(first); // 1
console.log(second); // 2
console.log(rest); // [3, 4, 5]
```

Object Destructuring

For objects, destructuring allows the extraction of properties into variables. The order of properties does not matter, and the syntax involves placing the property names within curly braces on the left-hand side of the assignment.

```
const person = { name: 'John', age: 30 };
const { name, age } = person;

console.log(name); // John
console.log(age); // 30
```

To assign properties to variables with different names, you can use the colon syntax:

```
const person = { name: 'John', age: 30 };
```

```
const { name: personName, age: personAge } = person;

console.log(personName); // John
console.log(personAge); // 30
```

Default values can be assigned to variables in cases where the destructured property does not exist or is ‘undefined‘:

```
const person = { name: 'John' };
const { name, age = 25 } = person;

console.log(name); // John
console.log(age); // 25
```

Nested objects can also be destructured by using nested curly braces:

```
const person = {
  name: 'John',
  address: {
    city: 'New York',
    zip: '10001'
  }
};
const { name, address: { city, zip } } = person;

console.log(name); // John
console.log(city); // New York
console.log(zip); // 10001
```

Function Arguments

Destructuring assignment can be particularly useful for handling function arguments, allowing for more readable and succinct code when passing objects with multiple properties.

```
function printPerson({ name, age }) {
  console.log(`Name: ${name}, Age: ${age}`);
}

const person = { name: 'John', age: 30 };
printPerson(person); // Name: John, Age: 30
```

This technique can be further enhanced with default values for function parameters:

```
function printPerson({ name, age = 25 } = {}) {
  console.log(`Name: ${name}, Age: ${age}`);
}

printPerson({ name: 'John' }); // Name: John, Age: 25
printPerson(); // Name: undefined, Age: 25
```

Moreover, for array arguments, destructuring can streamline the assigned values needed within a function:

```
function sum([a, b]) {
  return a + b;
}

console.log(sum([3, 4])); // 7
```

Practical Applications

Destructuring is widely used in JavaScript applications. For example, it can simplify the extraction of values from arrays and objects returned by APIs or other functions. When dealing with complex structures, destructuring allows for clear and organized code.

Handling multiple return values from a function typically involves returning an object; destructuring can then be used to simplify the assignment:

```
function getPerson() {
  return {
    name: 'John',
    age: 30,
    job: 'Developer'
  };
}

const { name, job } = getPerson();
console.log(`Name: ${name}, Job: ${job}`); // Name: John, Job: Developer
```

In situations involving React, destructuring props and state in functional components makes the code concise and readable. For example:

```
function Welcome({ name, age }) {
  return <div>Welcome, {name}! You are {age} years old.</div>;
}
```

Array destructuring also finds its use in iteration scenarios like processing multiple values returned from useState hooks in React:

```
const [count, setCount] = useState(0);
```

Understanding and effectively utilizing destructuring assignment enhances code readability and structure, streamlining the extraction of needed values from complex data structures.

10.10 Template Literals and Tagged Templates

Template literals are a feature introduced in ES6 that allows for easier string interpolation, multiline strings, and more readable code. Unlike traditional string literals defined with single quotes (' ') or double quotes (" "), template literals are enclosed by backticks (` `). This allows for embedding expressions directly within the string using the `$expression` syntax.

```
// Traditional string concatenation
const name = "John";
const age = 30;
const greeting = "Hello, my name is " + name + " and I am " + age + "
    years old.";

// Using template literals
const greetingTemplate = `Hello, my name is ${name} and I am ${age}
    years old.`;

console.log(greeting);
console.log(greetingTemplate);
```

Listing 10.26: Basic Template Literal Example

```
Hello, my name is John and I am 30 years old.
Hello, my name is John and I am 30 years old.
```

With template literals, including dynamic content becomes more straightforward, and the code reads more naturally. Template literals also support multiline strings, reducing the need for manual concatenation of strings split across multiple lines.

```
// Traditional multiline string using concatenation
const multilineString = "This is line 1.\n" +
                        "This is line 2.\n" +
                        "This is line 3.";

// Template literals for multiline strings
const multilineTemplateLiteral = `This is line 1.\nThis is line 2.\nThis
    is line 3.`;

console.log(multilineString);
console.log(multilineTemplateLiteral);
```

Listing 10.27: Multiline Strings with Template Literals

```
This is line 1.
This is line 2.
This is line 3.
This is line 1.
This is line 2.
This is line 3.
```

Template literals extend their utility by enabling tagged templates. Tagged templates are a more advanced feature of template literals, allowing a function to preprocess a template literal. This function, called a tag, is invoked with the processed template string and expressions, enabling custom string processing and even security use cases like sanitization.

```
function highlight(strings, ...values) {
    return strings.reduce((result, string, i) => {
        return `${result}${string}<strong>${values[i] || ''}</strong>`;
    }, '');
}

const name = 'Alice';
const occupation = 'developer';
const sentence = highlight`My name is ${name} and I am a ${occupation}.`;


console.log(sentence);
```

Listing 10.28: Basic Tagged Template Example

```
My name is <strong>Alice</strong> and I am a <strong>developer</strong>.
```

In this example, the `highlight` function is used as a tag for a template literal. It processes the literals and embeds the expressions within `<strong>` HTML tags. The `strings` array contains the static parts of the template, while the `values` array contains evaluated expressions. The `reduce` method assembles the final output by iterating over `strings` and inserting corresponding `values` appropriately.

Tagged templates offer different applications, such as creating safe HTML templates by escaping potential user-generated content to prevent XSS (Cross-Site Scripting) attacks. Here is an example of a tagged template for sanitizing inputs:

```
function sanitize(strings, ...values) {
    return strings.reduce((result, string, i) => {
        const value = values[i]
            .replace(/&/g, '&amp;')
            .replace(/</g, '&lt;')
            .replace(>/g, '&gt;')
            .replace(/"/g, '&quot;')
            .replace(/'/g, '&#39;');
        return `${result}${string}${value || ''}`;
```

```
    }, '');
}

const userInput = '<script>alert("Hacked!")</script>';
const safeString = sanitize`<div>${userInput}</div>`;

console.log(safeString);
```

Listing 10.29: Sanitize User Inputs with Tagged Templates

```
<div>&lt;script&gt;alert(&quot;Hacked!&quot;)&lt;/script&gt;</div>
```

The `sanitize` function cleans each expression within the template by replacing potentially harmful characters with their respective HTML entities, thus ensuring the final output is safe for embedding within a webpage.

Template literals and tagged templates significantly simplify and enhance string manipulation in JavaScript, providing a flexible and powerful toolset for developers. They are essential in modern JavaScript development, especially for constructing complex strings, enhancing code readability, and ensuring security in web applications.

10.11 Spread and Rest Operators

The spread and rest operators, introduced in ECMAScript 2015 (ES6), offer syntactic conveniences for handling arrays and objects. These operators enable more expressive and flexible function calls, array manipulation, and object handling. Let's delve into their usage and benefits, starting with their basic definitions.

The spread operator uses three consecutive dots (‘...‘) to expand an iterable (like an array or object) into individual elements. Conversely, the rest operator uses the same syntax to collect multiple elements and condense them into a single array.

Consider the spread operator first:

```
const arr1 = [1, 2, 3];
const arr2 = [...arr1, 4, 5];
console.log(arr2); // Output: [1, 2, 3, 4, 5]
```

In this example, the spread operator (i.e., ‘...arr1‘) expands the elements of ‘arr1‘ into the new array ‘arr2‘. This enables concise syntax for copying arrays or combining multiple arrays into one.

Beyond arrays, the spread operator extends its utility to objects:

```
const obj1 = {a: 1, b: 2};
const obj2 = {...obj1, c: 3};
console.log(obj2); // Output: {a: 1, b: 2, c: 3}
```

Here, '...obj1' spreads the properties of 'obj1' into 'obj2', effectively cloning 'obj1' and adding an additional property.

Spread operators are also useful in function calls, where an array can be expanded into individual arguments:

```
const numbers = [1, 2, 3];
function add(a, b, c) {
   return a + b + c;
}
console.log(add(...numbers)); // Output: 6
```

The array 'numbers'' elements are spread as individual arguments to the 'add' function.

Next, examine the rest operator, which aggregates multiple arguments into a single array. It is commonly used in function parameter lists to handle an arbitrary number of arguments:

```
function sum(...args) {
   return args.reduce((acc, cur) => acc + cur, 0);
}
console.log(sum(1, 2, 3, 4)); // Output: 10
```

In this example, the 'sum' function uses '...args' to collect all arguments into an array and then calculates their sum using the 'reduce' method.

The rest operator finds similar utility in array destructuring, enabling the capture of remaining elements:

```
const [first, ...rest] = [1, 2, 3, 4];
console.log(first); // Output: 1
console.log(rest); // Output: [2, 3, 4]
```

The variable 'first' captures the first element, while '...rest' captures the remaining elements as an array.

Applying rest properties in object destructuring is another typical use case:

```
const { a, b, ...others } = { a: 1, b: 2, c: 3, d: 4 };
console.log(a); // Output: 1
console.log(b); // Output: 2
console.log(others); // Output: { c: 3, d: 4 }
```

In this example, 'a' and 'b' extract specific properties, while '...others' groups the rest into a new object.

Combining spread and rest operators in practice results in highly flexible and concise code constructs. Consider their use in cloning and merging arrays or objects:

```
const originalArray = [1, 2, 3];
const cloneArray = [...originalArray];
console.log(cloneArray); // Output: [1, 2, 3]

const originalObject = { a: 1, b: 2 };
const cloneObject = { ...originalObject };
console.log(cloneObject); // Output: { a: 1, b: 2 }

const mergedArray = [...originalArray, 4, 5];
console.log(mergedArray); // Output: [1, 2, 3, 4, 5]

const mergedObject = { ...originalObject, c: 3, d: 4 };
console.log(mergedObject); // Output: { a: 1, b: 2, c: 3, d: 4 }
```

In these scenarios, the spread operator efficiently handles duplication and merging without invoking explicit loops or method calls.

The interplay between spread and rest operators fundamentally transforms handling and manipulating collections in JavaScript. Their judicious use promotes cleaner, more maintainable code across diverse scenarios, encompassing array and object manipulation, function invocation, and beyond.

10.12 Enhanced Object Literals

Enhanced object literals, introduced in ES6, offer several new shorthand syntaxes and features that make defining and enhancing objects more concise and readable. These improvements include property shorthand, method definitions, computed property names, and the ability to define prototypes directly within object literals.

Property shorthand allows for a more succinct way of initializing properties from variables. When a property name matches the variable name being assigned to it, we can use the shorthand syntax.

```
const name = 'John';
const age = 30;
const person = {
    name,
    age
```

```
};
console.log(person); // { name: 'John', age: 30 }
```

This code is equivalent to:

```
const person = {
   name: name,
   age: age
};
```

Method definitions within object literals have also been streamlined. Instead of specifying the `function`keyword, we can directly define the method using a more concise syntax.

```
const person = {
   name: 'John',
   sayHello() {
      return `Hello, my name is ${this.name}!`;
   }
};
console.log(person.sayHello()); // Hello, my name is John!
```

Computed property names enable dynamic property keys in object literals. By utilizing square brackets, any expression can be used as the property name.

```
const propName = 'age';
const person = {
   name: 'John',
   [propName]: 30
};
console.log(person.age); // 30
```

Object literal syntax enhancements also include the ability to define an object's prototype at the same time as creating the object. By using the `__proto__` property, we can set the prototype of an object directly within the literal.

```
const proto = {
   greet() {
      return 'Hello!';
   }
};

const obj = {
   __proto__: proto,
   name: 'Alice'
};

console.log(obj.greet()); // Hello!
```

Additionally, the object spread operator (...) merges object properties into a new object. This provides a shorthand way to copy objects and merge multiple sources of properties.

```
const obj1 = { a: 1, b: 2 };
const obj2 = { b: 3, c: 4 };
const mergedObj = { ...obj1, ...obj2 };

console.log(mergedObj); // { a: 1, b: 3, c: 4 }
```

The spread operator is helpful not only for merging but also for cloning objects.

```
const original = { a: 1, b: 2 };
const clone = { ...original };

console.log(clone); // { a: 1, b: 2 }
clone.a = 99;
console.log(original.a); // 1
```

Regular property assignment in objects can be overwritten by subsequent properties with the same name, as demonstrated, where `obj2`'s `b` value replaces `obj1`'s `b` value in `mergedObj`.

Enhanced object literals not only make the codebase more concise but also introduce more flexibility and ease in manipulating objects within modern JavaScript applications.

10.13 Classes and Inheritance in ES6

In ES6, the introduction of classes simplified the process of creating objects and managing inheritance. This functionality streamlined the development process, making JavaScript more familiar to developers coming from other object-oriented programming languages. ES6 classes allow for cleaner syntax and bring more intuitive structure to object creation and inheritance principles in JavaScript.

The `class` keyword was introduced to define classes. A class is a blueprint for creating objects with a specific design and set of functionalities. The structure of a class in ES6 is defined using the `class` keyword followed by the name of the class.

```
// Defining a simple class
class Person {
```

```
  constructor(name, age) {
    this.name = name;
    this.age = age;
  }

  // Method in the Person class
  greet() {
    console.log(`Hello, my name is ${this.name}.`);
  }
}

// Creating an instance of the Person class
const person1 = new Person('Alice', 30);
person1.greet(); // Output: Hello, my name is Alice.
```

The above example illustrates a basic ES6 class definition. The `constructor` method is a special method for creating and initializing objects with a class. When the `new` keyword is used to create an instance of the class, the `constructor` is called to set up the object with the provided parameters. Additionally, methods can be defined within the class to provide functionality accessible to class instances.

ES6 also supports inheritance, allowing a class to extend another class. The `extends` keyword is used to create a subclass that inherits properties and methods from a parent class. Subclasses can call the constructor of the parent class using the `super` keyword, enabling the preservation and augmentation of inherited functionalities.

```
// Defining a class that extends another class
class Employee extends Person {
  constructor(name, age, jobTitle) {
    // Call the parent class's constructor
    super(name, age);

    this.jobTitle = jobTitle;
  }

  // Method in the Employee class
  work() {
    console.log(`${this.name} is working as a ${this.jobTitle}.`);
  }
}

// Creating an instance of the Employee class
const employee1 = new Employee('Bob', 25, 'Engineer');
employee1.greet(); // Output: Hello, my name is Bob.
employee1.work(); // Output: Bob is working as an Engineer.
```

In this example, the `Employee` class extends the `Person` class, inheriting its properties and methods. The `super` function calls the constructor of the parent class, ensuring that the inherited properties are initialized correctly. The subclass is also capable of defining its own methods and properties, as shown with the `work` method and the additional `jobTitle` property.

ES6 classes also support static methods, which are called on the class itself rather than instances of the class. Static methods are useful for utility functions related to the class.

```
// Using static methods in ES6 classes
class Calculator {
  static add(a, b) {
    return a + b;
  }

  static subtract(a, b) {
    return a - b;
  }
}

// Calling static methods
console.log(Calculator.add(5, 3)); // Output: 8
console.log(Calculator.subtract(5, 3)); // Output: 2
```

Static methods are defined using the `static` keyword. They can be invoked without creating an instance of the class, as they belong to the class itself.

Furthermore, ES6 classes can utilize getters and setters for encapsulating data access within the class. Getters and setters can be defined to control the access and mutation of properties, ensuring a clean and controlled interface for object data.

```
// Using getters and setters in ES6 classes
class Rectangle {
  constructor(width, height) {
    this.width = width;
    this.height = height;
  }

  // Getter for the area property
  get area() {
    return this.width * this.height;
  }

  // Setter for the width property
  set width(value) {
    if (value <= 0) throw new Error('Width must be positive.');
    this._width = value;
```

```
  }

  get width() {
    return this._width;
  }

  // Setter for the height property
  set height(value) {
    if (value <= 0) throw new Error('Height must be positive.');
    this._height = value;
  }

  get height() {
    return this._height;
  }
}

// Creating an instance of the Rectangle class
const rect = new Rectangle(10, 5);
console.log(rect.area); // Output: 50

rect.width = 15;
console.log(rect.area); // Output: 75
```

In this snippet, the `Rectangle` class defines getters and setters for its properties. The getter for `area` calculates and returns the area of the rectangle. The setters for `width` and `height` enforce positive values, demonstrating encapsulation by controlling property values.

Using classes and inheritance in ES6 brings significant improvements to the readability and maintainability of JavaScript code. These enhancements align JavaScript with modern programming practices and enable developers to write more robust, modular, and reusable code.

10.14 Iterators and Generators

Iterators and generators provide a powerful mechanism for working with sequences of data in JavaScript. This section delves into the concepts of iterators and generators, explaining their purpose, usage, and the underlying mechanics that make them integral features of modern JavaScript programming.

An iterator is an object that enables traversal through a collection of values, such as an array or a set. It adheres to the iterator protocol, which defines a standard way to produce a sequence of values, one at a time. To create an iterator, an object must implement a `next()` method.

The `next()` method returns an object with two properties: `value` and `done`. The `value` property represents the next value in the iteration sequence, and the `done` property is a boolean indicating whether the iteration is complete.

The following code snippet demonstrates how to create a custom iterator:

```
const myIterator = {
  current: 0,
  last: 5,
  next() {
    if (this.current <= this.last) {
      return { value: this.current++, done: false };
    } else {
      return { value: undefined, done: true };
    }
  }
};

let result = myIterator.next();
while (!result.done) {
  console.log(result.value);
  result = myIterator.next();
}
```

```
0
1
2
3
4
5
```

Generators, introduced in ES6, simplify the process of writing iterators. A generator is a function that can pause its execution and return an intermediate result. The `function*` syntax is used to define a generator function. Inside the generator function, the `yield` keyword is used to pause the function and return a value. Upon subsequent invocation, the generator resumes execution immediately after the last `yield` statement.

Here is an example of a generator function:

```
function* countUpTo(max) {
  let current = 0;
  while (current <= max) {
    yield current++;
  }
}

const counter = countUpTo(5);
let result = counter.next();
```

```
while (!result.done) {
    console.log(result.value);
    result = counter.next();
}
```

```
0
1
2
3
4
5
```

Generators provide a more readable and concise way to implement iterators compared to the manual implementation demonstrated earlier. Additionally, they are particularly useful for dealing with asynchronous operations by enabling the writing of code that looks synchronous. This is achieved through the use of the `yield` keyword, which pauses the generator function and waits for a value to be returned asynchronously.

The following example illustrates an asynchronous generator function:

```
function* asyncGenerator() {
    const value1 = yield new Promise(resolve => setTimeout(() => resolve(
        'First Value'), 1000));
    console.log(value1);
    const value2 = yield new Promise(resolve => setTimeout(() => resolve(
        'Second Value'), 1000));
    console.log(value2);
}

const gen = asyncGenerator();
gen.next().value.then(value => {
    gen.next(value).value.then(value => {
        gen.next(value);
    });
});
```

```
First Value
Second Value
```

Using the `for...of` loop, you can easily iterate over the values produced by an iterator or generator. The `for...of` loop internally calls the `next()` method on the iterable to retrieve each value until the `done` property is `true`.

Here is an example using the generator function with the `for...of` loop:

```
function* countdown(start) {
    while (start >= 0) {
        yield start--;
    }
```

```
}

for (const value of countdown(5)) {
    console.log(value);
}
```

```
5
4
3
2
1
0
```

Additionally, JavaScript objects can be made iterable by implementing the `[Symbol.iterator]` method. This method should return an iterator. Below is an example of turning a custom object into an iterable:

```
const iterableObject = {
    data: ['a', 'b', 'c'],
    [Symbol.iterator]() {
        let index = 0;
        const data = this.data;
        return {
            next() {
                if (index < data.length) {
                    return { value: data[index++], done: false };
                } else {
                    return { value: undefined, done: true };
                }
            }
        };
    }
};

for (const value of iterableObject) {
    console.log(value);
}
```

```
a
b
c
```

Iterators and generators not only enhance the ability to work with sequences of data but also integrate seamlessly with new and existing JavaScript features. This combination empowers developers to write cleaner, more maintainable, and more efficient code that aligns with modern development practices.

10.15 Promises and Async/Await in Modern JavaScript

Promises and the `async/await` syntax constitute fundamental aspects of modern JavaScript for handling asynchronous operations. Understanding these concepts is critical to writing efficient, clean, and readable code. Promises represent objects that encapsulate asynchronous operations and their eventual results, either resolved or rejected. The `async/await` syntax offers a cleaner, more linear approach to asynchronous programming, reducing complexity and improving error handling.

A Promise is created using the `Promise` constructor, which accepts a single function argument known as an executor. This executor function takes two callback parameters, `resolve` and `reject`, to determine the operation's outcome.

```
const myPromise = new Promise((resolve, reject) => {
  // Perform some asynchronous operation
  let success = true; // This simulates the operation's outcome

  if (success) {
     resolve("Operation was successful!");
  } else {
     reject("Operation failed.");
  }
});
```

Promises have several methods to handle their results. The `.then()` method is used to process resolved values, whereas `.catch()` handles rejected values.

```
myPromise.then((resolvedValue) => {
  console.log(resolvedValue); // "Operation was successful!"
}).catch((error) => {
  console.error(error); // If operation failed, it would log "Operation
      failed."
});
```

For more advanced scenarios, `Promise.all()`, `Promise.race()`, `Promise.allSettled()`, and `Promise.any()` provide mechanisms to combine multiple promises.

```
const promise1 = Promise.resolve(3);
const promise2 = 42;
const promise3 = new Promise((resolve, reject) => {
  setTimeout(resolve, 1000, 'foo');
```

```
});

Promise.all([promise1, promise2, promise3]).then(values => {
    console.log(values); // [3, 42, "foo"]
});
```

The async/await syntax, introduced in ECMAScript 2017, provides an elegant way to handle Promises. The async keyword before a function declaration indicates that the function returns a Promise. Within an async function, the await keyword pauses execution until the Promise resolves, simplifying the handling of asynchronous code.

```
async function myAsyncFunction() {
    try {
        let resolvedValue = await myPromise;
        console.log(resolvedValue); // "Operation was successful!"
    } catch (error) {
        console.error(error); // If operation failed, it would log "
            Operation failed."
    }
}
```

The async/await syntax enhances readability and maintainability by flattening the promise chain, avoiding the so-called "callback hell." Consider the transformation of nested Promises into a clean, linear structure with async/await:

```
function getData() {
    return new Promise((resolve => {
        setTimeout(() => resolve("Data received!"), 1000);
    }));
}

// Using .then() and .catch()

function fetchData() {
    getData()
        .then(result => {
            console.log(result);
            return "Processing Data";
        })
        .then(processed => {
            console.log(processed);
        })
        .catch(error => {
            console.error(error);
        });
}
fetchData();
```

Versus the more readable `async/await` approach:

```
async function fetchData() {
   try {
      let result = await getData();
      console.log(result); // "Data received!"
      let processed = "Processing Data";
      console.log(processed); // "Processing Data"
   } catch (error) {
      console.error(error);
   }
}
fetchData();
```

Error handling with `try/catch` blocks in `async` functions is generally more intuitive than chaining `.catch()` onto each Promise. This provides a single location to manage potential failures.

```
async function fetchDataWithError() {
   try {
      let result = await getData(); // Assume getData throws an error
      console.log(result);
   } catch (error) {
      console.error("Error:", error);
   }
}
fetchDataWithError();
```

Combining `async/await` with Promise combinators allows handling complex scenarios involving multiple concurrent operations easily. For example:

```
async function fetchMultipleData() {
   try {
      let [result1, result2, result3] = await Promise.all([
         promise1, promise2, promise3
      ]);
      console.log(result1, result2, result3); // Outputs combined
          results
   } catch (error) {
      console.error("One of the promises failed:", error);
   }
}
fetchMultipleData();
```

By understanding Promises and `async/await`, developers can effectively manage asynchronous tasks, ensure more predictable control flows, and enhance overall code quality. They are indispensable tools in the modern JavaScript ecosystem, indispensable for building scalable and robust applications.

10.16 New Built-in Methods (Array, Object, String, etc.)

Modern JavaScript introduces several new methods for Array, Object, and String. These built-in methods streamline common tasks, making code more readable and efficient.

Array methods have evolved significantly, offering robust functionalities for array manipulation. Among the most notable are `Array.prototype.includes`, `Array.prototype.flat`, and `Array.prototype.flatMap`.

```
let array = [1, 2, 3, 4];
console.log(array.includes(2)); // true
console.log(array.includes(5)); // false
```

Listing 10.30: Usage of Array.prototype.includes

The `includes` method checks if an array contains a specified element, returning a boolean value. It provides a more readable alternative to `indexOf` for this purpose.

```
let nestedArr = [1, 2, [3, 4, [5, 6]]];
console.log(nestedArr.flat()); // [1, 2, 3, 4, [5, 6]]
console.log(nestedArr.flat(2)); // [1, 2, 3, 4, 5, 6]
```

Listing 10.31: Usage of Array.prototype.flat

The `flat` method creates a new array with sub-array elements concatenated into it recursively up to the specified depth. By default, the depth is 1.

```
let arr = [1, 2, 3, 4];
console.log(arr.flatMap(x => [x, x * 2])); // [1, 2, 2, 4, 3, 6, 4, 8]
```

Listing 10.32: Usage of Array.prototype.flatMap

The `flatMap` method first maps each element using a mapping function, then flattens the result into a new array. This method is useful for combining map and flat operations efficiently.

Object methods have similarly grown in number and capabilities. Important new additions include `Object.entries`, `Object.values`, and `Object.fromEntries`.

```
let obj = { a: 1, b: 2, c: 3 };
console.log(Object.entries(obj)); // [['a', 1], ['b', 2], ['c', 3]]
console.log(Object.values(obj)); // [1, 2, 3]
```

Listing 10.33: Usage of Object.entries and Object.values

The `entries` method returns an array of a given object's own enumerable string-keyed property [key, value] pairs. The `values` method returns an array of a given object's own enumerable property values.

```
let entries = [['a', 1], ['b', 2], ['c', 3]];
console.log(Object.fromEntries(entries)); // { a: 1, b: 2, c: 3 }
```

Listing 10.34: Usage of Object.fromEntries

The `fromEntries` method transforms a list of key-value pairs into an object. It is the reverse operation of `Object.entries`.

String methods have been enhanced to include `String.prototype.startsWith`, `String.prototype.endsWith`, and `String.prototype.repeat`.

```
let str = 'JavaScript';
console.log(str.startsWith('Java')); // true
console.log(str.endsWith('Script')); // true
```

Listing 10.35: Usage of String.prototype.startsWith and String.prototype.endsWith

The `startsWith` method checks if a string begins with the specified characters, while the `endsWith` method checks if a string ends with the specified characters.

```
console.log('hello'.repeat(3)); // 'hellohellohello'
```

Listing 10.36: Usage of String.prototype.repeat

The `repeat` method constructs and returns a new string that contains the specified number of copies of the string it was called on, concatenated together.

These methods represent just a subset of the numerous enhancements in modern JavaScript that improve developer productivity and code clarity without compromising functionality.

10.17 Optional Chaining and Nullish Coalescing

Optional chaining and nullish coalescing are two recent additions to the JavaScript language, introduced in ECMAScript 2020 (ES11). These features enhance code readability and reduce the likelihood of runtime errors when dealing with deeply nested objects or values that may be null or undefined.

Optional chaining allows for safe access to nested object properties without explicitly checking for the existence of each level in the hierarchy. It accomplishes this by short-circuiting and returning ‘undefined‘ if any part of the chain is ‘null‘ or ‘undefined‘.

The syntax for optional chaining uses the ‘?.‘ operator. Let’s consider an example where we have an object representing a user, which may or may not contain an address property:

```
// Define a user object without the address property
const user = { name: "Alice" };

// Accessing properties using traditional chaining
let city = user.address.city; // Throws an error: Cannot read property 'city' of
    undefined

// Accessing properties using optional chaining
city = user?.address?.city; // Evaluates to undefined instead of throwing an error
```

Here, if ‘user.address‘ is not defined, the expression ‘user?.address?.city‘ will safely return ‘undefined‘ rather than throwing an error. This reduces the need for explicit checks:

```
// Traditional way with explicit checks
let city = user && user.address && user.address.city; // Evaluates to undefined

// Using optional chaining - more concise and readable
city = user?.address?.city; // Also evaluates to undefined
```

Optional chaining can be used with function calls as well. If the function does not exist, it will return ‘undefined‘ instead of throwing an error:

```
const user = {
    name: "Alice",
    greet: function() { return "Hello" }
};

// Traditional check before calling greet function
let greeting = user.greet ? user.greet() : undefined; // Calls the function if
    defined

// Using optional chaining
```

```
greeting = user.greet?.(); // Calls greet if it exists, otherwise evaluates to
    undefined
```

Another use case is safely handling arrays and their properties. Consider an array of users where we want to access a specific user's property:

```
const users = [{ name: "Alice" }, { name: "Bob" }];

// Accessing the name of the third user using traditional checks
let userName = users[2] && users[2].name; // Evaluates to undefined

// Using optional chaining
userName = users[2]?.name; // Also evaluates to undefined
```

Nullish coalescing, introduced with the '?¿ operator, provides a way to handle default values only when dealing with 'null' or 'undefined'. It is particularly useful when you want to distinguish between 'null'/'undefined' and other falsy values like '0', 'NaN', or an empty string ("").

The nullish coalescing operator '?¿ allows setting a default value only if the initial value is 'null' or 'undefined':

```
let user = {
   name: "Alice",
   age: 0,
   status: null
};

// Using || operator - it considers falsy values
let age = user.age || 18; // Evaluates to 18, which is incorrect
let status = user.status || "active"; // Evaluates to "active"

// Using ?? operator - only null or undefined triggers the default value
age = user.age ?? 18; // Evaluates to 0
status = user.status ?? "active"; // Evaluates to "active"
```

Combining optional chaining and nullish coalescing can be powerful in handling nested configurations safely with default values:

```
const config = {
   user: {
      settings: {
         theme: null
      }
   }
};

// Accessing theme setting with default value
let theme = config.user?.settings?.theme ?? "light"; // Evaluates to "light"
```

In this example, 'config.user?.settings?.theme' will safely return 'null' if any part of the chain is missing. The '?¿ operator then ensures that if 'theme' is 'null', the default value '"light"' is used.

These features together significantly enhance the readability and robustness of JavaScript code, especially when dealing with complex objects and optional configurations. By effectively using optional chaining and nullish coalescing, developers can write more concise and error-resistant code, avoiding unnecessary checks and improving maintainability.

10.18 The Fetch API for Network Requests

The Fetch API provides an interface for fetching resources (including network requests) in a more powerful and flexible manner than the traditional 'XMLHttpRequest' (XHR). The Fetch API is promise-based, enabling a more streamlined approach to asynchronous operations. In this section, we will discuss the basic syntax and usage of the Fetch API, handling responses, and various options available for making network requests.

Basic Syntax and Usage:

To perform a basic fetch request, you can use the global 'fetch' function. The 'fetch' function takes a URL as its argument and returns a Promise that resolves to the Response object representing the response to the request.

```
fetch('https://api.example.com/data')
  .then(response => response.json())
  .then(data => console.log(data))
  .catch(error => console.error('Error:', error));
```

In the above example, the 'fetch' function initiates a request to the specified URL. The response is then processed with the '.json()' method, which returns a Promise resolving to the JSON content of the response. The data is logged to the console, and errors are handled using the '.catch()' method.

Handling Responses:

The Response object provides several methods to handle different types of content. Here are some common methods used to parse the response:

```
fetch('https://api.example.com/data')
  .then(response => {
    if (!response.ok) {
```

```
    throw new Error('Network response was not ok');
  }
  return response.json();
})
.then(data => console.log(data))
.catch(error => console.error('Fetch error:', error));
```

In this example, the 'response.ok' property is checked to ensure the request was successful. If the response was not ok, an error is thrown. Otherwise, 'response.json()' is called to parse the JSON content.

Other methods of the Response object include:

- `response.text()` - Returns a Promise resolving to the body as a string.
- `response.blob()` - Returns a Promise resolving to a Blob object.
- `response.formData()` - Returns a Promise resolving to FormData.
- `response.arrayBuffer()` - Returns a Promise resolving to ArrayBuffer.

Request Options:

The Fetch API supports a wide array of options to customize the request. The optional 'init' parameter can be used to specify method, headers, body, mode, credentials, cache, and other properties.

```
fetch('https://api.example.com/data', {
  method: 'POST',
  headers: {
    'Content-Type': 'application/json'
  },
  body: JSON.stringify({
    name: 'John',
    age: 30
  })
})
  .then(response => response.json())
  .then(data => console.log('Success:', data))
  .catch(error => console.error('Error:', error));
```

In this example, a POST request is made with a JSON body. The 'headers' property is used to specify the content type. The body of the request is created by serializing a JavaScript object to a JSON string.

Advanced Usage:

The Fetch API also supports more advanced usage scenarios like handling streaming responses, aborting requests, and using request/response objects for more control.

```
const controller = new AbortController();
const signal = controller.signal;

fetch('https://api.example.com/data', { signal })
  .then(response => response.json())
  .then(data => console.log(data))
  .catch(error => {
    if (error.name === 'AbortError') {
      console.log('Fetch aborted');
    } else {
      console.error('Fetch error:', error);
    }
  });

// Abort the fetch request after 5 seconds
setTimeout(() => controller.abort(), 5000);
```

In this example, an 'AbortController' is created to enable the ability to cancel the fetch request. The 'signal' property of the controller is passed to the fetch configuration, allowing the request to be aborted after 5 seconds.

The Fetch API for network requests provides a modern, ease-to-use, and versatile approach for handling HTTP requests, making it a cornerstone of contemporary JavaScript web development. Its full potential can be realized by integrating it with other modern JavaScript features and patterns.

Made in the USA
Monee, IL
04 November 2026

67384073R00213